Regulation of Passenger Fares and Competition among the Airlines

"Regulation of Passenger Fares and Competition among the Airlines"

Edited by
Paul W. MacAvoy
and John W. Snow

Ford Administration Papers on
Regulatory Reform

American Enterprise Institute for Public Policy Research
Washington, D.C.

Paul W. MacAvoy is professor of economics at Yale University and an adjunct scholar at the American Enterprise Institute.

John W. Snow is a visiting fellow at the American Enterprise Institute.

Library of Congress Cataloging in Publication Data
Main entry under title:

Regulation of passenger fares and competition among the
    airlines.

    (AEI studies in government regulation ; 158)
    "Ford administration papers on regulatory reform."
    1. Airlines—United States—Rates.   I. MacAvoy,
Paul W.   II. Snow, John W.   III. Series: American
Enterprise Institute for Public Policy Research.
AEI studies ; 158.
HE9783.55.U5R43   387.7'1   77-2797
ISBN 0-8447-3256-7

AEI Studies 158

Printed in the United States of America

CONTENTS

FOREWORD

Early in 1975, I called for the initiation of a major effort aimed at regulatory reform. Members of my administration, and the Congress, were asked to formulate and accelerate programs to remove anti-competitive restrictions in price and entry regulation, to reduce the paper work and procedural burdens in the regulatory process, and to revise procedures in health, safety and other social regulations to bring the costs of these controls in line with their social benefits.

My requests set in motion agency and department initiatives, and a number of studies, reorganization proposals, and legislative proposals were forthcoming last year. A number of these resulted in productive changes in transportation, retail trade, and safety regulations. Nevertheless, much remained to be done, in part because of the time required to complete the analysis and evaluation of ongoing regulations.

This volume provides one set of the analytical studies on regulatory reform that were still in process at the end of 1976. Necessarily, these studies would have undergone detailed evaluation in the agencies and the White House before becoming part of any final reform program. They do not necessarily represent my policy views at this time, but they do contribute to the analyses that must precede policy making. I look forward to the discussion that these papers will surely stimulate.

Gerald R. Ford

GERALD R. FORD

PREFACE

In October 1975, the Ford administration submitted to Congress its proposal to reform economic regulation of the airline industry, the Aviation Act of 1975. The Aviation Act called for the most comprehensive legislative changes in airline industry regulation since the Civil Aeronautics Act established the basic federal airline regulatory system in 1938.

In submitting the legislation, President Ford stated that its objective was "to ensure that we have the most efficient airline system in the world providing the American public with the best possible service at the lowest possible cost." The proposal was designed to give airline carriers greater pricing flexibility and greater freedom to enter and exit markets. It also proposed to eliminate the Civil Aeronautics Board's authority to approve anticompetitive agreements. In short, the Aviation Act sought to substitute competitive market forces for the public utility type of regulation established in the 1938 legislation and administered by the Civil Aeronautics Board.

This, however, was not the only initiative. Major aviation reform proposals were introduced by Senator Howard W. Cannon (Democrat, Nevada), Senator Edward M. Kennedy (Democrat, Massachusetts), and Congressman Glenn M. Anderson (Democrat, California). The CAB itself submitted a proposal calling for reduced control over entry and pricing. Hearings on aviation reform were held in both the Senate and the House during the 94th Congress. A number of similar proposals have been introduced in the 95th Congress.

The Carter administration has publicly stated its support for aviation regulatory reform. Hearings have been held on this issue in the Senate and have begun in the House. Aviation regulatory reform promises to be a major issue in the 95th Congress.

This volume makes available a number of background studies and analyses done within the Ford administration bearing upon the issue of aviation reform. They illustrate the kind of applied research undertaken by the Ford administration in connection with the aviation reform effort and the important role played by such research and analysis in that effort. Moreover, they provide some insight into the most important issues which arose in the deregulation debate and they provide the latest analysis developed to deal with those issues. One of the interesting lessons drawn from the debate over regulatory reform is that the legislative system imposes a heavy burden of proof which advocates of reform are expected to meet. These papers provide some insight into the nature of that burden and illustrate how the advocates of aviation reform tried to meet it. The CAB itself undertook a number of important studies on the need for economic regulation. In fact, a major staff study concluded that the economic structure of the industry did not require regulation to achieve good performance.

In developing the Aviation Act, the Ford administration drew upon a number of important academic studies on the economics of airline regulation. Of particular importance were the industry study by Richard Caves, the pathbreaking work on airline pricing by George W. Douglas and James C. Miller III, and the analysis of the intrastate California experience by William A. Jordan. By and large, these studies dealt with the broad impacts of regulation on the performance of the aviation industry. They presented an assessment of the social losses resulting from regulation, and they analyzed how the aviation regulatory system interfered with efficient resource allocation so as to produce these losses.

The papers in this volume have a different focus, however. In general, they address particular questions on the effects from deregulation which came up in the congressional consideration of the Aviation Act: the applicability of the intrastate experience in predicting deregulation effects on the interstate air system; financial effects from opening up markets on the industry and on particular carriers; likely adjustment patterns in service offerings by individual airlines; and, most importantly, whether there would be loss of service to small communities as a result of deregulation. These issues have a narrower focus than the questions addressed in the academic literature, but they were of major concern to the Congress. The congressman faced with the contention that his district would lose its air service as a result of the proposal was rarely satisfied with a reference to the literature on the social welfare loss resulting from regulation. The academic literature was of great significance in developing the Ford administration's basic aviation reform policy. In the actual debate over the proposal, however, the need arose to supplement the academic research with studies addressing the issues of specific effects from decontrol, and the papers presented here were prepared to fill that need.

It is our hope that these materials will be useful to students of aviation regulatory reform and will contribute to the continuing debate on proposals for legislative reform in this industry. Whatever the outcome of that debate, President Ford's statement in his October 8, 1975, Message to Congress still stands: "The rigidly controlled regulatory structure now serves to stifle competition, increase costs to travelers, make the industry less efficient than it could be, and deny large segments of the American public access to lower cost air transportation."

PAUL W. MacAVOY
Yale University

JOHN W. SNOW
American Enterprise Institute

May 1977

PART ONE
INTRODUCTION TO THE ISSUES

The Ford administration's aviation reform proposal, the Aviation Act of 1975, proceeded from the view that the aviation industry was too heavily regulated by the Civil Aeronautics Board and that the industry would operate more efficiently in a less regulated environment. Thus, the proposal sought to reduce CAB control over entry into the industry and over pricing by airline carriers. The first paper in this volume reviews the major problems associated with the regulatory system administered by the CAB and the benefits of putting greater reliance on competitive market forces in aviation. The paper then reviews a number of issues that came up in the debate over aviation deregulation—issues that are addressed in much greater detail in subsequent papers in the volume.

1

THE PROBLEMS OF AIRLINE REGULATION AND THE FORD ADMINISTRATION PROPOSAL FOR REFORM

John W. Snow

Aviation industry regulatory reform is one of the most important and controversial questions facing the aviation community today. It would not be an exaggeration to say that we are at a watershed for aviation regulation. I shall first describe the bill proposed by the Ford administration and then discuss some of the allegations made by its opponents.

The Ford Administration's Proposal

The present system of airline regulation is seriously deficient. Its most serious deficiency is that it causes air fares to be considerably higher than they would be otherwise. It also results in a serious misallocation of resources, discourages innovations in service, denies consumers the range of price and service options which they would prefer, and creates a chronic tendency towards excess capacity in the industry.

The Civil Aeronautics Board (CAB) has historically used its broad powers to forbid competitive pricing and lower fares. Unable to compete on the basis of price, carriers have been forced into costly service competition, and the costs of these services have been passed on to the consumer. On review of the evidence, one is forced to conclude that the present regulatory system is hindering, not advancing, the original statutory objectives of "adequate, economical and efficient service by air carriers at reasonable charges." The present regulatory system has become a major obstacle to the provision of air service at the lowest cost consistent with the furnishing of such service. Ironically, airline profit levels are not increased by this regulatory system, and they may indeed be made more volatile than otherwise.

This paper is edited from testimony before the U.S. Congress, House, Subcommittee on Aviation of the Committee on Public Works and Transportation, May 11, 1976.

These defects result from the policies the CAB has adopted with respect to entry into the market and pricing. They flow naturally from the artificial suppression of competitive market forces. The deficiencies can only be corrected by modification of the present regulatory system to allow wider operation of competitive market forces. The most pressing problems in the airline regulatory field cluster in two broad areas: pricing flexibility and market entry. A third set of problems concerns anticompetitive agreements, which must be prohibited.

Only through fundamental changes in the present law with respect to these matters will the airline industry be able to operate in a workably competitive fashion. Only by allowing the industry to operate in this fashion will the basic defects of its performance be corrected.

Pricing. The administration's Aviation Act is designed to obtain the increased pricing flexibility that is essential to improve the performance of the aviation industry. Under the bill, carriers will be given substantially more freedom to increase or reduce fares free from the fear of suspension. In addition, explicit time limits will be placed on CAB action in fare cases, and management will be given much greater freedom to reduce rates without fear that the rate reduction ultimately will be found unlawful.

The CAB's power to suspend or set airline fares is statutory. The Federal Aviation Act of 1958 requires air carriers to file and observe just and reasonable tariffs. If the board finds a rate unjust, unreasonable, unjustly discriminatory, unduly preferential, or unduly prejudicial, it may suspend the tariff. After investigation, the board may determine and prescribe a different fare, or maximum or minimum charges, or both.

Under the statute, carriers are free to file fares with the CAB which are different from those of their competitors, and this might be thought to create considerable pricing competition. As a practical matter, however, there is little real price competition. Airline fares have been generally uniform in all markets of equal distance, regardless of costs, supply, seasonality, or traffic density. The only important exception is that the board has given local service carriers the right to charge 130 percent of the formula fare—but only where they are monopolists!

Carriers that file tariffs reflecting moderate price decreases for particular types of service have had to answer to competing carriers who have generally complained to the board that the rate reduction is unreasonably low. The cost, the uncertainty, and the delay of board suspension proceedings have had a chilling effect upon individual carrier rate-making initiatives. Because carriers anticipate the difficulty of obtaining approval, many reductions are never filed in the first place.

The board's use of industry average costs and of an assumed demand elasticity equal to less than unity for all traffic for all rates leads to an upward bias in fare determination. The details of this bias were discussed in the extended testimony of William T. Coleman, Jr., the secretary of transportation, before the House Subcommittee on Aviation, and they need not be repeated here. Suffice it to say that the board's actions have caused fares to be too high and that this bias is a natural result of the kind of price regulation the board feels it must use.

The Aviation Act of 1975 is designed to increase carrier pricing flexibility by reducing the regulatory hurdles to innovative pricing. First, it amends section 1002(d) to provide that a rate above "direct costs" may not be found unjust or unreasonable on the basis that it is too low. Direct costs are defined as those costs which vary directly with output—that is, overhead, fixed costs, and nonvariable costs are excluded. By limiting the board's minimum rate-making authority in this way, the act provides for considerable downward pricing flexibility. The board's present authority with respect to the ultimate lawfulness of rate increases is not affected.

Second, the act amends section 1002(g) to create a "no-suspend zone." The board's rate-making procedures have two parts: a suspension proceeding and a hearing about ultimate lawfulness. After a rate is introduced, the board can "suspend" the rate, pending a full hearing. Suspension, however, does not mean that the rate will ultimately be found to be unlawful. It simply postpones the effective date of the rate. If the rate is suspended, the board then proceeds to a hearing, and it is at this hearing that the lawfulness of the rate is decided. Although the suspension proceeding does not decide the ultimate lawfulness of a rate, it does add to the regulatory lag. It is almost certain that an innovative rate will be suspended, and this denies the carrier the ability to respond quickly to changing markets. Also, if a rate is suspended, it means that the hearing cannot be based on actual experience, but must be based on hypothetical assumptions about the consequences of putting the rate into effect. To reduce this lag and to ensure that hearings are based on fact, the bill proposes substantial restrictions on the present suspension procedures.

Rate increases may be suspended under the administration's

bill, but only if they exceed 10 percent of the rate in effect one year prior to the proposed change. Rate decreases may be suspended, but only if there is a clear and convincing reason to believe that they do not cover the direct costs of the service at issue or if the resulting rate decrease exceeds certain limits. In the first year after enactment, the board may not suspend a rate which provides for less than a 20 percent decrease in the rate in effect on the date of enactment. In the second year after enactment, the board may not suspend a rate which provides for less than a 40 percent decrease in the rate in effect on the date of enactment. During the third and succeeding years, the board may not suspend any proposed rate reduction unless there is clear and convincing evidence to believe on the basis of a preliminary finding that the rate is likely to be below operating costs. The direct-operating-costs criterion is a protection against predatory pricing. It should be emphasized that this zone relates only to suspensions and does not affect the board's authority to rule on the ultimate lawfulness of a rate.

The act also amends section 1002(e) to place increased emphasis on the need for price competition as a means of promoting a healthy air transportation industry responsive to the public needs. Finally, the act provides a time limit for rate cases. If the board has not completed its proceedings within 180 days of the time the rate was scheduled to take effect, the tariff goes into effect and is deemed lawful without further proceedings.

The foregoing changes in the Aviation Act will create considerable opportunities for increased pricing flexibility. It should be added that the bill just introduced by Senator Edward M. Kennedy (Democrat, Massachusetts) also includes an increase in pricing flexibility as one of its key features. Pricing flexibility is a necessary condition to improve the performance of the airline industry. Problems of excess capacity, high air fares, and the narrow range of price service options are directly related to the absence of effective price competition in the airline industry. In intrastate markets, such as Texas and California, where entry and pricing have been less restricted, prices have been considerably lower than in comparable interstate markets. Commuter airlines, operating completely free of controls over entry and price, and using equipment which is more costly per passenger mile, tend to charge comparable or lower fares than regulated carriers on flights of similar distance.

Market Entry. The Federal Aviation Act grants the board wide discretion in determining entry and route awards. Under section 401 of the Federal Aviation Act, the board is given authority to determine which carriers may operate in scheduled interstate service and on which routes they may operate. The applicant must be found fit, willing, and able to perform the service properly, and the transportation must be required by public convenience and necessity. The board has interpreted the entry provisions of the act so as to create unnecessarily high barriers to entry into the industry. Reducing the barriers to entry into the commercial aviation business is a second essential condition to improve its performance.

Moreover, increased pricing flexibility and liberalized entry go hand-in-hand. Thus, any proposal relating to price must be combined with one relating to entry into air transportation markets. The present system of blockaded entry reduces the pressure on existing carriers to price competitively. This, in turn, contributes to the problem of high fares, low load factors, and excessively high costs. As the board's staff has correctly pointed out in their excellent study,[1] with the number of competitors essentially fixed, regulation of the maximum fare and the minimum quality of service may be necessary. But with liberalized entry and pricing, carriers will be under competitive pressure to provide a range of services desired by the public at prices which reflect the actual cost of producing the service without regulation of the maximum fare. The threat of potential competition will police carrier behavior and will provide the needed incentive for carriers in existing markets to keep prices at a level low enough to forestall entry of competitors. Potential competition is a vitally important force in producing desirable market results, that is, in assuring that firms are diligent about providing the type of service and price/quality options that the public desires.

Relaxation of entry is essential to police the Aviation Act's provisions for pricing flexibility. Pricing flexibility unaccompanied by entry relaxation—as desired by airlines—would create a serious danger of higher fares, exacerbation of the overcapacity problem, and an even poorer economic performance by the airline industry.

The Aviation Act of 1975 is designed to reduce substantially the barriers facing qualified firms that wish to enter into air transportation, expand into new markets, or offer new varieties of service. Enactment of the legislation, however, will not necessarily lead to the addition of new carriers on each domestic route, nor even to the addition of new carriers on a majority of the domestic routes. The basic result will be the introduction of potential competition. The lib-

---

[1] Civil Aeronautics Board, *Report of the CAB Special Staff on Regulatory Reform*, Washington, D.C., July 1975.

7

eralized entry will place firms at the edge of the market, able and ready to step into that market when consumers are dissatisfied with the existing service and price levels. Because such dissatisfaction would attract new entrants, the existing firms will have an incentive to price competitively and to offer the type of price service options which consumers desire. Certainly, there will be occasions when an outsider will come into the market. This will occur where the new entrant provides a type of service not available from existing carriers and where the new firm is simply more efficient than existing firms. The more important result, however, will be the introduction of potential competition, which in turn will produce more competitive results by existing firms.

The proposed act contains a number of provisions designed gradually but substantially to reduce the barriers to entry into air transportation while providing adequate time for existing carriers to rationalize their operations and adjust to the changing economic environment. Eight major provisions of the act regarding market entry are outlined below.

Policy changes. The board's present declaration of policy, written some thirty-eight years ago, was framed in the context of an infant industry in need of protection, rather than a mature industry capable of operating in a competitive environment. The board has, in the past, relied on its declaration of policy to limit competition. In contrast, the Aviation Act of 1975 proposes to revise this declaration to stress the desirability of competition and to deemphasize the protection of established carriers. The bill proposed by Senator Kennedy has a similar provision and the testimony of John E. Robson, chairman of the Civil Aeronautics Board, before the Senate subcommittee indicates that the CAB also favors this change in the law. It might be added that the Kennedy bill also contains many of the other administration proposals with respect to entry. It should further be noted that the administration is submitting a clarifying amendment to the proposed policy declaration that directs the board to take into account any special factors or circumstances that it finds affects foreign air transportation.

Procedural changes. The board has often refused to hear applications and to render decisions within a reasonable period of time—a violation of the present Federal Aviation Act, which requires that applications be set for hearing and that the issues be resolved "as speedily as possible." It has been able to do so by using procedural motions to settle substantive questions—thus avoiding judicial review.

The Aviation Act of 1975 deals with these matters by proposing procedural changes which ensure that the board will comply with the already existing requirement to hear and decide cases speedily. To speed the disposition of cases the board will be given the option of dismissing any cases it chooses not to hear. However, any cases dismissed will be dismissed for cause and will be reviewable by the court of appeals—thus ending the practice of denying applications by inaction and leaving the applicant with no recourse to court review.

Certificate restrictions. Over a period of years, the board has attached numerous types of conditions and restrictions to the operating certificates held by air carriers. Viewed as a comprehensive whole, the primary effect of these restrictions is to protect the markets of estabished air carriers by preventing other carriers from offering services they would like to provide. These operating restrictions have a particularly pernicious effect: they increase the operating costs (and/or decrease the revenues) of the restricted carrier. Consequently, they permit the restricted carrier's competitors either to operate inefficiently, or to become poor marketers, or to earn monopoly profits.

The Aviation Act of 1975 directs the board to undertake a proceeding to eliminate all existing certificate restrictions within a five-year period and specifically prohibits the board from imposing such restrictions as closed-door stops, single-plane service, mandatory stops, et cetera. The board will be directed to proceed carefully in phasing out the existing restrictions, keeping an eye toward the effects on the carriers and on the traveling public. The phasing of the restriction removal program is dictated by the desire to provide all existing carriers with adequate opportunity to increase their efficiency and adjust their operations to the requirements of a more competitive environment.

Supplemental versus scheduled service. For years doubt has existed about whether paragraph 401(d)(3) of the Federal Aviation Act was intended to prevent supplemental carriers (that is, charter carriers) from also applying for authority to provide scheduled service. The board has recently addressed this question and decided that a supplemental carrier could not hold operating authority as a scheduled carrier. Partly as a result of this legal ambiguity, no supplemental carrier has ever been permitted to undertake scheduled service even though qualified in every other respect. The Aviation Act of 1975 amends paragraph 401(d)(3) so that supplemental air carriers will be allowed to apply for authority to provide scheduled service. This provision is important because it places at the edge of the market a group of carriers that are clearly fit, willing, and able to provide airline service. Mr. Robson has also favored this provision.

Charter service. In the past, the board has generally placed such strict limitations on charter services that their growth has been impaired. Legislation presently before Congress (S. 421 and H.R. 6625) would substantially broaden the availability of charter services. In response to this legislation and substantial public criticism, the board has recently expanded charter availability on its own initiative. The Aviation Act of 1975 incorporates the essential features of S. 421 and H.R. 6625 in order to guarantee the continued availability of charter services which are not unduly restricted. The liberalizing of charter rules is important for two reasons. First, there is no good economic reason to inhibit the provision of service which people are willing to buy and which can profitably be provided. Second, the availability of charter services as a viable alternative to travelers will provide a further competitive check on the prices charged by airlines.

Unserved markets. Under present law, a board finding of public convenience and necessity is required even though the applicant is otherwise fit, willing, and able to serve a particular market and service is not being provided by established firms. When qualified firms are prevented from offering service which established firms are not willing to provide, no useful function is served—not even the dubious function of protecting existing firms, except insofar as their less desirable, roundabout, or indirect service may be protected. The Aviation Act of 1975 deals with this problem by requiring the board to grant approval for qualified applicants wishing to provide nonstop service between points not receiving such service from certificated carriers.

Liberalized exemptions. In 1952 the board exempted operators of small aircraft from the detailed economic regulation administered by the board. So long as they operated aircraft smaller than 12,500 pounds (approximately nineteen seats), commuter air carriers were free to charge whatever price they wished to set and to operate where and when they chose. In 1972 the board increased the exemption to thirty passengers or 7,500 pounds of payload.

The Aviation Act of 1975 liberalizes the exemption from thirty seats to fifty-five. This provision will enable commuter carriers to purchase larger turboprop pressurized aircraft and should materially expand their scope of operations. It will enable these carriers to improve service to small points not attractive to certificated carriers and will foster the development of new aircraft in the thirty- to fifty-five-seat range.

Sale of certificates. The Aviation Act of 1975 provides that after January 1, 1978, a carrier may sell, transfer, or lease any portion of its operating authority to another carrier so long as the purchaser is fit, willing, and able to undertake the transportation and so long as the transfer does not diminish competition. In effect, this provision provides an alternative to the normal requirement for market entry by qualified air carriers, namely, that the transportation be required by public convenience and necessity.

This provision provides carrier management with the opportunity to improve their route network, and it also provides an additional way for new firms to enter the business of scheduled air transportation. Any firm found to be fit, willing, and able to provide air service by the board may purchase route authority from an established carrier. In particular, this may be expected to help the supplemental air carriers who for years have sought to provide scheduled service. This provision will open markets for new firms and will permit existing firms to rationalize their own systems. Since the transfer of operating authority will result in one carrier's authorization being substituted for another's, it will not increase the number of carriers authorized in any market unless an existing certificate holder is not using its route authority.

Discretionary mileage. To ensure a fully efficient air system, some measure of flexibility and entry will be needed in the long term in addition to that provided by the removal of current certificate restrictions. The final provision of the Aviation Act of 1975 dealing with entry is aimed at providing this flexibility over the longer term.

Following the completion of the certificate restriction removal program, the Aviation Act of 1975 will allow each carrier to provide a limited amount of scheduled service in addition to those services specified in its operating certificate. Carriers will be able to use this authority for a gradual expansion and rationalization of their route systems. The expansion process will be gradual since the total amount of new authority created each year will be limited to approximately 5 percent of system operations. Following a period of satisfactory service in markets entered under the discretionary mileage rule, the points served can be added automatically to the carrier's operating certificate without cumbersome procedures.

The entry provisions of the bill serve a number of important objectives:

- They allow the development of low-cost air service tailored to the needs of the market.

- They eliminate waste and inefficiencies associated with past CAB certification practices.

- They allow the threat of potential entry to police the pricing flexibility provisions of the act.

- They insure competitive market behavior under which an appropriate mix of price/service options will be offered to the flying public.

Taken together with the pricing flexibility provisions of the act, the entry provisions will allow competitive forces in the airline industry to set fares, determine service patterns, and police market behavior. In short, the Aviation Act's entry and pricing provisions will substitute the market place for the Civil Aeronautics Board's judgment on crucial issues of air fares and service levels.

Anticompetitive Agreements. A third broad area of present regulatory policy affected by the Aviation Act of 1975 is the Civil Aeronautics Board's grant of antitrust immunity to carrier agreements and to carrier mergers. We have indicated in other parts of this paper the problem with such mergers and agreements, especially capacity agreements. The Aviation Act addresses the problem of antitrust immunity by providing new standards and procedures by which to judge such agreements and mergers. Capacity limitation and pooling agreements will be barred. For mergers, the act provides that all restructurings be judged first by a standard similar to that used in the Clayton Act. Unlike the Clayton Act, however, there will be a weighing of the anticompetitive effects against the transportation convenience and the needs of the communities. Specifically, the amendment provides that a restructuring may not be approved if it would result in a monopoly in any part of the United States or if its effect in any part of the country may be to lessen competition substantially or to tend to create a monopoly. An exception would be if the board finds that the anticompetitive effects are outweighed by the transportation convenience and the needs of the communities and that such needs may not be met in a less anticompetitive manner. Both of these changes will do a great deal to bring airline merger and agreement policy in step with other areas.

Abandonments. Finally, the Aviation Act provides for a new abandonment procedure and, more important, for a new subsidy system. The abandonment provision, in many ways, ratifies the present practice whereby the board has broad powers to control exit from service. The bill in essence provides that a carrier may exit an unprofitable point after sufficient notice to the community and time for adjustment. (Carriers can already exit from almost any unprofitable *market* so long as doing so does not entirely terminate their service to one of the points involved.) The main purpose of introducing this amendment was to ensure that the board at some future date did not change its policy and force carriers to remain in unprofitable points. It was also introduced to encourage carriers to enter new markets, some of which might be marginal. If exit were restricted, carriers would hesitate to enter such markets for fear of being locked in.

Even though the bill's abandonment provision does little to change the existing abandonment practice of the board, it has created a degree of concern in some small towns and cities that carriers will take advantage of the law's new abandonment provisions and leave these communities without air service.

As detailed below, there is little basis for these concerns about the administration's bill. For more than a decade, regulated airline service to small communities has continued to decline. Regulated carriers have dropped nearly one-third of the points they once served.

The answer to this problem, however, is not to stop this abandonment. Carriers should not be forced to serve unprofitable markets. A party forced to provide service will seek to minimize the amount of service it provides, and losses in one community will have to be made up in excess profits in other communities. In addition, it is important to remember that as the regulated carriers left many small markets, their place was taken in most instances by the more efficient and unregulated commuter carriers. What was unprofitable for the regulated was profitable for the commuters, and the willing commuters often provided more frequent and generally better service than the certificated carriers.

The administration has proposed as an amendment to the Aviation Act of 1975 a provision that clearly and simply guarantees air service to all those communities presently served by certificated carriers for up to ten years. The provision also calls for a study to examine both the program created by the administration's proposal and the existing program. Since the subsidy provision was not submitted with the original bill, it would be helpful to outline the major features of the proposal.

13

Guarantee. The proposal guarantees essential air service to all those communities that received such service from a certificated carrier on January 1, 1976.

Effective date. The amendment becomes effective immediately upon signing into law by the President. Within 180 days of enactment, the CAB must announce procedures for applying for subsidies and general definitions of what constitutes "essential service."

Who may apply? Any community now receiving service from a certificated carrier may apply if it feels it is in danger of losing essential service without assistance. Final determination of a community's eligibility for subsidy will be made by the CAB.

What airlines may be subsidized? Any airline the CAB finds to be "fit, willing, and able" to provide service, whether certificated or not, may enter into agreements with the CAB. The board may not give preference to carriers already serving the community in question. It is anticipated that most of the carriers that will receive subsidy will be commuters, but any carrier will be eligible.

Contractual terms. Agreements can be for up to three years and may be renewed up to 1985.

At least annually, the CAB will review average daily enplanements at subsidized points. At points where average daily enplanements are five passengers or less for the preceding twelve months, the community will, after one additional year, be required to pay half the costs of the subsidy. If local or state sources do not provide sufficient assurance that they will make up the difference, the CAB's subsidy obligation will cease.

Service may be discontinued prior to 1985 "only in exceptional circumstances if continued operation is not practical or the need for the service has declined to the point that continued operation is not in the public interest." Agreements must specify maximum rates, types of service, frequency, schedules, and equipment.[2]

Amount of subsidies. Subsidies will be determined by the board on the basis of the costs of providing specific service to specific communities and on the basis of negotiations with interested carriers. The agreement price may not be increased for the benefit of an air

---

[2] Agreements entered into pursuant to this provision must be in conformity with the Federal Property and Administrative Services Act of 1949. That act provides that awards must be made to the person whose offer is "most advantageous to the Government, price and other factors considered." 41 U.S.C., section 253.

carrier, unless cost increases are attributable to action of the federal government.

In summary, the amendment will ensure continued air service to even the smallest communities.

The Arguments Used to Oppose Regulatory Reform

Several arguments have been advanced against the administration's Aviation Act by opponents of regulatory reform. The administration has attempted to answer these arguments on a number of occasions. The Department of Transportation has undertaken research and a number of studies which are directly responsive to these arguments. Despite the fact that we have carefully and, I believe, successfully responded to each of these arguments, they continue to be repeated in the same form and with all the original defects. I would like to review the arguments and the evidence prepared by the administration.

Service to Small Communities. There is a myth that less regulation will result in widespread loss of service—especially to small communities. Although this myth is widespread and is fostered by the aviation industry, it is simply not true. Rather, the present system of economic regulation has permitted the withdrawal of certificated service to many small communities. In contrast, the Aviation Act will be most beneficial to small communities. This section will outline the myth, the true situation, and what the proposed Aviation Act will do for service to small communities. The department has an extensive report on this issue, and this testimony only summarizes that report.

Route certification and restriction. The Civil Aeronautics Board is prohibited by law from controlling either equipment or schedules. The obligations for service contained in the present statute are minimal and, as a result of this factor and of the board's statutory inability to control equipment and scheduling, the board seldom requires that any particular route be flown. In other words, the board requires that a community receive "some" service, not that it receive ten flights a day, or that it be connected to three other communities.

The service may be nonstop, multiple stop, or connecting service. Service between any two points on a carrier's system may be so poor that connecting schedules are not even published in the *Official Airline Guide*. In addition, the board has been quite liberal in allowing carriers to drop points entirely. The result is that all carriers have a large amount of discretion in choosing the markets they wish to enter and the level of service they wish to provide in each market they serve. They do not have to use all of their route authority, and most serve only a tiny fraction of the authority theoretically available to them. This implies that, within constraints imposed by the board, the level of service provided by the airline industry and the markets served are established by market demand rather than by dictates issued by the board. Service is not being provided now because it is a condition of route certification. Carriers will continue to serve profitable routes regardless of whether the regulatory system is changed. On virtually all unsubsidized routes today, air service is profitable. Therefore, we do not expect any reduction of service on the vast majority of the routes because of the Aviation Act. Indeed, as we will demonstrate, service will be greatly improved and the proposed bill contains a guarantee that no community presently served by a certificated carrier will lose air service for ten years.

The easiest way to illustrate the point that the present system provides little help to small communities is to look at one certificate. One of the simplest route certificates is that of Air New England, whereby the company is authorized to serve the thirteen points shown in Figure 1-1. The privilege of serving those thirteen points carries with it an obligation to provide some minimal level of service to each point. This has generally been interpreted by the board to mean that each point must receive one or two daily flights (weekends excluded). So long as it provides one or two flights per day to each point, Air New England may provide service among any city-pairs or to any series of points named on its certificate unless explicitly prohibited by restrictions in the certificate. Air New England has two restrictions: it may not provide nonstop service in the Burlington-New York market, and it may not provide nonstop or single-stop service in the Boston-New York market.

Air New England might serve its cities by establishing a hub at Keene, New Hampshire, for example, and serve every other city from there. This "hub and spoke" type of arrangement would allow Air New England to serve each point with a minimum of twelve flight segments. Alternatively, Air New England could provide nonstop service between all of the seventy-six city-pairs it is authorized to serve.[3]

---

[3] Since Air New England serves thirteen points, it could provide service, in the absence of restrictions, to seventy-eight unduplicated city-pairs. The general formula is $\frac{n(n-1)}{2}$, where n represents the number of points. Since two markets are restricted, Air New England can therefore provide service in seventy-six different city-pair markets.

Figure 1-1

ROUTE CERTIFICATE OF AIR NEW ENGLAND

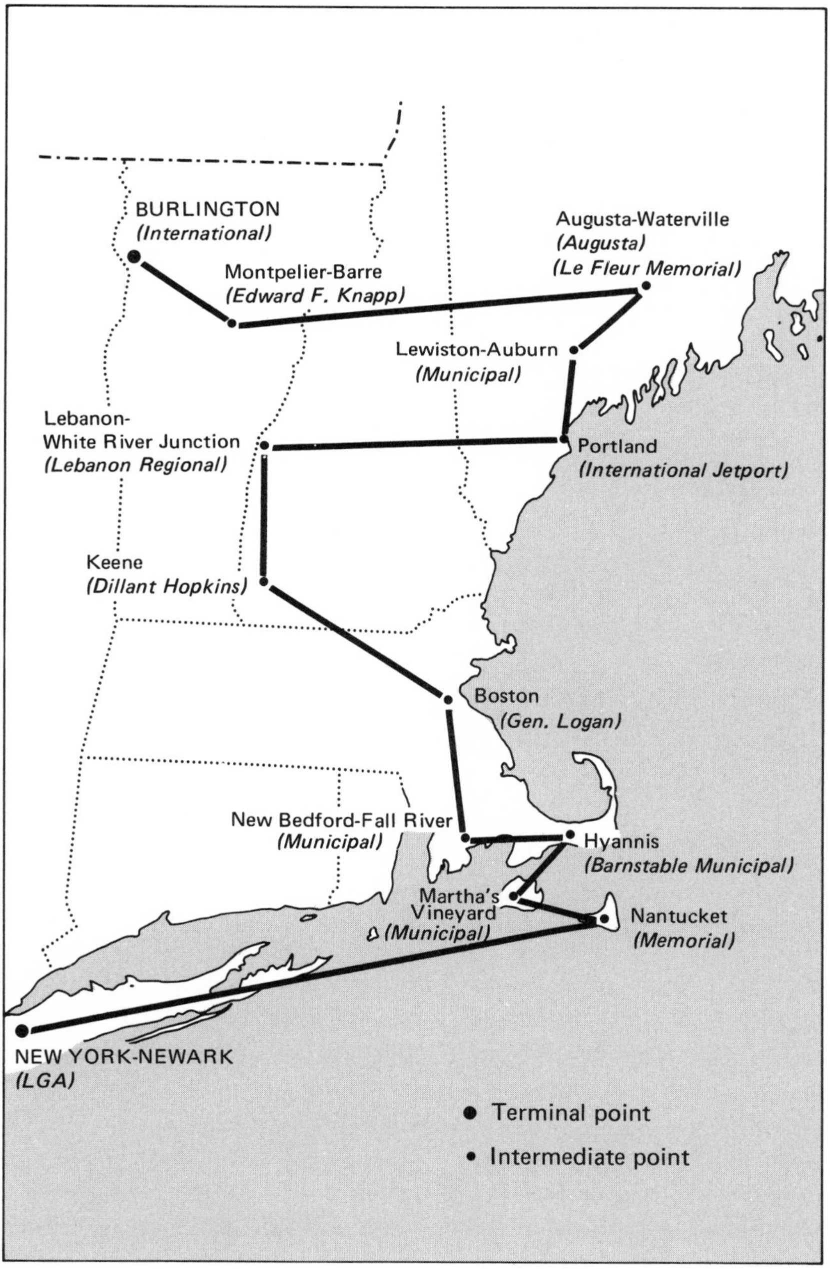

BURLINGTON
(International)

Augusta-Waterville
(Augusta)
(Le Fleur Memorial)

Montpelier-Barre
(Edward F. Knapp)

Lewiston-Auburn
(Municipal)

Lebanon-
White River Junction
(Lebanon Regional)

Portland
(International Jetport)

Keene
(Dillant Hopkins)

Boston
(Gen. Logan)

New Bedford-Fall River
(Municipal)

Hyannis
(Barnstable Municipal)

Martha's
Vineyard
(Municipal)

Nantucket
(Memorial)

NEW YORK-NEWARK
(LGA)

● Terminal point

• Intermediate point

17

In August 1975, Air New England actually served the twenty-four flight segments shown in Figure 1-2. It did not serve fifty-two potential nonstop routes which they were free to serve without restriction.

Several features of the route certificate, the obligations imposed, and the resulting service pattern should be noted.

First, Air New England has a great deal of latitude in choosing the markets it wishes to serve. It may add or drop city-pair markets without board approval. Since any city-pair market can be dropped by Air New England, the only guarantee of service for the points on Air New England's system is that one or two flights per day will continue to be provided. The flights may be to or from any other point served by Air New England; they may arrive at any hour the carrier chooses and with any equipment the carrier chooses. Thus, the obligation imposed on the carrier is minimal, as is the value of the "guarantee" to the community being served.

Second, Air New England has a great deal of unused route authority. It uses only one-third of its potential nonstop authority.

Third, the restrictions applied to Air New England serve to prevent competition rather than to guarantee service. For example, consider the first of Air New England's restrictions—that it must make at least two stops in providing service between Boston and New York. Six other carriers (American, Delta, Eastern, National, Trans World, and United) now provide approximately fifty daily nonstop trips in each direction between Boston and New York. In the face of this competition, Air New England is not likely to become a viable competitor with two-stop service, and it simply does not attempt to participate actively in the market. Thus, the restriction does little to aid the four points (New Bedford, Hyannis, Martha's Vineyard, and Nantucket) which might benefit by forcing Boston-New York traffic to stop through those points. Furthermore, even if the restriction were intended to force traffic through small points, the restriction would help only two of the four points. These would ordinarily be the two largest points. The two smallest points presumably most in need of protection would receive little or none. Air New England's other restriction, that nonstop service may not be offered in the Burlington-New York market, has the identical characteristics of limiting competition without guaranteeing or protecting service.

The restrictions imposed by the board on carriers are aimed basically at keeping competitors out of the markets served by other airlines rather than at compelling service that would not otherwise be provided. North Central Airlines offers an excellent example.

Figure 1-2

FLIGHT SEGMENTS SERVED BY AIR NEW ENGLAND,
AUGUST 1975

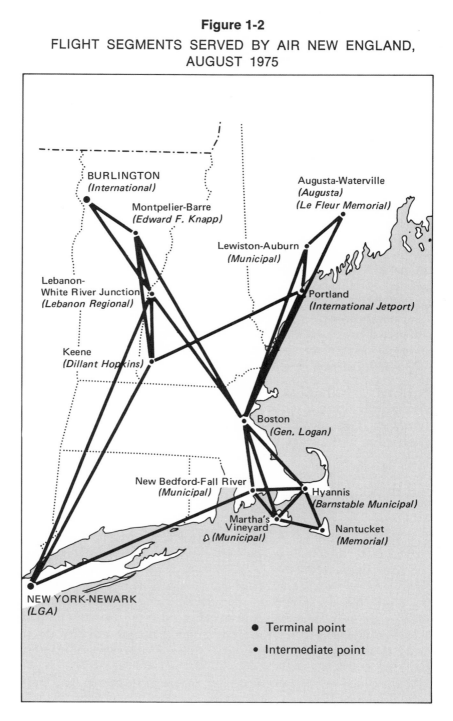

North Central serves thirty-nine points where it is the only certificated air carrier. In each of those thirty-nine monopoly points it faces no route restriction of any kind. It can provide any type of service between each of those monopoly points and any other point on its system. And it can provide any level of service to each of those points it chooses. The only restriction is that one or two daily flights must be scheduled into each point. In contrast, North Central serves twenty-eight points which are also served by other airlines. At each of these points where North Central is not a monopolist, it faces restrictions on the type of service it can provide. In general, the more potential competitors North Central faces at a point and the larger the point is in terms of traffic generated, the more restrictions North Central has in its certificate.

This is the nature of the present system of restrictions imposed by the board—the restrictions limit competition, keep airlines out of competitors' markets, and tell the airlines what they may *not* do. The restrictions imposed by the board do not compel service in particular markets. The net result is that the board is *permissive* in allowing a carrier to provide whatever service it desires in the markets it is authorized to serve. The board is *restrictive* in keeping carriers out of the markets of competitors. By removing those restrictions, the proposed legislation would result in more, not less, air service.

Cross-subsidy. The argument is made by some that regulatory reform will disrupt service to small towns by eliminating cross-subsidies. The contention is that trunk airlines (those airlines not eligible for direct federal subsidy) serve unprofitable markets now because they are able to support such service with profits from other markets. The increased competition fostered by regulatory reform will eliminate the excess profits used to cross-subsidize service in unprofitable, low-density markets, and some communities will lose trunk airline service as a result.

To be persuasive, this argument requires evidence that trunk airlines both lose money on some routes and elect voluntarily to subsidize this unprofitable service out of excess profits earned elsewhere. As seen earlier, airlines have considerable latitude in restricting or eliminating service in unprofitable markets. And, of course, there is no regulatory requirement that they use excess profits to subsidize unprofitable service and certainly no incentive to do so. Thus, it would be surprising to find widespread prevalence of cross-subsidized trunk line service.

For trunk services, the board has not for years encouraged cross-subsidies and has attempted to eliminate them where they do exist.

There is no reason to believe that substantial cross-subsidies exist, first, because airlines are generally free to discontinue unprofitable services and, second, because the airlines have never been able to prove such cross-subsidies.

In response to a request from the Subcommittee on Administrative Practice and Procedure of the Senate Judiciary Committee, United Air Lines provided information on alleged cross-subsidization within its system. When costs and revenues were first allocated, half of United's 327 city-pairs were labeled as unprofitable and a loss of $142 million in serving these city-pairs was estimated. However, only 58 of the city-pairs were unprofitable in the sense that the revenue generated failed to cover incremental costs. The remaining city-pairs, while not covering fully allocated costs, did have revenues which more than covered incremental costs and United had no intention of dropping them. Of the 58 unprofitable city-pairs, 4 were flown for the purpose of repositioning aircraft, 17 were flown because of their traffic-generating ability, 8 were shorter than 60 miles in length (and in no need of trunk service), and the remaining 29 were the only ones which might be detrimentally affected by even total deregulation.

As the Senate subcommittee's report pointed out, these twenty-nine flight segments accounted for only 0.5 percent of United's revenue passenger miles, and the annual loss associated with those routes was only $5.5 million. This estimate is, incidentally, equal to only 0.3 percent of United's system-wide revenues, and equal to only 3 percent of United's overall profits for 1974. Thus, the amount of cross-subsidy in United's system is quite small. We agree with the Senate subcommittee and with others that this is typical of the industry in general.

Abandonment. What is the situation at small communities? Trunk airlines operate jet airplanes with ninety or more seats. The smallest aircraft operated by local service carriers usually have more than fifty seats. Many of the local service carriers are converting to aircraft with ninety or more seats. Realizing that it is uneconomic for a large aircraft to stop to pick up one or two passengers, the CAB has generally permitted carriers, especially unsubsidized carriers, to abandon service to most unprofitable cities—those where only few passengers board. As a result, many small towns have lost certificated air service. Since 1962, more than 170 points have lost such service, and certificated carriers now serve only about 400 communities in the forty-eight states.

What caused this decline in service and loss of service at many points? A variety of factors are involved, including the development of the Interstate Highway System, which made regional airports more attractive and eliminated the need for many nearby airports. But other important factors are associated with the present system of economic regulation and the present subsidy program. The board's route-strengthening program was designed to let local service carriers participate in larger markets. The goal was to allow such carriers to earn profits with which to cross-subsidize other routes. The board's 1972 study of air service to small communities could find no evidence of cross-subsidies resulting from the route-strengthening program. However, it did transform the local service carriers into miniature trunk line carriers—shifting their emphasis away from service to small towns towards service on major routes with larger aircraft.

A second factor in the decline of service to small communities is the present subsidy system which has at times provided carriers incentives to procure ever larger aircraft.[4] As local service carriers have hastened to convert to all-jet fleets, service to small communities has become less attractive to them. Thus, the present regulatory system has not protected air service to small communities. Indeed, if anything, it has hastened abandonments of service at many points.

The withdrawal of certificated service from small points is continuing rapidly, and it may be increasing in tempo. Between 1970 and 1975 the number of communities with populations under 100,000 receiving certificated service declined by about 14 percent. Weekly flight frequencies dropped by about 25 percent. At the start of 1975, certificated carriers served forty-three points in the continental forty-eight states which boarded ten or fewer passengers per day. Fifteen months later, certificated service had been discontinued at one-third of those points, and abandonment or suspension proceedings were under way for several other points. As local service carriers continue to increase the proportion of jet aircraft in their fleets, service to small communities will become increasingly expensive, along with subsidy needs. As a result, the pressures to abandon the smallest points will continue to increase.

Growth of commuter service. Fortunately, at a time when certificated service is declining in many areas, many small communities are getting better air service than ever before. They receive service from unregulated commuter air carriers. These carriers, flying small aircraft and exempt from board regulation, are able to enter or leave

---

[4] George C. Eads, *The Local Service Airline Experiment* (Washington, D.C.: The Brookings Institution, 1972), pp. 134-35.

markets as they choose and to set their own prices free of board interference. Although still tiny in comparison with the certificated carriers, commuter carriers have grown far faster than certificated carriers during recent years. In many ways they offer service superior to that of the regulated carriers at small points. They tend to offer greater flight frequency and lower fares over short distances. The larger commuters have typically been in the industry between ten and twenty years, offer excellent reliability, and are far less likely to abandon small points than are certificated carriers, even though they are under no theoretical obligation to continue service at a small point. Commuter air carriers now provide scheduled and unsubsidized service to 230 communities with a population under 100,000. At 150 of these communities, commuter carriers provide the only scheduled air service. These cities—which tend to be the smallest receiving scheduled air service—receive service not because of economic regulation. Rather, the smallest communities receive service only because of an exemption from economic regulation. If these smallest of cities were to depend solely upon certificated air carriers for service, many would be receiving no service at all.

Small communities will benefit from enactment of the proposed legislation. As air travel throughout the nation increases, so will the "feeder" traffic generated by small communities. The result will be a "trickle down" or "bootstrap" effect—more people will travel from small points to use the more heavily traveled parts of the system, resulting in greater flight frequencies and still more traffic being generated. The liberalization in the size-of-aircraft restriction applicable to commuter airlines will help all but the very smallest of our communities.

Subsidized service. The present subsidy program was intended to guarantee service to small, isolated communities. The widespread abandonment of service by certificated carriers attests that it has not served this purpose. The unsubsidized commuter airlines are the bulwark of service to small communities. And much of the current subsidy pays for services that the market would be willing to provide at no cost to the government.

The Aviation Act makes an important change in the current subsidy system. For those communities receiving certificated service, the present subsidy program is retained, although it has not had a noticeable effect in encouraging carriers to continue service to the smallest of communities. But beyond this, the legislation contains a meaningful guarantee of continued service to small communities. Every community now receiving service from regulated carriers will be guaranteed a continuation of scheduled air service for ten years. In the event that a regulated carrier abandons a point and that point would be left with no scheduled air service, the board is empowered and directed to contract with a commuter air carrier to provide continued air service to that community. This guarantee of continued service at small points is immensely superior to the prospects faced by such communities today. If certificated carriers abandon today, there is no guarantee of continued service.

In summary, air service to small communities is not endangered by this legislation. Indeed, the decline of air service to small communities under the present regulatory system (and the fact that the present regulatory system has often hastened that decline) is one of the reasons why this legislation is necessary. The proposed legislation will enhance the situation of small communities both by improving the health of the aviation system in general and by providing a guarantee of continued service to the smallest of points for ten years.

Market Chaos. The myth that regulatory reform will lead to "market chaos" consists of a series of allegations which seem intended to frighten or to confuse. A picture is painted of an industry responding to increased management discretion by rushing around in blind confusion, with all carriers concentrating on a few markets, abandoning scores of others, and generally destroying each other. It is alleged that passengers will be unable to make reservations; that nobody will know from day to day which airline flies which routes and at what fares; that airlines will not transfer baggage or make interline reservations; that airport operators will not know which carriers will use their facilities; that long-range planning will be impossible; and that chaos will result. In short, the market will not function.

Why the airline industry is so different from other industries that are not regulated and are not bent on self-destruction is not clear, but the argument is made nevertheless. There is no justification for such an argument. But this chaos argument is often made as a defense or as an excuse for continued anticompetitive practices. For example, in the historic electrical equipment conspiracy cases in the early 1960s, the claim was made that without price-fixing and market-sharing agreements among suppliers, the markets for turbines, generators, and similar equipment would become chaotic. Prices would fluctuate excessively and electrical utilities would be deprived of stable sources of supply. The court was unconvinced.

Most markets are unregulated and these markets function in a generally efficient way without chaos. Firms make long-run commitments and customers are able to secure services. It is in the suppliers' interest to give orderly and dependable service. The unregulated portions of the airline industry operate in this fashion. Commuter airlines are not subject to economic regulation, but they make reservations, adhere to schedules, and make long-run plans. Their fares are known, they transfer baggage, and in every respect they render service the public wants and is willing to pay for. Service in intrastate markets is also available for comparison. There is no chaos there.

The argument that there will be a headlong rush to provide service only on well-traveled routes is clearly refuted by the service rendered by commuter airlines and by the experience in the intrastate markets. Unregulated and unsubsidized commuter airlines have actively moved into low-density markets. They have done so because people are willing to pay for airline service in these markets, not because of regulatory requirements. There are now some 200 commuter airlines carrying some 7 million passengers annually, mostly in low-density markets. Their air fares, moreover, are comparable to certificated carriers' fares on comparable routes. Commuter traffic is the fastest growing segment of the airline industry.

Where price and entry regulation has been relaxed in the California and Texas intrastate markets, service has not bunched into a few major routes. In fact, in Texas, service to relatively small communities such as Harlingen has improved markedly. And intrastate carriers have taken the lead in dispersing traffic out of the major hub airports. Service from satellite airports benefits passengers by reducing their total door-to-door travel time. In California, for example, instead of service being concentrated at the major San Francisco and Los Angeles airports, it has been dispersed to twelve airport pairs.

A final refutation of the chaos myth is that airlines today use far less of their operating authority than they could. This proves that airline managements are fully capable of assessing markets. They would not respond to a lessening of economic controls by rushing about blindly to the detriment of all. To put this in perspective, carriers now use less than 20 percent of their certificate authority and often do not use all of their certificate authority even in major markets (see Table 1-1). So, considerable discretion and flexibility does exist in the system today. Not enough, to be sure, and not necessarily in the right places, but a significant amount. And this has not led to chaos.

Predatory Practices and Cutthroat Competition. Some opponents of regulatory reform contend that the act will lead to predatory price

Table 1-1
TOP-RANKED MARKETS WITH UNUSED NONSTOP AUTHORITY

Market	Rank	Annual O&D Passengers [a]
New York–Washington	3	1,638,310
Chicago–Detroit	13	590,490
Boston–Washington	15	579,360
Buffalo–New York	19	526,670
Boston–Philadelphia	27	409,360
New York–Rochester	28	408,030
Los Angeles–Seattle	31	376,670
Miami–Philadelphia	57	260,600
Boston–Los Angeles	62	252,900
New Orleans–New York	63	252,860
Boston–Miami	69	238,970
Detroit–Los Angeles	71	237,600
Miami–Washington	72	236,680

[a] O&D refers to "origin and destination" passengers.
Source: Civil Aeronautics Board, *Origin-Destination Survey of Airline Passenger Traffic*, for the 12 months ended March 31, 1975, table 6.

cutting as firms try to drive others out of the market. This will not occur under the Aviation Act, and in fact the bill will reduce the prospect of predatory actions.

The provisions of the bill for price flexibility will change the form of competition rather than increase its intensity. Airlines now rely principally on service competition to attract passengers from competitors. The Aviation Act will allow them to compete on the basis of both price and service. Thus, price flexibility will change the emphasis of competitive efforts, but there is no reason to believe it will lead to ruinous conditions in the industry, that is, a condition under which rates are chronically below fully allocated costs.

Equally important, the provisions of the bill for entry greatly reduce the prospects for predatory conduct. Since predatory competition entails certain short-term losses, a rational firm would engage in such conduct only where there existed a strong prospect of obtaining monopoly profits either by driving other firms from the market or by disciplining the market. Two conditions are essential for predatory pricing: (1) the predator firm must have superior resources which give it greater staying power to achieve the purpose of driving the rivals out of the market; and (2) there must be high barriers to entry to enable the predator firm to recoup its losses.[5] In other words, the prospect of eventually realizing monopoly profits from the predatory conduct must be high. Where entry or reentry can occur relatively easily whenever prices return to levels at or above cost, the incentive to engage in such behavior is eliminated. By reducing the barriers to entry, the Aviation Act will also reduce the prospect of successful predation. There are no effective entry barriers other than regulatory barriers in the airline industry.

Finally, actual experience in markets where price competition and entry have been allowed confirms these conclusions. The experience of the California and Texas intrastate carriers certainly suggests that price competition in the airline industry does not have destructive results.

The underlying economic characteristics of the industry along with the reduction in the barriers to entry resulting from the Aviation Act indicate that predatory pricing does not pose a serious problem in the airline industry. In addition, it should be noted that the Aviation Act itself prohibits rates below variable cost and, of course, remedies under the antitrust statutes or under section 411 of the Federal Aviation Act, which prohibits unfair competition, will continue to apply.

Regulatory Reform Will Lead to Monopoly. It is sometimes argued that regulatory reform will eventually lead to monopoly. This would only happen if there were significant economies of scale in the industry. Such cost conditions do not exist in the airline industry. It is sometimes claimed that scale economies are present in the industry because large aircraft have lower costs per seat-mile than small aircraft. But both small and large airline firms are able to purchase large aircraft. They will do so to take advantage of aircraft-related scale economies in markets where large aircraft are justified.

The issue of scale economies in the airline industry has been extensively researched, and practical experience confirms the research findings that small firms can operate as efficiently as large ones. The report by the Subcommittee on Administrative Practice and Procedure notes, for example, that a thorough search of the literature by Pro-

---

[5] See the extended discussion in Phillip Areeda and Donald F. Turner, "Predatory Pricing and Related Practices Under Section 2 of the Sherman Act," *Harvard Law Review*, vol. 88 (1975), p. 697.

fessor Sam Peltzman reveals unanimity of view on this point.[6] The intrastate experience of small airlines like Pacific Southwest Airlines (PSA), Air California, and Southwest Airlines competing successfully with major trunk carriers is also convincing.

Moreover, for industry concentration to lead to monopoly abuses, the surviving firms would have to be able to bar new entrants. Otherwise, competing firms would reenter markets when the existing firms tried to raise prices. But other than regulatory barriers, there are no effective entry barriers in this industry. The relevant technology is generally available. Aircraft can be acquired. Airport facilities can be leased. The necessary management structure can be created. All this may not be easy, but it can be done by corporations where there are prospects of future long-term profitability. It is important to recognize that under competitive conditions there may be only a few competitors on some low- and medium-density routes. But they will not be able to exploit their monopoly power because the potential of entry will discipline their market actions. This is the reason that the bill provides for both price and entry flexibility. The Air Transport Association of America (ATA) wishes to continue severe entry restrictions while allowing price flexibility. Their intent is obvious. Such a policy would ensure that airline monopoly power on low- and medium-density routes would not be restrained by the threat of competition from new entrants.

In short, this is not an industry which is inherently monopolistic, and the fear of monopoly emerging is unfounded. Ironically, the present regulatory system is the only "hope" for monopoly. As Professor Richard Caves said at a recent seminar on air transportation:

> The preclusion of entry by new airlines has greatly reduced competitive pressure on the certificated carriers for efficiency and performance, and the preclusion of entry into individual city-pair markets—whether by newcomers or airlines established elsewhere—has removed the one ultimately effective curb on the tendency to high concentration in the individual city-pair market. These entry restrictions are all the more damaging to the industry in the long run because airlines sometimes disappear from natural causes, and indeed the mortality rate is increased by the rigidities of the certificated route structures that consign some carriers to unprofitable route structures and promote "failing-firm" mergers.

[6] U.S. Congress, Senate, Subcommittee on Administrative Practice and Procedure of the Judiciary Committee, *Report on Civil Aeronautics Board Practices and Procedures*, 94th Congress, 1st session, February 1975.

Therefore the regulated industry has a long-run tendency toward fewer and fewer airlines.[7]

Airlines Are Like Public Utilities. Opponents of regulatory reform have argued that the present restrictive regulatory system is required by the public utility aspects of the airline industry.

This claim has two possible facets. One is that airlines, like utilities, are natural monopolies and thus must be regulated to prevent monopoly abuses. The natural monopoly argument, however, requires that there be long-run economies of scale among airline firms. Only if unit costs decrease with firm size can a few large firms drive out the competition in a freely competitive market and establish monopoly power. Where there are substantial economies of scale, economic regulation is often felt to be in the public interest.

But as indicated above, airlines are not subject to increasing returns to scale. There is widespread agreement among scholars of airline economics that small firms can be as efficient as large ones so that numerous firms would coexist in a competitive industry. These findings of academic scholars are reinforced by actual experience in many markets. Small and large firms compete head-to-head in many markets, with large firms having no particular cost or marketing advantage. There is simply no substance to the argument that airlines are natural monopolies and thus should be regulated like public utilities.

It is also alleged that the current system of regulation is required because the industry, like a public utility, has an obligation to provide service. Public utilities are regulated because they have a natural monopoly. Because of this monopoly they are required to provide service to all customers and prices are regulated. The obligation to serve is imposed because the consumer has no alternative to turn to, and price regulation is required because otherwise customers would be exploited by the monopoly. In other words, utilities are not regulated because they are required to serve; they are regulated and required to serve because they are monopolies. This is not the airline situation because airlines are not natural monopolies.

The facts regarding the airline's obligation to serve also contradict the "public utility" argument. As indicated earlier, airlines have great discretion over the type of service they choose to provide to a given point. They also have great latitude in deciding whether to

---

[7] Richard Caves, remarks at Conference on Regulatory Reform and the Aviation Act of 1975, Transportation Center, Northwestern University, Evanston, Illinois, February 29-March 1, 1976.

serve points on their system at all. Of the 543 points served in 1963 by certificated carriers, only 394 now receive certificated service. Most of the points abandoned by certificated carriers are now served by commuter airlines that are unregulated by the CAB. Thus, it is clear that the "obligation to serve" is not what ensures continued service.

Airlines Are Unique. Some have argued that the airline industry is somehow a unique or different industry—that other industries can exist without regulation, but not the airline industry. Sometimes this is stated in terms of the complexity of the airline system, and the specific examples given are the need to interline and to maintain elaborate reservation and baggage systems. Another point is the inability of the industry to inventory a finished product. Once the plane departs, all the empty seat capacity is gone. Other industries can inventory in slack times and then sell their inventory and make their profits in better times. The airline industry cannot "inventory." And the airline industry is subject to large changes in demand, and to the changing wants and pocketbooks of tourists.

The airline industry is not unique. It is a service industry, and it has the same problems and opportunities as many other service industries. The airline industry's unique characteristic among service industries (excluding other transportation modes) is that it is regulated.

As an example, the hotel/motel industry is much like the airline industry. It is large, nationwide, has the same "inventory" problem, has a complex reservation system, and is subject to the whims of tourists. Obviously, there are many differences, but the similarities are there.

One of the differences is that the hotel/motel business is not regulated. As a result, one of these service industries is constantly before the federal government for one reason or another, while the other industry devotes its skills and energies to business management; one of the industries offers the consumer a wide variety of product offerings at a wide variety of prices, while the other industry does not.

The essential point is: The special circumstances of the airline industry are the result of regulation, not of any inherently unique features of the business.

How Can Fares Drop If Costs Do Not Drop? The Air Transport Association has argued that it is illusory to think that fares will be lower under regulatory reform. The argument is that fares cannot drop if the prices of fuel, labor, aircraft, and other supplies purchased by the industry do not drop.

Fares will decrease with a lessening of economic controls not because the costs of inputs will decrease but because fewer inputs will be used per passenger. With increased emphasis on price competition, costly service competition will decrease. Air carrier productivity will therefore increase, and this will provide the basis for fare decreases.

Of course, fares will not come down in every market. Also, in an economic environment characterized by continuing inflation, costs will tend to rise. But the important point is that these costs will increase less in a more competitive environment than they would have increased if the present regulatory system were continued. As carriers achieve efficiencies, the pricing and entry/exit provisions of the act will assure that any cost savings resulting from those efficiencies will be passed on to travelers and shippers. Average prices will be lower, as a result, than they would be under a continuation of the present regulatory system.

Carriers will be less likely to compete for customers by overscheduling flights. As a result, planes will fly more fully loaded, and the costs per passenger will drop. Wasteful route restrictions will be eliminated, and carriers will be allowed gradually to rationalize their systems through the discretionary mileage and the certificate transfer provisions of the act. This will further increase the efficient utilization of resources and reduce per-passenger costs, even though the prices of inputs stay the same or rise gradually.

The experience in the California and Texas intrastate markets shows that the reduction of economic controls can, under certain market conditions, lead to substantially lower fares. The intrastate carriers have been faced with the same rising fuel, equipment, construction, and labor costs as interstate carriers, yet their fares are considerably lower for comparable routes.

Safety. Some carriers have argued that increased competition will lead to lower profits, which will lead airlines to cut costs and the amount they spend for safety. Safety is a primary concern for all, and the Aviation Act of 1975 will not in any way endanger safety. The basic assurance that airlines will fly safely is not provided by economic regulation, but rather by strict enforcement of federal safety regulations. Congress has recognized this separation between safety and economic matters by giving the economic regulation to the

CAB and the safety regulation to the Department of Transportation and the Federal Aviation Administration. The Congress has also established the National Transportation Safety Board as one independent agency for monitoring transportation safety and for fact-finding purposes. The department and the administration have repeatedly stated that they will not permit any diminution in the strict enforcement of the safety regulations. The Aviation Act only affects economic regulation.

The Aviation Act of 1975 continues in its declaration of policy the mandate that the board consider "the importance of the highest degree of safety in air commerce" as being in the public interest and in accordance with the public convenience and necessity.

Airline Financing. Some have argued that airlines will not be able to obtain needed financing under a new system of regulation. The argument takes two forms. Some claim that airlines must always be strictly regulated or they will not be able to attract capital. Others argue that the current financial difficulties of certain airlines coupled with the large future capital requirements of the industry are so serious as to preclude at this time regulatory modernization. Both arguments are faulty.

It is clear that, under the present regulatory system, insulation of the industry from the functioning of competitive market forces has not resulted in high industry profitability. In fact, returns in the airline industry have been low, and there are questions today about the industry's basic financial health. Effective public service can only be provided by an industry that is financially strong. The industry must be able to compete for funds in the capital markets in order to replace aging equipment and to satisfy future growth requirements.

Although air carriers have been able to attract needed capital in the past, the performance of the present regulatory system does not provide confidence in the future. Regulation has contributed to a cyclical pattern of carrier earnings. Only twice in the past eighteen years has the industry's return on investment exceeded 10 percent. The average return on investment in this period has been less than 6 percent. Although industry revenues grew in this period from $2.3 billion to more than $15 billion annually, this growth was not matched by growth in profitability.

Each successive cyclical downturn in the last ten years has left several carriers weaker. The industry and its regulator can no longer count on long-term growth rates high enough to shield each and every carrier from temporary downturns in traffic. The prospects are for lower rates of growth and unfortunately, under the current regulatory system, for continued low profits. If something is not done to correct the situation, we may not be as fortunate in the next cyclical downturn as we were in this most recent one.

Public statements by lenders indicate their apprehension about financial prospects for the airline industry. Certainly, the present system of airline regulation is not creating lender or investor confidence. The industry is now emerging from the low part of a business cycle. The current difficulties faced by some air carriers in obtaining financing must be attributed primarily to the industry's cyclical history of generally poor financial performance. The poor profitability of airlines gives investors and lenders little encouragement that weaker carriers will be able to achieve reasonable and consistent average earnings in the future. This poor past performance took place during a period of rigid government regulation.

The roller coaster cycle of airline earnings and investment is costly and leads to inefficiencies. The need is to reform regulation in a way that will result in more earnings stability and that will encourage more even investment patterns. The problem with an industry which is as dynamic and as naturally competitive as the airline industry is that, under present regulation, there is no way to assure a stable, guaranteed return and a consistent pattern of capital investment, while at the same time to encourage efficient, reasonably priced air service that is properly adapted to market needs.

As has been pointed out above, the existing airline regulatory system does not work well. This is particularly so in an inflationary, mature-growth environment because managers do not have enough flexibility in pricing to adjust to cost changes, test their markets, or price in response to differing conditions in different markets. Nor has the regulatory system shown itself able to cope adequately with a dynamic industry whose fortunes follow the economy.

Although immediate airline expansion needs are modest on average, the industry will need significant numbers of new aircraft in the next ten years.[8] In addition to replacement of older, noisier, and less efficient equipment, the industry needs to secure a new generation of quieter, more efficient aircraft, and to acquire additional capacity to satisfy normal growth in demand for air travel.

---

[8] In the next three years, we estimate that the investment requirements for the airline industry will average about $1.5 billion annually, primarily to replace older, less economical aircraft. The need for industry-wide financing through earnings and external capital sources will increase after 1978, when continued traffic growth will create a need for major additions to airline capacity. Estimated annual industry capital investment in 1979 and beyond will be more than $3.5 billion.

33

The phased price and entry/exit provisions of the Aviation Act, including the flexibility to sell and exchange routes, will allow air carrier managements to improve their financial position. This will enable them to attract the capital required in the next decade. The regulatory reform provided in this bill is necessary if the industry is to be fully responsive to the public demand for its services during this period.

The bill is phased to avoid near-term disruptions of airline finances. Pricing flexibility is gradually phased in over three years. The liberalized entry provisions do not become fully effective until the sixth year. During the transition period, the industry will be profitable and gains in productivity from the elimination of regulatory inefficiencies should be passed on to the public in the form of fares lower than they would otherwise be.

This is an ideal time to initiate regulatory reform. Under the phased program of the Aviation Act of 1975, the transition to a more competitive and less regulated industry will occur during a period in the airline financial cycle when excess capacity does not exist. Corporations and managements will be able to accommodate to change in an orderly manner without financial turbulence or disruption in service. The industry will be buoyed by rising demand and tight industry capacity. Carriers will be able to adapt their route structures to become more efficient, and they will be able to price to reflect cost and demand conditions.

In the transition period and beyond, managements that are able to convince investors and lenders of their efficiency and their ability to earn market-required financial returns will be able to secure equity and debt financing, and their firms should prosper and expand. Less efficient managements, unable to earn adequate returns, will not be able to attract capital. This is as it should be. Corporations in this position will have strong incentives to acquire more efficient managements, or gradually to shrink their operations by withdrawing from unprofitable routes and by selling assets. The working of competition in the marketplace will ensure that the benefit of improved efficiency in air transportation is passed on to consumers through the medium of lower rates.

Carrier managements will be encouraged not to expand excessively and not to compete for market share if by so doing their corporations become insufficiently profitable to obtain needed financing. By the same token, the public will be protected because competition will prevent excess profits.

This result does not equate to instability and chaos. It does represent a requirement that more reliance be placed on the discipline of the marketplace in regulating efficiency and productivity. Under a less regulated environment, financial requirements will undoubtedly be as stringent for airlines as they are for other industries. The high-forecast long-term capital requirements and the heavy competition for funds will force air carriers to be profitable if they are to be able to grow in meeting the public demand for air service. There is no substitute for earnings if the industry is to attract capital. This requires that air carriers be able to earn financial returns related to the risk associated in creditors' and investors' minds with the industry. The market will set the required rate of return, and air carriers will be able to attract needed capital.

Airport Financing. Air transportation regulatory reform will not result in erratic air service nor will it undermine the stability of airport/airline financial arrangements which are needed to finance airport facilities.

An argument has been raised that enactment of the Aviation Act will make airport planning and financing difficult. This assertion is based on the assumption that major dislocations and disruptions will accompany implementation of the Aviation Act. This assumption is inconsistent with the phasing provision of the act, does not take into account the improved health of the industry which will result from the act, and ignores the prospect of increased traffic.

In the end, it is the traffic generated by the carriers serving a community that is the basic guarantor of airport revenues. Airports are generally financed by bonds which are guaranteed by the revenues that the airport generates. The Aviation Act, by promoting greater productivity and efficiency in the air transportation system, and by passing on savings from greater productivity in the form of lower prices, will promote greater travel and growth in the system. This will increase the traffic base which supports airport financing.

The air service will be increased throughout the system under the Aviation Act of 1975—from large metropolitan areas to small communities. Service to the public will be greater at large, medium, and small hub points as well as nonhub airports. Thus, all categories of airports will potentially be able to depend on a large traffic base.

Where congestion and capacity limits exist at some large hub airports, growth can be handled at less congested or underutilized facilities, or by means of new traffic-connecting complexes. This will improve the financial viability of satellite airports.

Today, airports are generally financed through revenue bonds. These bonds are purchased on the strength of long-term (fifteen- to thirty-year) obligations of the carriers serving an airport. Airline contracts generally contain limited termination provisions. An airline obligation to underwrite an airport bond is only as strong as the basic financial strength of the carrier. A guarantee from a weak carrier even under today's system may be no guarantee at all. Moreover, today if service becomes uneconomical, carriers will withdraw despite the guarantee.

Nothing in the act limits the right of airport owners to require a carrier to assume a long-term financial obligation before operating out of an airport. Airports will continue to have the power to protect their financial arrangements. Entry and exit, in this respect, will not be "free" from the point of view of an airline management. Just as corporations assume long-term aircraft leases and building leases, so must they assume responsibility for long-term airport facilities leases. The act does not change this. But by creating a healthier, more financially stable airline industry, the act will strengthen the ability of carriers to service their airport obligations. The airport obligations themselves will remain as an important stabilizing influence on air service, in that carriers will tend to plan and operate for the long term, thus allowing airport managers to plan and finance for the long term.

The federal government itself must plan airport and airway facilities for the long-term future. The administration believes that this act could well ease the planning task. Airline service will be stable. The air transportation system will continue to grow and evolve to meet developing public needs. Airport and airway planning will be required to reflect, as they do today, public needs. Reliance on competitive market forces rather than on regulators' perceptions will allow a better air system to evolve—responsive to the public need and with less regulatory lag.

The contention that a lessening of economic controls will result in erratic service reflects a lack of perspective or unfamiliarity with unregulated markets. Most industries are not regulated, yet they provide stable and dependable service at known prices. They do so because it is in their self-interests to supply orderly and dependable service. A direct comparison can also be made with intrastate airlines and airport concession holders. They are not regulated by the board and they make long-run commitments for airport facilities. Indeed the experience of intrastate airlines strongly suggests that the reduction of federal regulation would result in more extensive use of airports. In both California and Texas there is far greater flight frequency than in comparable interstate markets.

The regulatory system has not provided stability and continuity of service on which airport operators can base long-range plans. Regulated carriers have discontinued service at many airports. Of the 543 points served by regulated air carriers in 1963, only 394 now receive certificated service. In most of the abandoned points commuter airlines stepped in and provided service after the regulated carriers left. Thus, airports receive air service only if there is an economic demand for the service. Airport operators will be able to plan and finance airport facilities for which there is an economic demand. They are not protected by the regulatory system.

PART TWO

THE INTRASTATE MARKET AND COMMUTER AIRLINE INDUSTRY EXPERIENCE

Advocates of reduced economic regulation of the airline industry frequently cited the experience in the Texas and California intrastate markets to show the desirable results of less regulation: frequent service, lower fares, and higher load factors. Critics answered that these intrastate markets were unique and did not provide a sound basis for the view that reduced regulation would result in lower air fares in the interstate markets. The first paper in this part is the summary report from a study reviewing the intrastate experience and comparing it to interstate markets.

The experience of the commuter airline industry was also drawn upon in the debate over aviation regulatory reform. Service provided in aircraft with fewer than thirty seats is exempt from economic regulation by the CAB. Operating within this exemption, a vigorous and rapidly growing industry of more than 200 commuter airlines has developed to provide service for smaller communities not served by the certificated carriers. This experience was cited by advocates of aviation reform as indicative of efficient, low-cost service that would follow in larger markets from reduced CAB regulation. Critics responded that in fact commuters were high-cost carriers and did not operate as efficiently as the certificated carriers. The second paper in this part analyzes this issue.

2

THE INTRASTATE AIR REGULATION EXPERIENCE IN TEXAS AND CALIFORNIA

Simat, Helliesen and Eichner, Inc.

The Intrastate Air Carrier Experience

Although the intrastate portion of the revenue air passenger miles carried by U.S. carriers accounts for less than 2 percent of all U.S. air traffic, this small sector attracted a great deal of attention during 1975. Much of the interest focused on three small carriers, in California and Texas, which succeeded in earning profits and providing a high level of service, while keeping fares well below those charged by the larger interstate carriers. This phenomenon is particularly striking, because these three carriers are not subject to regulation by the U.S. Civil Aeronautics Board (CAB), which controls both the rates and the routes of the trunk and local service carriers. Rather, these intrastate carriers fall within the jurisdiction of the California Public Utilities Commission (PUC) and the Texas Aeronautics Commission (TAC), respectively. These agencies have objectives, processes, and powers which differ significantly from those of the CAB, and they have produced a regulatory environment within each state which is distinctly different from that maintained by the CAB. It is the intent of this study to analyze the intrastate experience as compared to other domestic services, and thereby to assess the impact of differing regulatory environments on the aviation system.

Intrastate Operations in California. California is currently served by two major intrastate carriers, Pacific Southwest Airlines (PSA) and Air California. PSA, which initiated operations in 1949 and is by far

This paper is edited from *An Analysis of the Intrastate Air Carrier Regulatory Forum*, vol. 1, *Summary Report*, prepared for the Department of Transportation, Office of the Secretary, Air Transportation Policy Staff, January 1976.

Table 2-1

DIFFERENTIAL BETWEEN INTRASTATE AND
INTERSTATE FARES IN CALIFORNIA, 1972

Length of Haul	Intrastate Fares Per Mile	Interstate Fares Per Mile	Percent Interstate Above Intrastate
Very short haul (65 miles)	16.923¢	23.585¢	39.4
Short haul (109 miles)	9.363¢	16.858¢	80.0
Short-medium haul (338–373 miles)	5.021¢	9.685¢	92.9

Source: Simat, Helliesen and Eichner, Inc., *An Analysis of the Intrastate Air Carrier Regulatory Forum,* vol. 2, table 10, p. 47.

the larger of the two, serves a total of twelve points, with the focus of its operations centered between Los Angeles, Burbank, Ontario, and Long Beach on the one hand, and the San Francisco Bay area on the other.[1] Air California, which began operations in 1967, serves a total of ten points, and its largest market is between Santa Ana and the San Francisco Bay area.[2]

These carriers are characterized by a distinctive combination of features which have drawn national attention to their operations. In particular:

- They have offered the public fares substantially below those offered in similar interstate markets.

- They have provided high levels of service and have maintained excellent safety records.

- They have generated dramatic increases in traffic volume.

- At the same time, the carriers themselves have been profitable.

The fare differential between California intrastate fares and those for markets of similar length in other parts of the country is graphically illustrated in Table 2-1. These figures, drawn from a 1973 Western Airlines exhibit, show that fares in a sample of CAB-regulated domestic markets outside of California range from 39 to 93 percent higher than those in effect in California intrastate markets of comparable length.

---

[1] PSA also serves Sacramento, San Diego, Fresno, Stockton, and Lake Tahoe.

[2] Air California also serves Los Angeles, Ontario, Sacramento, San Diego, Palm Springs, and Lake Tahoe.

Table 2-2

REVENUE-PER-PASSENGER DIFFERENTIAL BY MARKET
BETWEEN INTRASTATE AND INTERSTATE CARRIERS
IN CALIFORNIA, 1972

Market	Intrastate	Interstate	Percent Interstate Above Intrastate
Ontario–Palm Springs	$11.53	$10.20	13.0
Los Angeles–Palm Springs	13.55	11.59	16.9
Los Angeles–San Diego	21.65	8.00	58.1
Los Angeles–Oakland	20.53	14.14	45.2
Los Angeles–San Francisco	30.10	14.22	111.7
Long Beach–San Francisco	22.53	15.39	46.4
Ontario–San Francisco	23.32	15.73	48.3
Los Angeles–Sacramento	24.64	15.78	56.1

Source: Simat, Helliesen and Eichner, Inc., *An Analysis of the Intrastate Air Carrier Regulatory Forum*, vol. 2, table 11, p. 48.

Moreover, the average passenger fare received by PSA and Air California is below that received by interstate carriers in the same markets, as shown in Table 2-2. Although substantial fare increases have occurred in all markets in the past few years, intrastate fares have remained well below the level of interstate fares.

The low fares have been accompanied by a high level of service. PSA alone offers an average of fifty-six nonstop flights per day from the San Francisco Bay area to the Los Angeles Basin, in addition to four flights per day by Air California. Air California offers an average of eleven nonstop flights per day in its prime market from Santa Ana to the three San Francisco area airports. Most of the flights operated by the two carriers are Boeing 727s and Boeing 737s.

The passenger response to this service has been highly positive. The intrastate carriers in California have experienced substantial traffic growth, which has had a significant impact on the overall growth of California markets. Between 1965 and 1971, traffic on the California intrastate carriers increased by more than 250 percent, an average of 23.3 percent per year. In contrast, the average annual growth in all domestic short-haul markets under 500 miles was only 4.7 percent during the same period. As a result, total intra-California traffic has grown almost 11 percent per year, more than twice the rate of all U.S. passenger markets under 500 miles.

This traffic growth has enabled intrastate carriers to maintain high load factors in the major intrastate markets. For example, Air California's system load factor was 70.2 percent in 1974 and 70.6 percent in the first nine months of 1975. PSA operated with load factors of more than 60 percent in six of its seven largest markets, which accounted for almost two-thirds of its available seats in 1974.

The lower fares are, of course, a major factor in generating traffic volume. However, the development of satellite airports by the intrastate carriers has also played a significant role in generating traffic growth. For example, most of Air California's services have a satellite airport (Santa Ana, Ontario, Oakland, or San Jose) as either an origin or a destination, while a substantial portion of PSA's traffic travels via Burbank, Oakland, or San Jose. By 1971, almost 60 percent of Los Angeles Basin-San Francisco Bay area traffic used a satellite airport on at least one end of the trip, and the two intrastate carriers were carrying more than 91 percent of that satellite traffic. As a result, PSA and Air California carried 75 percent of all intra-California traffic in 1971, compared to only 29 percent in 1961.

The substantial traffic gains of the intrastate carriers have more than offset the low revenue yields per passenger, and both PSA and Air California earned profits in 1972, 1973, and 1974. Air California, in particular, was very successful in those three years, earning a return on operating investment of more than 24 percent in each year, with a yield well below those of the local service industry and as low as those of long-haul trunk carriers.

Intrastate Operations in Texas. The primary Texas intrastate carrier, Southwest Airlines, began operation in 1971, after more than three years of litigation. It currently serves four markets in Texas with Boeing 737 aircraft: Houston-Dallas, Dallas-San Antonio, Houston-San Antonio, and Houston-Harlingen. Like the California carriers, Southwest has been an aggressive competitor, offering the public low fares and frequent service, resulting in dramatic traffic increases as well as profits for the carrier.

A distinctive feature of Southwest's pricing is its "two-tier" fare structure, consisting of a weekday "Executive Class" fare and an evening and weekend "Pleasure Class" fare. As shown in Table 2-3, these fares have been set substantially below the corresponding interstate fares. The "Executive Class" fares are approximately 30 to 40 percent below the corresponding coach fares, and the "Pleasure

Table 2-3

COMPARISON OF INTERSTATE AND INTRASTATE FARE
LEVELS IN SELECTED TEXAS MARKETS, DECEMBER 1, 1975

Fare Type	Dallas–Houston	Dallas–Harlingen[a]	Dallas–San Antonio	Houston–Harlingen[a]
CAB Interstate				
First Class	$48.00	. . . .	$51.00	. . . .
Coach[b]	35.00	$57.00	37.00	$42.00
Economy	32.00	51.00	33.00	38.00
Southwest Intrastate				
"Executive Class"	25.00	40.00	25.00	25.00
"Pleasure Class"	15.00	25.00	15.00	15.00

[a] Also applicable for interstate carriers to Brownsville and McAllen.
[b] "Y" refers to jet coach or "S" jet custom class service.
Note: All fares include tax.
Source: *Official Airline Guide*, December 1, 1975.

Class" fares are reduced 37 to 40 percent more. The former are somewhat higher than in intra-California markets of similar length, but the latter are the lowest generally available off-peak fares for scheduled short-haul air transportation in the United States (see Figure 2-1).

Southwest has complemented its innovative fare structure with a strong service pattern, offering as many as sixteen daily Dallas-Houston roundtrips and six daily Dallas-San Antonio roundtrips, Monday through Friday.

The stimulative effects of Southwest's operations on traffic growth have been dramatic. During the years 1970 to 1974, a sample of other high-density domestic markets similar to Dallas-Houston grew an average of only 9.8 percent. During the same period, traffic in the Dallas-Houston market increased 127.5 percent, resulting in a market 2.1 times the size it would have been had it grown at the average growth rate of the other high-density markets. A similar sample of representative medium-density markets, approximately the size of the Dallas-San Antonio market, grew 22.6 percent between 1970 and 1974. During the same period, Dallas-San Antonio traffic increased 154.1 percent, resulting in a market 2.1 times the size it would have been at the average growth rate of the other medium-

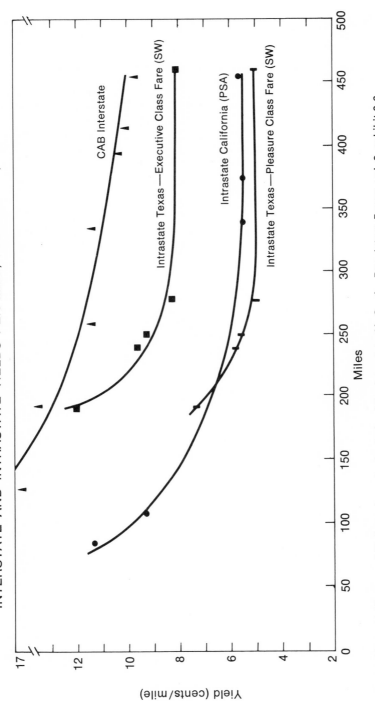

Figure 2-1

INTERSTATE AND INTRASTATE YIELDS PER MILE, FEBRUARY 1, 1975

CAB Interstate

Intrastate Texas—Executive Class Fare (SW)

Intrastate California (PSA)

Intrastate Texas—Pleasure Class Fare (SW)

Yield (cents/mile)

Miles

Source: Simat, Helliesen and Eichner, Inc., *An Analysis of the Intrastate Air Carrier Regulatory Forum*, vol. 2, exhibit 3-6.

density markets. This rapid traffic growth, coinciding with Southwest's entry into the market, is clearly shown in Figures 2-2 and 2-3. Thus, by 1974, Southwest was carrying more than 60 percent of the local traffic in the Dallas-Houston and Dallas-San Antonio markets.

Additional evidence of the impact of Southwest's intrastate operations is provided by recent experience in the Rio Grande Valley markets, which Southwest began serving in February 1975. Between May and July of that year, 43 percent more passengers boarded aircraft in the Rio Grande Valley than in the same months in 1974.

As in the case of California, selection of airports has had a significant effect on Southwest's development. The carrier now uses only Love Field in Dallas and Hobby Airport in Houston, both of which are close-in airports. The interstate carriers, on the other hand, serve the Dallas area exclusively through Dallas-Fort Worth Regional Airport and serve the Houston area via Houston Intercontinental Airport, northwest of Houston. The move by the interstate carriers to a less convenient airport placed them at a disadvantage in attracting short-haul travelers, since it is not convenient for people to travel the extra distance and to spend the extra time and money to journey to the regional airport simply to make a one-day business trip from Dallas to Houston or San Antonio. As a result, the Dallas-Houston and Dallas-San Antonio traffic of the interstate carriers dropped sharply in 1974, following the opening of Dallas-Fort Worth Regional Airport in January 1974. At that time, the carriers abandoned Love Field and left Southwest as the only carrier providing scheduled intrastate service in short-haul markets from the close-in Love Field.

After an initial period of low load factors and heavy losses, Southwest has steadily improved its passenger load factor, reaching 58.4 percent in 1974 and 62.2 percent for the first nine months of 1975. As a result, the carrier has earned a net profit in each quarter since April 1973, producing a net profit of $2.1 million in 1974 and $2.6 million in the first nine months of 1975. Its 1974 return on operating investment was 12.6 percent.

Application of the Intrastate Experience. The California and Texas experience clearly indicates that there is a potential for low-fare, high-volume services in short-haul, high-density markets. It also suggests that the regulatory environment is likely to play a significant role in determining whether such services can be developed elsewhere, since the regulatory system in each of these two states is unique within the domestic system. In order to assess better the effects of various regulatory procedures on a national scale, the Department of

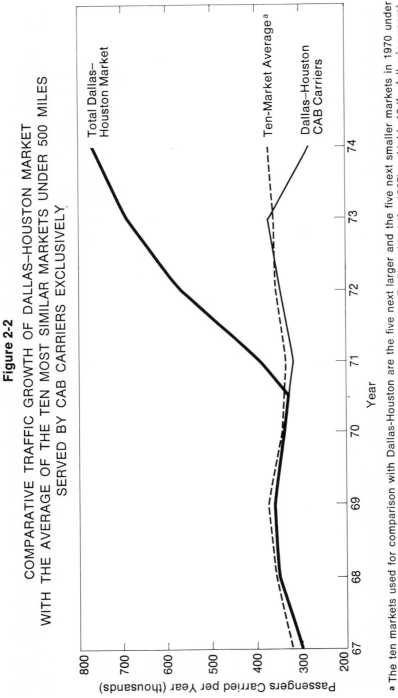

Figure 2-2

COMPARATIVE TRAFFIC GROWTH OF DALLAS–HOUSTON MARKET
WITH THE AVERAGE OF THE TEN MOST SIMILAR MARKETS UNDER 500 MILES
SERVED BY CAB CARRIERS EXCLUSIVELY.

Total Dallas–
Houston Market

Ten-Market Average [a]

Dallas–Houston
CAB Carriers

Passengers Carried per Year (thousands)

800
700
600
500
400
300
200

67   68   69   70   71   72   73   74

Year

[a] The ten markets used for comparison with Dallas-Houston are the five next larger and the five next smaller markets in 1970 under 500 miles in length. See CAB, *Origin-Destination Survey of Airline Passenger Traffic*, table 1 (for 1967) and table 10 (for following years).

Source: Civil Aeronautics Board, Docket 28068, Service to Harlingen Case, exhibits HRL-R-256 and TXIA-SRT-2.

Figure 2-3

COMPARATIVE TRAFFIC GROWTH OF DALLAS–SAN ANTONIO MARKET WITH THE AVERAGE OF THE TEN MOST SIMILAR MARKETS UNDER 500 MILES SERVED BY CAB CARRIERS EXCLUSIVELY

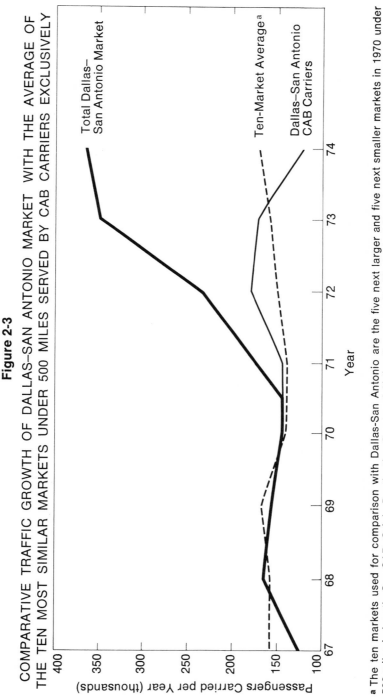

a The ten markets used for comparison with Dallas-San Antonio are the five next larger and five next smaller markets in 1970 under 500 miles in length. See CAB, *Origin-Destination Survey of Airline Passenger Traffic*, table 1 (for 1967) and table 10 (for following years). **Source:** Civil Aeronautics Board, Docket 28068, Service to Harlingen Case, exhibit HRL-R-263; Texas International Airlines v. Texas Aeronautics Commission, District Court of Travis County, Texas, number 229, 971, exhibit SW-6-82.

Transportation asked Simat, Helliesen and Eichner, Inc. (SH&E) to review the California and Texas experience, and to compare the state regulatory processes and their results with those of the CAB. In addition, SH&E was asked to analyze the evidence gathered by the Senate Subcommittee on Administrative Practice and Procedure in its report on regulatory reform.

The key observations and conclusions drawn from this study are summarized in this paper.[3] The following section reviews the statutory bases for the two state regulatory systems, as well as for the Civil Aeronautics Board. Later sections explore the practices and the policies of the respective agencies, the impact they have had on the development of intrastate services, and the implications of the intrastate experiences for national regulatory policy.

Regulatory Objectives and Enabling Acts

The objectives as defined in the enabling acts of the three regulatory agencies being compared in this study (the U.S. Civil Aeronautics Board, the California Public Utilities Commission, and the Texas Aeronautics Commission) all indicate a concern for the enhancement and the development of aviation, but they vary substantially in their nature and specificity.

The Civil Aeronautics Board. The objectives which the CAB must pursue are set forth in the Federal Aviation Act of 1958. Among other things, the board is directed to "foster sound economic conditions" in air transportation; develop a system that meets the needs of foreign and domestic commerce; "promote adequate, economical, and efficient service by air carriers at reasonable charges"; encourage competition; and promote civil aeronautics. As has often been noted, the objectives of the act dealing with the public convenience and necessity (PC&N) are somewhat contradictory, and each has been used to justify, at least temporarily, decisions reflecting diametrically opposed policies.

These often conflicting objectives have resulted in considerable controversy over the value of individual policy elements. For example, "low fares," achieved through high productivity of both capital and labor, are obviously beneficial to the public, but they may be viewed as detrimental to the system if they lead to bankruptcies of less

---

[3] The detailed data and analysis that support this summary are contained in vol. 2, *The Technical Report.*

50

efficient air carriers, loss of employment, loss of economic services on light-density routes, or increased federal subsidy.

The California and Texas Agencies. The regulatory experience in California can be analyzed only with an understanding of the objectives of the California intrastate system. Section 2739 of the Air Carriers Act gives the California Public Utilities Commission the statutory responsibility to promote an "orderly, efficient, economical, and healthy intrastate air passenger network." This 1965 act, in effect, makes "stability," "low fares" (relative to those charged by interstate airlines), and frequent service in high- and medium-density markets the aviation objectives of the PUC.[4] It appears to be subject to somewhat less contradiction than the federal regulatory environment.

In Texas, the statutory responsibility of the Texas Aeronautics Commission is "to further the public interest and aeronautical progress by providing for the protection, promotion, and development of aeronautics."[5] Air carriers are required to obtain a certificate of public convenience and necessity from the TAC.

Although both of these state mandates are more limited than the federal regulatory legislation, neither of them is specific about the nature of the air transportation system to be operated. Thus, the differences between the intrastate and interstate systems appear to be a function more of the interpretations of policy by the regulators than of the legislation itself.

Intrastate and Federal Regulatory Patterns

Regulation in California. California represents the oldest and largest example of intrastate regulation of air transportation. Although all the interstate certificated carriers have been subject to CAB regulation, the California constitution gives jurisdiction over intrastate scheduled air service and rates to the California Public Utilities Commission (PUC). The enactment of Assembly Bill 413 on September 17, 1965, added to the authority of the PUC, giving it control over entry, exit, and to some degree scheduling practices of the intrastate carriers, in addition to the jurisdiction over rates and fares which it had previously held.

---

[4] For a discussion of the objectives of intrastate air regulation in California, see California Public Utilities Commission, Decision No. 84544 to Application No. 55160, June 17, 1975, especially p. 30 of the opinion and the dissents by commissioners Holmes, Symons, and Ross.

[5] Texas Rev. Civ. Stat. Ann., article 46c-2, "Declaration" (as amended in 1969).

We shall concentrate here on the contrasts between the pre-1965 and the post-1965 periods and on the distinctions between California and federal regulation during this time.

Entry and exit. Regulation of entry and exit, as regards both new carriers and new routes, has passed through three phases in California: free entry and exit prior to 1965; liberalized entry and exit between 1965 and 1969; and more restrictive entry in the 1970s, similar to that under the CAB. During the period of free entry (1946–1965), sixteen intrastate carriers began operations, of which nine lasted less than a year and only two are still operating.[6] Since then, only two new carriers have initiated operations, of which only one has survived—Air California. In fact, no new carrier has entered the market since 1967. Between 1965 and 1970, there was a substantial increase in the route authority available to intrastate carriers, although there has been little change since that period.

Thus, state regulation has not produced completely open competition in California, but rather it has led to the evolution of specialized intrastate carriers serving specific—and mostly separate—markets. The PUC has fostered this development in several ways:

- The PUC has been exemplary in certificating service to the satellite airports of the Los Angeles Basin and the San Francisco Bay area. Oakland International, for example, possesses intrastate authority comparable to that of San Francisco International to each of the airports in the Los Angeles area.

- The PUC route award policy has been one of noncompetition between intrastate carriers. Today, a certificated duopoly exists in place of the uncertificated monopoly that evolved early in 1965 (prior to PUC control of entry). To a large extent, the PUC's route grants have encouraged development of a specialized carrier at each satellite rather than granting "area" authority to each carrier.

- Maximum and minimum limits on flight frequencies, which are mandatory for the carrier receiving new authority, have been imposed concurrent with PUC route awards. It appears that frequency restrictions were adopted in an attempt to prevent excessive competition by carriers which serve the same city through competing airports. The California carriers have opposed these frequency impositions, and there is no evidence of any beneficial results from the practice.

[6] Pacific Southwest Airlines (PSA) and Mercer Enterprises.

- The PUC has an explicit exit policy, which was summarized by Holiday Airlines in its prospectus:

  Service over a route authorized by the PUC may not be discontinued by an airline without PUC approval unless operations over the route are unprofitable. Operations may then be discontinued upon 30 days notice to the PUC and to such other persons as the PUC may require, unless within the 30-day period the PUC, after hearing, finds that such operation is not profitable and orders its discontinuance.[7]

Procedures. The PUC is unique among the three regulatory bodies discussed in this report, in that air transportation regulation is only a small part of its duties, which include the regulation of surface transportation and public utilities. There appear to be a number of shortcomings in various PUC procedures, including: (1) a "normal" timetable of twenty-four to thirty months in route proceedings; (2) lack of prehearing conferences; (3) lack of flexibility to deal with applications that are unopposed or that a carrier wishes to withdraw; and (4) the lack of economists in the air regulatory sections.

Fare and rate making. Under PUC rules of practice and procedure, rates are to be determined under the same procedures for all regulated utilities, including both intrastate and interstate air carriers.[8] However, the PUC has paid particular attention to the development of specialized operators in the aviation field, and has tended to set rates at a level where PSA could operate profitably.[9] The result, as described by United Air Lines, is that "as a practical matter, intrastate fares in markets where the interstate carriers wished to remain competitive with PSA could not be increased until PSA filed and justified such increases."[10]

Regulation in Texas. When it was originally established in 1945, the Texas Aeronautics Commission (TAC) was granted no regulatory powers. In 1961 the statute was amended to allow the TAC to regulate intrastate air carriers through the issuance of economic and safety regulations and certificates of public convenience and necessity.

---

[7] Holiday Airlines, *Prospectus*, May 22, 1969, pp. 7, 9, and 14; and Holiday Airlines, *First Annual Report 1969.*

[8] California Public Utilities Commission, *Rules of Practice and Procedure*, article 6, Applications for Authority to Increase Rates, and article 2, Formal Requirements for All Pleadings and Briefs.

[9] There are indications that charges of inefficiency against PSA may result in Air California's becoming the new "rate-making" carrier.

[10] Civil Aeronautics Board, Docket 24779, *Interstate and Intrastate Fares in California and Texas Markets*, Exhibit U-DT-1, June 1973, p. 1.

The Texas Aeronautics Statute, amended to its present form in 1969 and 1973, authorizes the TAC to issue certificates of public convenience and necessity, to issue economic and safety regulations, and to extend its jurisdiction to cover unscheduled carriers. The Texas Aeronautics Commission differs from the California PUC by virtue of the fact that it has not exercised control over the rates of CAB or intrastate carriers. The interstate carriers are thus free to change their intrastate tariffs at will, without filing with any state or federal regulatory body. Thus, regulation in Texas involves only control over entry by intrastate carriers, with rates remaining unregulated.

Entry and exit. The chief regulatory activity of the TAC has been the control over entry by scheduled non-CAB carriers,[11] since the TAC lacks jurisdiction over routes, rates, or entry of CAB carriers in Texas markets, and since it has exercised no control over the rates, fares, or expenses of intrastate carriers.[12] Since the appellate process in Texas allows an existing carrier to challenge decisions involving potential competition in the courts, the judicial system itself has become a major part of the regulatory process in Texas. Not only must the TAC be wary of court review in its decision making, but it must itself take an advocacy position to ensure that its regulatory objectives are met. The net result of this regulatory environment has been relatively restricted entry for non-CAB carriers seeking new route awards.

Fare and rate making. Southwest has been free to experiment with fare innovations since the TAC has exercised no control over fares. As a result, Southwest has developed the "two-tier" fare structure described earlier, which has produced the lowest generally available off-peak fares for scheduled short-haul transportation in the United States.

To the delight of consumers, the lack of control over fares resulted in all-out price warfare and the firm establishment of a "two-tier" structure. Although Southwest Airlines did not introduce the concept of off-peak pricing, it has gone considerably farther in its development than CAB carriers have gone, particularly as regards short-haul markets, in which the CAB and its carriers have long considered demand to be relatively price inelastic and in which there has been only limited pricing experimentation.

---

[11] Most of these intrastate airlines (Metro, Davis, Rio, Amistad, and Maverick) are operators of small aircraft under 30,000 pounds gross weight.

[12] With the possible exception of its ordering Southwest Airlines to serve Love Field.

Regulation by the Civil Aeronautics Board. Regulation as practiced by the CAB is characterized by virtually no new entry combined with tight rate regulation in the relatively long-haul and relatively high-density scheduled trunk industry. The local service carriers, characterized by short-haul route structures similar to the large intrastate carriers reviewed in this study, are subject to slightly less restrictive entry, more flexible rate regulation on increases, and close regulation on rate decreases.

An alternative to the existing pattern has been suggested in the *Report on Civil Aeronautics Board Practices and Procedures,* released on February 21, 1975, by the Subcommittee on Administrative Practice and Procedure of the Senate Judiciary Committee. The subcommittee's report concludes that CAB regulation has been defective in the past, reflecting the inherent difficulty of applying classical route and entry regulation to a competitive, economically volatile industry.[13]

The subcommittee's procedural recommendations for route regulation include:

- Abandonment of procedures used to formulate and administer the "route moratorium."

- Abandonment of the use of a procedural motion (the motion for an expedited hearing) to set substantive policy.

- Revision of standards governing ex parte communications, particularly concerning possible rule making or hearings.

- Establishment of a strict set of time limits for processing and acting upon route applications.[14]

Its recommendations for route and rate regulatory policy include institution of a legislative and regulatory program that gradually liberalizes entry requirements and allows carriers the flexibility to set their own fares within a ceiling set by the CAB. Removal of a ceiling should occur only when entry rules become sufficiently liberal for the threat of new competition to hold prices down.[15] The subcommittee favors automatic allowance of those discount fares that reflect cost savings and, also, latitude for carriers to experiment with

---

[13] U.S. Congress, Senate, Subcommittee on Administrative Practice and Procedure of the Judiciary Committee, *Report on Civil Aeronautics Board Practices and Procedures,* 94th Congress, 1st session, February 1975, p. 19.

[14] Ibid., pp. 182-83.

[15] Ibid., p. 20. A lower bound on prices would be set by the prohibition in the antitrust laws against predatory pricing; ibid., p. 185.

other discounts that respond to a widely held need of the traveling public.[16]

The recommended abandonment of the CAB route moratorium has already occurred, and the second and third procedural recommendations, regarding improper use of procedural motions and ex parte communications, have no state regulatory counterpart and can be implemented as an internal CAB reform at any time the board chooses. The fourth recommendation, concerning the establishment of strict time limits for CAB procedures, could also be applied to Texas and California, where route applications are subject to lengthy proceedings. The normal time period for processing an application in California has been between twenty-four and thirty months, while in Texas nineteen months were consumed in ruling on Southwest's only application since its original certification in 1968. This nineteen months was "expedited" only because Texas International was on strike. Four years of hearings and appellate litigation would appear to be "normal" in Texas.

The timing of the CAB application processing is more uneven. There is no set procedure for setting an application for hearing, and it may take years before an application is processed. On the other hand, CAB hearings, once begun, are not usually subject to serious delays. In this regard, federal regulation appears superior to that of the state bodies, at least in carrying out the process between the prehearing conference and the point of initial decision by the law judges. The greatest delays usually occur in setting an application for hearing, or between the initial decision of the administrative law judge and prior to oral argument, or between oral argument and final CAB decision.

The subcommittee's report indicates that liberalized entry and exit exist in California and Texas. It must be recognized, however, that during the last three years, at least, this has not been the case.

With regard to rate regulation, the subcommittee recommends that carriers be allowed flexibility to charge the prices they desire, subject only to a rate ceiling which would be removed when route awards are liberalized to the point where the threat of entry will hold down prices. This appears sound, because limited pricing flexibility, restricted by a floor 10 percent to 20 percent below existing fares, is not likely to result in rate reductions substantial enough to generate the increases in traffic volume that are necessary to make lower fares economically viable. Wide latitude to set rates would appear necessary in order to accomplish those objectives.

---

[16] Ibid., pp. 140-41 and 185.

Implications of the Intrastate Experience

The experience of the intrastate carriers provides some indications of the effects of the various types of regulation practiced by the CAB and the state agencies. However, the factors that have enabled the intrastate carriers to provide their service profitably at low rates have not always been clearly understood. For example, aircraft utilization is not one of those factors, since the utilization achieved by the intrastate carriers is similar to and in some cases lower than that of interstate carriers operating similar types of aircraft.[17]

However, the intrastate carriers are distinguished from their short-haul interstate counterparts by certain measures of productivity. In particular, they are carrying almost twice as many revenue ton-miles per employee and boarding 1.7 to 2.2 times as many passengers per employee as the average short-haul carrier—despite the fact that the number of aircraft departures performed and the number of hours flown per employee are, for the most part, below average (see Table 2-4). In the case of Southwest, for example, its total operating expense per employee in 1974 was approximately the same as that of the local service industry, but it carried 62 percent more revenue ton-miles per employee and, as a result, produced 31 percent more operating revenue per employee. Thus, revenue productivity is the key factor that differentiates the intrastate carriers from other short-haul operators.

The carriers have been able to achieve their productivity gains as a result of a number of actions on their part:

- They have concentrated their operations in *short-haul markets.* A new service has three potential sources of traffic: new travelers attracted by the price or the quality of service, who would not have traveled otherwise; passengers diverted from other air carriers or other routes; and passengers diverted from other modes (for example, automobile, bus, train). Although the first two sources are common to all types of markets, only in relatively short-haul markets are there substantial numbers of travelers using other modes of transportation. Thus, specialization in short-haul markets has enabled the intrastate carriers to tap this potential market, which is relatively price-sensitive.

- They have operated primarily in *medium- and high-density markets.* This provided them with a substantial traffic potential,

---

[17] Utilization measures the average number of hours per day an aircraft is used.

Table 2-4

SELECTED PRODUCTIVITY INDEXES, JULY 1974–JUNE 1975

Airline	Per Employee				Average		
	Revenue ton-miles	Hours flown	Departures performed	Passengers boarded	Aircraft seats	Aircraft haul-miles	Passenger trip-miles
PSA[a]	80,009	23.29	35.83	2,733	163.0	245	308
Southwest	73,606	30.64	45.25	2,820	110.0	241	251
Air California	79,762	29.48	45.94	2,113	115.0	211	363
Allegheny	46,748	30.35	42.49	1,338	86.0	229	315
North Central	34,326	31.95	65.84	1,323	73.7	131	227
Southern	44,376	31.34	53.73	1,177	72.5	170	286
Frontier	42,798	33.20	52.23	1,007	73.1	191	385
Ozark	35,474	31.95	55.33	1,136	74.5	157	273
Aloha	33,897	13.60	36.41	2,369	114.9	122	138
Texas Int'l.[b]	36,450	30.56	45.84	982	71.9	211	342
Hughes Airwest	40,916	24.86	37.67	1,036	86.5	227	383
Hawaiian	32,521	13.03	34.52	2,071	114.5	122	136
Average	40,835	29.61	48.52	1,271	80.7	186	296

[a] PSA figures are for calendar year 1974.

[b] Texas International's traffic has been increased 50 percent to normalize the period the airline was on strike. Employees are the average employed during the period the carrier was in operation.

Sources: direct testimony of George Mitchell, prepared for Pacific Southwest Airlines, October 1975, tables 3, 4, 5, 6, 7, and 8; Civil Aeronautics Board, *Air Carrier Traffic Statistics*, December 1974; International Air Transport Association, *World Air Transport Statistics*, 1974; Pacific Southwest Airlines, Annual Report, 1974; "The Regional Airlines—Peas In a Pod? A Comparison of the Local Service, Hawaiian and Intrastate Carriers," *Avmark*, October 15, 1975, pp. 3-4.

capable of supporting frequent service at high load factors. It also enabled them to achieve high productivity from their ground employees and maximum impact from marketing efforts.

- They have generated a substantial volume of new traffic and have penetrated the existing market by charging *low fares* and offering *frequent service*. Southwest, in particular, has sought to maximize the volume of new traffic, while minimizing the total cost of accommodating that traffic, by instituting a "two-tier," peak/off-peak pricing system.[18]

- They have made extensive *use of satellite or close-in airports*, where they were able to generate substantial traffic volumes, with little or no direct competition from the larger interstate carriers. As noted earlier, PSA and Air California carried more than 91 percent of Los Angeles-San Francisco satellite traffic in 1971, while Southwest obtained a significant advantage from its exclusive service at Love Field in Dallas and at Hobby Airport in Houston.

- They have operated their aircraft at a *higher seating density* than the interstate carriers. For example, PSA has 18 percent to 33 percent more seating density on its aircraft than United or Western, and has an average seating density far above that of any other short-haul carrier (Table 2-4). Both Southwest and Air California also average substantially more seats per aircraft than any local service carrier.

Although the carrier managements were, of course, responsible for all of these actions, the regulatory environment had a significant bearing on what they were able to accomplish. First, regulation of entry had to be sufficiently flexible so as to permit the emergence of new carriers with the authority to provide competitive service on high- and medium-density routes. Second, the new carriers had to be able to price their services so as to generate a substantial volume of new traffic. Finally, these specialized carriers had to have the opportunity to develop their new markets without predatory competition from other new carriers.[19]

---

[18] As a result, Southwest has a higher percentage of seats occupied on its off-peak and weekend "Pleasure Class" services than on its peak period "Executive Class" services.

[19] For example, there is general agreement that Air California would not have survived if placed in direct competition with PSA in identical markets. The PUC's route award policy has been to encourage the carriers to "specialize" in different satellite markets.

Obviously, these conditions were met sufficiently in both Texas and California for PSA, Air California, and Southwest Airlines to develop and flourish. However, the regulatory environments in the two states have a number of limitations which will affect future developments in the states and which have implications for national regulatory policy. Entry in both states is tightly restricted, as a result of the judicial review process in Texas and of PUC policy in California. Although this provides some advantages to the existing intrastate carriers, it restricts their potential growth and limits the possible future development of new carriers. Furthermore, while Texas carriers have full pricing flexibility, the California system relies on stringent control of rates, based on the experience of the lowest cost carrier. This limits the opportunities for pricing innovation and experimentation, and it would be difficult to implement for a nation-wide system.

On a national level, significant pricing flexibility would require a major departure from the present CAB-regulated system. Over the past three decades, the national aviation system has been based on a significant amount of cross-subsidization from profitable to less economic routes. Recently, the CAB has made a major effort to reduce cross-subsidization of short-haul routes by long-haul routes by introducing a substantial cost-based taper into the fare structure.[20] As a result, fares in short-haul markets have risen sharply (see Figure 2-4), dampening traffic growth.

However, the CAB fare structure is not attuned to the volume of traffic in individual markets; it is based solely on market distance. As a result, interstate carriers have not had the opportunity to use low fares as a basis for achieving the potential productivity gains in short-haul, high-density markets. Interstate fares in such markets are there-fore higher than economically necessary. The specialized intrastate carriers, on the other hand, have been able to charge lower fares and still remain profitable, through the achievement of significant produc-tivity improvements.

The introduction of pricing flexibility nationally, resulting in lower fares in high-density markets, would also affect markets with lower density, as carriers might adjust fares or service levels to reflect appropriately the higher unit costs that often exist in such markets. In fact, explicit subsidies or more economic forms of service might be required in order to maintain current service levels in these markets. However, greater pricing flexibility would also provide an opportunity

---

[20] In Phase 9 of the *Domestic Passenger Fare Investigation.* See Civil Aeronautics Board, Docket 216866-9, March 18, 1974, and December 1974.

Figure 2-4

INTERSTATE CARRIER YIELDS PER MILE IN SELECTED MARKETS, 1955 AND 1975

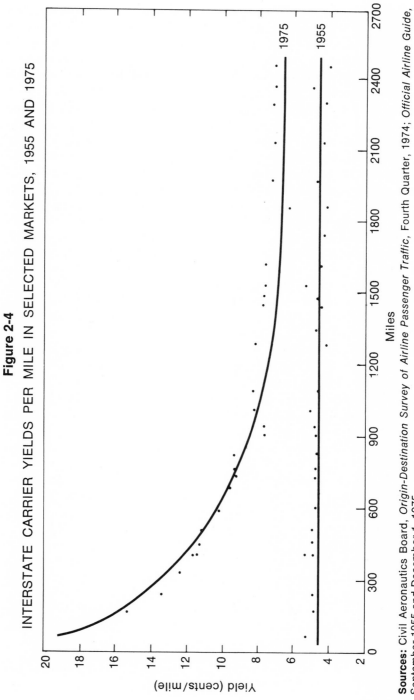

Sources: Civil Aeronautics Board, *Origin-Destination Survey of Airline Passenger Traffic*, Fourth Quarter, 1974; *Official Airline Guide*, September 1955 and December 1, 1975.

for imaginative pricing in high-density markets, such as that developed by Southwest Airlines. The present CAB policy of discouraging differentiated pricing through a greater reliance on cost-based pricing appears to have hurt the personal and family travel market in particular. It fails to allow for varying elasticities of demand in markets of different lengths, traffic composition, and stages of development.[21] It ignores the possibility, as evidenced in the intrastate markets, that large fare changes may create a traffic response at a much greater rate than small changes. Furthermore, the elimination of some discounts has accentuated daily and weekly demand fluctuations. In contrast, Southwest's "two-tier" structure has increased the carrier's productivity by stimulating additional traffic and by encouraging travel in off-peak hours. As a result, Southwest has been able to reduce its unit costs below the levels that would otherwise have been attainable.

It should be noted that, even in circumstances where some flexibility has existed, interstate carriers have failed to take advantage of the service and pricing opportunities available to them. For example, any interstate carrier operating in Texas could offer service between any city-pair within the state at any price it wished. Yet, no interstate carrier has taken advantage of this "loophole," except in markets competitive with Southwest. This lack of initiative on the part of the interstate carriers may be because of the operational and economic difficulties of establishing a specialized service as part of a much larger operation, or because of a lack of innovative spirit stemming from a highly structured regulatory environment. However, the Texas experience indicates that small, specialized carriers can take advantage of a flexible regulatory environment to produce service and pricing improvements in short-haul, medium- and high-density markets.

The development of such operations on a national scale would have significant effects on the aviation system. Nationwide, there are seventy-two short-haul, high- and medium-density markets at least as large as Dallas-San Antonio.[22] These markets, listed in Table 2-5, account for 16.8 percent of originating domestic passengers on interstate carriers. Of the 22.2 million passengers in the seventy-two markets, 2.3 million fly on CAB carriers in the seven markets where low intrastate fare levels already exist,[23] or in an eighth market which has

---

[21] The CAB has used a compromise overall elasticity factor of -0.7 in regulatory decisions for the past three years.

[22] Dallas-San Antonio has 125,000 annual origin and destination (O&D) passengers.

[23] Los Angeles-San Francisco; Dallas-Houston; Los Angeles-San Diego; Los Angeles-Sacramento; Fresno-San Francisco; Fresno-Los Angeles; Dallas-San Antonio.

Table 2-5

CAB ORIGIN–DESTINATION PASSENGER TRAFFIC IN MAJOR SHORT-HAUL CITY-PAIR MARKETS, 1974

Market	True O&D Passengers	Nonstop Mileage	1975 "Y" or "K" Fares[a]	Cents Per Mile	1975 Intrastate Fare ("K" only)[a]	Cents Per Mile
Boston–New York	1,842,600	191	29.63	15.5		
New York–Washington	1,680,800	215	31.48	14.6		
Los Angeles– San Francisco	957,240	347	40.74	11.7	20.83	6.0
Las Vegas–Los Angeles	654,060	236	31.48	13.3		
New York–Pittsburgh	621,480	329	40.74	12.4		
Chicago–Detroit	620,890	238	33.33	14.0		
Chicago–Minneapolis	597,110	344	41.67	12.1		
Boston–Washington	595,160	406	47.22	11.6		
Cleveland–New York	585,880	410	47.22	11.5		
Honolulu–Kauai	570,640	102	19.44	19.1		
Buffalo–New York	553,010	291	37.96	13.0		
Chicago–St. Louis	469,810	256	34.26	13.4		
Hilo–Honolulu	465,780	216	25.93	12.0		
New York–Rochester	428,170	253	34.26	13.5		
Boston–Philadelphia	421,580	271	37.04	13.7		
Honolulu–Maui	401,520	100	19.44	19.4		
Chicago–Cleveland	380,670	311	39.81	12.8		
Los Angeles–Phoenix	352,860	370	37.96	10.3		
New York–Syracuse	333,240	199	30.56	15.4		
Philadelphia–Pittsburgh	331,750	265	36.11	13.6		
Dallas–Houston	295,740	222	29.63	13.3	13.89	6.3
Chicago–Kansas City	290,150	407	41.67	10.2		
Chicago–Pittsburgh	287,150	412	47.22	11.5		
Los Angeles–San Diego	274,540	109	20.37	18.7	10.79	9.9
Portland–Seattle	256,510	132	25.00	18.9		
Houston–New Orleans	251,750	304	35.19	11.6		
Seattle–Spokane	247,060	223	32.41	14.5		
Columbus–New York	242,410	473	52.78	11.2		
Detroit–Washington	228,060	391	46.30	11.8		
Miami–Tampa	214,710	198	30.56	15.4		
Chicago–Cincinnati	206,480	254	35.19	13.9		
New York– Raleigh/Durham	204,560	425	48.15	11.3		
Los Angeles–Sacramento	196,140	373	39.81	10.7	22.92	6.1
Atlanta–Tampa	194,270	412	47.22	11.5		
Baltimore–New York	194,130	179	28.70	16.0		
Detroit–Philadelphia	187,550	452	50.93	11.3		
Chicago–Columbus	186,140	287	37.96	13.2		
Reno–San Francisco	182,780	188	29.63	15.8		
Miami–Orlando	181,720	196	30.56	15.6		
New York–Norfolk	179,010	290	37.04	12.8		
Greensboro–New York	178,930	455	50.93	11.2		
Las Vegas–San Francisco	176,850	420	46.30	11.0		
Chicago–Indianapolis	176,610	167	27.78	16.6		
Cleveland–Detroit	176,420	94	22.22	23.6		
Dallas–New Orleans	172,620	437	50.00	11.4		

Table 2-5 (continued)

Market	True O&D Passengers	Nonstop Mileage	1975 "Y" or "K" Fares[a]	Cents Per Mile	1975 Intrastate Fare ("K" only)[a]	Cents Per Mile
Pittsburgh–Washington	164,600	185	30.56	16.5		
Fresno–San Francisco	162,780	165	25.93	15.7	13.84	8.4
Chicago–Memphis	162,350	485	52.78	10.9		
Baltimore–Boston	161,830	370	43.52	11.8		
Kansas City–St. Louis	161,110	233	33.33	14.3		
Cleveland–Philadelphia	157,250	363	43.52	12.0		
Denver–Salt Lake City	154,960	381	44.44	11.7		
Cleveland–Washington	154,600	297	38.89	13.1		
Albany–New York	152,620	139	25.93	18.7		
New York–Providence	151,570	150	25.93	17.3		
Fresno–Los Angeles	149,590	213	30.56	14.3	17.64	8.3
Atlanta–Jacksonville	148,650	270	36.11	13.4		
Boston–Pittsburgh	147,420	490	53.70	11.0		
Hartford–Washington	146,300	317	39.81	12.6		
Los Angeles–Salinas/Monterey	145,340	267	36.11	13.5	25.32	9.5
Austin–Dallas	141,480	183	25.93	14.2		
Atlanta–Orlando	139,150	400	47.22	11.8		
Chicago–Des Moines	137,570	306	38.89	12.7		
New York–Richmond	135,670	286	37.04	13.0		
Los Angeles–Tucson	133,390	451	44.44	9.9		
Atlanta–Memphis	133,180	332	40.74	12.3		
Chicago–Omaha	132,540	423	48.15	11.4		
Honolulu–Kona	131,550	169	23.15	13.7		
Atlanta–Charlotte	128,920	227	32.41	14.3		
Chicago–Louisville	127,940	276	37.04	13.4		
Chicago–Dayton	125,570	231	33.33	14.4		
Dallas–San Antonio	125,220	247	30.56	12.4	13.89	5.6
Total	22,159,690					

a "Y" refers to "coach class"; "K" refers to "thrift class."

Sources: Civil Aeronautics Board, *Origin-Destination Survey of Airline Passenger Traffic,* for the 12 months ended December 31, 1974, table 6; *Fares Official Aviation Guide,* North American edition, December 1, 1975.

intrastate fares offered by a certificated carrier.[24] In these intrastate markets, stimulation because of lower fares and higher frequencies has already occurred. In addition, four of the seventy-two markets are intra-Hawaiian markets, which already have a specialized form of service.[25] The remaining 18.3 million passengers travel in sixty markets where two of the prerequisite conditions exist for successful specialization: short distance and high density.

[24] Los Angeles-Monterey.
[25] The four markets have 1.6 million passengers annually.

If the regulatory environment permitted or encouraged some new competition in each market so that there would be at least one carrier in each market lacking sufficient market share at present but possessing the means to go after it, and if a differentiated fare structure could be employed,[26] then passenger volumes would be likely to increase to at least twice their present level, assuming a continuation of the fare and cost trends of the 1970–1974 period. Thus, with the evolution of specialized operations in the sixty key potential markets, and with fare and service patterns comparable to those found in Texas and California, more than 18 million additional air passengers could be generated each year.

There are a number of cities that offer promise as a base for the development of this type of short-haul market. These include New York, Chicago, Washington/Baltimore, Boston, Pittsburgh, Atlanta, Cleveland, Philadelphia, and Detroit (Table 2-6). In some cases, development could be constrained by congestion at major airports (for example, La Guardia and Washington National), but even this problem could be solved by application of the regulatory policies initiated by California in combination with the pricing flexibility available in Texas. California was very successful in stimulating satellite services by the designation of separate airports in various metropolitan areas. Texas has followed suit. If the new services were certificated from satellite airports (for example, Midway, Baltimore, Love, and Hobby), a system of specialized high-density, short-haul operations could be implemented without congestion and access constraints. For example, in the New York area, Newark could be tried as the designated airport for the low-fare services. La Guardia would, in effect, become a higher priced product, and the carriers serving La Guardia could price so as to take advantage of the superior convenience of that airport.

There are some areas, however, in which the impact of a substantial improvement in pricing and services in short-haul, high- and medium-density markets is unclear. For example, a significant increase in passenger volumes would impose additional burdens, and thus costs, on the airport and airways system.[27] Also, there are energy trade-offs that would result from a shift from automobile to air travel.

---

[26] Wherein the off-peak fare would be between 40 and 50 percent of the Phase 9 fare levels, and the peak fares would be no more than 140 to 160 percent of the off-peak fares.

[27] The system costs would not increase in proportion to the increase in traffic volume. Rather, the nature of the new services would improve the productivity of the system, through higher seating density, increased load factors, the use of satellite airports, and the application of peak/off-peak pricing differentials. Of course, additional tax revenues would also be generated.

Table 2-6

SHORT-HAUL HIGH-DENSITY MARKETS SORTED BY HUBS

Hub	Markets	
New York (15)	Boston	Raleigh
	Washington	Baltimore
	Pittsburgh	Norfolk
	Cleveland	Greensboro
	Buffalo	Albany
	Rochester	Providence
	Syracuse	Richmond
	Columbus	
Chicago (14)	Detroit	Columbus
	Minneapolis	Indianapolis
	St. Louis	Memphis
	Cleveland	Des Moines
	Kansas City	Omaha
	Pittsburgh	Louisville
	Cincinnati	Dayton
Los Angeles (8)	San Francisco[a]	Sacramento[a]
	Las Vegas	Fresno[a]
	Phoenix	Monterey[a]
	San Diego[a]	Tucson
Washington (6)	New York	Pittsburgh
	Boston	Cleveland
	Detroit	Hartford
Atlanta (5)	Tampa	Memphis
	Jacksonville	Charlotte
	Orlando	
Boston (5)	New York	Baltimore
	Washington	Pittsburgh
	Philadelphia	
Cleveland (5)	New York	Philadelphia
	Chicago	Washington
	Detroit	
Pittsburgh (5)	New York	Washington
	Philadelphia	Boston
	Chicago	
Dallas (4)	Houston[a]	Austin
	New Orleans	San Antonio[a]
Detroit (4)	Chicago	Philadelphia
	Washington	Cleveland
Philadelphia (4)	Boston	Detroit
	Pittsburgh	Cleveland
San Francisco (4)	Los Angeles[a]	Las Vegas
	Reno	Fresno[a]
Baltimore (2)	New York	Boston
Columbus (2)	New York	Chicago
Fresno (2)	Los Angeles[a]	San Francisco[a]

Table 2-6 (continued)

Hub	Markets	
Houston (2)	Dallas[a]	New Orleans
Kansas City (2)	Chicago	St. Louis
Las Vegas (2)	Los Angeles	San Francisco
Memphis (2)	Chicago	Atlanta
Miami (2)	Tampa	Orlando
New Orleans (2)	Dallas	Houston
Orlando (2)	Atlanta	Miami
St. Louis (2)	Chicago	Kansas City
Seattle (2)	Portland	Spokane
Tampa (2)	Atlanta	Miami
Albany (1)	New York	
Austin (1)	Dallas	
Buffalo (1)	New York	
Charlotte (1)	Atlanta	
Cincinnati (1)	Chicago	
Dayton (1)	Chicago	
Denver (1)	Salt Lake City	
Des Moines (1)	Chicago	
Greensboro (1)	New York	
Hartford (1)	Washington	
Indianapolis (1)	Chicago	
Jacksonville (1)	Atlanta	
Louisville (1)	Chicago	
Minneapolis (1)	Chicago	
Monterey (1)	Los Angeles[a]	
Norfolk (1)	New York	
Omaha (1)	Chicago	
Phoenix (1)	Los Angeles	
Portland (1)	Seattle	
Providence (1)	New York	
Raleigh (1)	New York	
Reno (1)	San Francisco	
Richmond (1)	New York	
Rochester (1)	New York	
Sacramento (1)	Los Angeles[a]	
Salt Lake City (1)	Denver	
San Antonio (1)	Dallas[a]	
San Diego (1)	Los Angeles[a]	
Spokane (1)	Seattle	
Syracuse (1)	New York	
Tucson (1)	Los Angeles	

[a] Market with intrastate carrier or fare.

Note: Included in this list are markets under 500 miles, with more than 125,000 passengers in 1974 (excluding intra-Hawaiian markets).

Source: Table 2-5.

In addition, within the aviation system itself, it is important to determine the service requirements and true subsidy need of light-density markets. To the extent that carriers adjust fares or services in these markets, provision may be required for alternative forms of subsidy or more economic forms of service on such routes. These areas require study before a full assessment of short-haul services can be completed.

Summary

Although the regulatory environments in Texas and California differ substantially, each has resulted in the establishment of carriers which are specialized in their desire and ability to serve medium- and high-density, short-haul markets. Further, each has allowed these carriers to pursue a marketing and operational philosophy which has enabled them to achieve improved productivity and, as a result, to charge lower fares. Airport selection (particularly satellite airports), aircraft configuration, and frequency of service have all played key roles in the carriers' development. The pricing flexibility permitted under Texas regulation has been particularly effective in encouraging pricing experimentation, and has led to the development of a "two-tier" pricing structure which has clearly stimulated the personal segment of the air travel market on Texas routes.

CAB regulation, on the other hand, has produced both tight control of entry and tight rate regulation, and has required equal fares for markets of the same distance. Consequently, there has been no development of specialized interstate carriers serving short-haul routes of density comparable to those served by the intrastate carriers. Moreover, existing CAB carriers have failed to take initiative even in those intrastate markets where they have entry and pricing flexibility. Instead, they have only responded to pricing innovations instituted by the intrastate carriers.

Each system of regulation contains both beneficial aspects and serious flaws, and none, therefore, stands as a perfect model for future regulation. However, the state regulatory environments have produced a type of operation which has significant potential for the aviation system. Nationally, there are sixty interstate markets similar in distance and density to the Texas and California intrastate markets. Application of a "two-tier" pricing system, along with improved frequency, would be expected to double the traffic volume in these markets, generating more than 18 million additional air passengers each year. At an estimated average savings of $11 per passenger, this would produce annual savings of more than $200 million for travelers at existing traffic levels.

There are a number of cities that offer promise as a base for this type of market development, including New York, Chicago, Washington/Baltimore, Boston, Pittsburgh, Atlanta, Cleveland, Philadelphia, and Detroit. Of course, no two markets are precisely the same, and different conditions may well require different types of operations. Therefore, regulatory efforts should be directed at producing conditions under which carriers have the incentive and the ability to experiment and provide services appropriate to each market. With such a favorable regulatory environment, there are substantial opportunities for specialized short-haul carriers to develop the type of high-volume, low-fare operations that exist in the intrastate markets.

3

ANALYSIS OF COMMUTER AIRLINE FARE STRUCTURES

Regulatory Policy Staff, U.S. Department of Transportation

It has been argued by a number of observers that CAB regulation has tended to cause airline fares to be higher than they would be in an environment where fares and entry were subject to competition. There exists a segment of the airline industry, namely commuter carriers, which is not subject to CAB regulation in terms of fare or entry control. One might therefore logically suggest that, "if competition works, commuter fares should be lower than the CAB-regulated fares of certificated carriers."

Of course, commuter air carriers are subject to substantial regulation of another sort, namely, that by definition they cannot utilize aircraft which carry more than thirty passengers. In addition, intrastate fares are regulated in some states. Certificated carriers, on the other hand, tend to use larger aircraft (even though they are not required to do so). It is generally true that larger aircraft are more efficient to operate on a per-seat per-mile basis once in the air. The major cost advantage of smaller aircraft is that their "terminal" or fixed costs are lower, and their total costs per flight are lower.

Thus, commuters should tend to enjoy a cost advantage in shorter haul and low-density markets. Over sufficiently short distances, the per-mile advantages of larger aircraft would be offset by the higher terminal (or fixed) costs. In sufficiently "thin" markets, it might simply be impossible to fill enough seats per plane for the economies of scale of the larger aircraft to be realized.

It is not generally contended that CAB-regulated fares do not reflect the cost advantages of larger aircraft, but rather that they have

This paper was prepared in June 1976 by the regulatory policy staff in the Office of the Secretary, U.S. Department of Transportation. The principal author was Bruce N. Stram, an economist with the DOT.

not allowed these advantages to be fully achieved. Therefore, one could not rationally judge the performance of competitive versus regulated markets by comparing overall fares of commuter carriers to overall fares of certificated carriers.

Further, fares may not fully reflect costs. Many local service carriers receive subsidies for serving particular points on thin routes; thus, a fare lower than fully allocated costs might be charged. Certificated carriers may also charge fares lower than fully allocated costs in certain markets in order to gain a competitive advantage in carrying "beyond traffic." Neither of these advantages is generally available to commuter carriers. Despite these qualifications, however, if the competitive market does work, one might still expect a range of short, less dense markets where commuters do tend to offer lower fares.

In actuality, commuter air carriers do serve short-haul, less dense markets. For the year ended June 30, 1975, the average distance of the commuter-served market was 104 miles. More than three-fourths of the markets served by commuters enplaned fewer than ten passengers per day (see Table 3-1). This latter statistic is somewhat exaggerated because commuters which provided service for less than a full year "average out" to fewer daily enplanements than they actually provided during a period of operation.

With regard to comparisons of per-distance fares between commuters and certificated carriers, two informal studies are of interest and must be examined in detail.

Short Haul Versus Long Haul

The first study is by James C. Miller III and Leroy Laney of the Council of Economic Advisers.[1] For a random sampling of commuter markets, Miller and Laney performed a regression analysis which estimated commuter fares (F) as a fixed charge plus a mileage (M) charge:

$$F = 10.755 + 0.111\ M.$$

That is, on average, commuter fares can be represented by a formula containing a fixed charge of $10.75 plus a charge of 11.1 cents a mile.[2] This fare "formula" was compared to a linear approximation of the CAB fare formula (for December 27, 1974). This approximation was:

$$F = 17.02 + 0.062\ M.$$

[1] James C. Miller III and Leroy Laney, "Evidence on Regulated and Unregulated Air Fares," memorandum prepared for the Council of Economic Advisers, dated July 15, 1975.

[2] For commuter fares for fifty-one markets selected at random from the June 1975 *Official Airline Guide.*

Table 3-1

DISTRIBUTION OF COMMUTER PASSENGER MARKETS
BY MILEAGE AND PASSENGERS PER DAY
(year ended June 30, 1975)

Nonstop Mileage	City-pair Markets	Total O&D Passengers	Total Passenger Miles	Number of Markets by Passengers per Day										Avg. Trip
				0–0.9	1–4.9	5–9.9	10–14.9	15–19.9	20–24.9	25–29.9	30–34.9	35–39.9	40+	
0–24	51	91,137	1,548,132	35	7	1	2	—	1	2	1	1	1	17
25–49	159	1,343,163	53,474,934	82	23	19	9	3	3	3	—	1	16	40
50–74	179	1,089,850	68,114,223	90	27	16	8	6	2	2	6	2	20	62
75–99	159	1,275,473	109,885,043	71	25	15	5	6	4	4	2	3	24	86
100–124	152	1,046,604	117,955,099	58	29	10	10	11	6	3	2	4	19	113
125–149	125	583,649	78,443,193	50	28	11	12	4	5	1	2	1	11	134
150–174	127	453,409	73,641,819	50	31	16	10	8	1	3	2	—	6	162
175–199	104	374,194	69,911,830	43	19	11	9	7	1	2	2	4	6	187
200–224	68	196,607	41,622,411	24	14	10	9	5	1	—	1	2	2	212
225–249	65	185,627	44,629,517	31	13	10	3	—	3	2	—	—	3	240
250–274	37	63,164	16,317,660	21	7	3	3	1	—	—	—	—	2	258
275–299	38	22,856	6,563,300	22	13	2	1	—	—	—	—	—	—	287
300–324	17	21,389	6,727,051	13	2	1	—	—	—	—	—	1	—	315
325–349	31	24,604	8,216,719	19	4	7	1	—	—	—	—	—	—	334
350–374	7	590	216,767	7	—	—	—	—	—	—	—	—	—	367
375–399	10	3,020	1,156,474	8	1	1	—	—	—	—	—	—	—	383
400 and over	38	17,897	9,577,098	28	7	2	—	1	—	—	—	—	—	535
Totals	1,367	6,793,233	708,001,270	652	250	135	82	52	27	22	18	19	110	104

Note: Based on 365 days regardless of number of days actually served.
Source: Civil Aeronautics Board, Form 298-C, Schedule T-1.

They also observed that local service carriers are permitted to charge up to 130 percent of the coach fare as their "standard" fare, and they tend to do so in markets where they do not compete with trunk carriers. The corresponding 130 percent fare formula would be:

$$F = 22.24 + 0.081\ M.$$

These results led Miller and Laney to suggest that commuters charge fares lower than trunk carriers up to 126 miles and fares lower than local service carriers up to 312 miles if local service carriers were to charge the full 130 percent of the basic fare as permitted. However, the CAB fare formula consists of a fixed terminal charge and a mileage charge which decreases as mileage increases. Therefore, it would seem more proper, since commuters offer very few flights over 500 miles, to compare the CAB formula over the first 500-mile segment to the estimated commuter formula. The CAB formula for the first 500 miles, concurrent with the Miller-Laney study, is:

$$F = 13.85 + 0.078\ M.$$

Adjusted to 130 percent, this would be:

$$F = 18.005 + 0.101\ M.$$

The use of these fare formulas suggests that commuters charge lower fares up to 94 miles if the basic formula is used and up to and beyond 500 miles (873 precisely) if the maximum 130 percent standard fare is used.

These results suggest that commuters on average charge lower fares at least up to 100-mile distances. However, a second, more recent informal study by the CAB staff resulted in an estimate that commuter fares were lower only up to distances of twenty miles.[3] This result is obtained by estimating equations after the fashion of Miller and Laney for the top (in market density) twenty-five certificated carrier markets under 250 miles and the top twenty-five commuter markets.[4] The resulting equations are:

$$F = 14.44 + 0.073\ M \text{ for certificated carriers}$$
$$F = 13.42 + 0.124\ M \text{ for commuters.}$$

However, the data for certificated carriers in fact include six intrastate fares. This results in an estimated certificated formula which is *lower* than the current CAB formula for distances under 500 miles, which is:

$$F = 15.13 + 0.0827\ M.$$

Inclusion of these intrastate fares would seem to be unsupportable if one wishes to compare certificated fares and commuter fares. Exclu-

[3] Civil Aeronautics Board, "Comment on Commuter Fares," internal document prepared in June 1976.
[4] Based on data from the March 1, 1976, *Official Airline Guide.*

sion of these six markets from the sample yields the following equation:

$$F = 15.73 + 0.0825 \, M.$$

This is essentially the basic CAB formula. (Incidentally, this exclusion raises the R^2 from 0.15 to 0.61.) Use of the corrected formula suggests that commuters charge lower fares on average up to 56 miles. This figure corresponds roughly to the 94 miles obtained using the Miller and Laney formula. They are not strictly comparable because the 94-mile estimate is based on a random selection of markets, not on a comparison of dense markets.

These nineteen markets all have competition between trunk carriers and local service carriers, so local service carriers must presumably use the basic CAB fare formula to meet trunk fares. If one wishes to compare commuter fares to markets where local service carriers charge up to 130 percent of the basic CAB formula, one obtains the following formula:

$$F = 19.669 + 0.108 \, M.$$

This suggests that commuters charge lower fares than the local service standard fares up to 370 miles. These distances are lower than those obtained by Miller and Laney, but they are still substantial.

Market Density

Commuters would also seem to offer lower fares or enjoy a competitive advantage over certificated carriers in low-density markets. The CAB identified eighty-two markets (as of June 30, 1974) in which certificated carriers and commuters competed. Table 3-2 shows that on July 1, 1974, in the thirty of these markets averaging fewer than forty-five enplanements per day, commuters charged lower fares in fourteen markets and certificated carriers in twelve (four were the same). In markets averaging more than forty-five enplanements per day, certificated carriers had the lower fares in thirty-six cases, and commuters in twenty-eight (fourteen were the same). However, these fares in existence at a given point in time may not support reasonable profits over the longer run.

In Table 3-3 these same markets are reexamined for March 1, 1976. The results are startling. As of that date, commuters charged lower fares in twelve markets averaging fewer than forty-five enplanements per day; certificated carriers charged lower fares only in four. Further, nine certificated carriers had dropped out of these markets; whereas only two commuters had dropped out. Thus, over time,

Table 3-2

CERTIFICATED CARRIER FARES VS. COMMUTER FARES IN COMPETITIVE MARKETS, STRATIFIED BY MARKET SIZE, JULY 1, 1974

Enplanements Per Day[a]	Commuter Fare Lower	Local Carrier Fare Lower	Same Fare
Under 10	1	2	0
10–15	2	4	1
15–20	2	2	0
20–25	1	1	0
25–35	2	1	0
35–45	6	2	3
Under 45	14	12	4
45–60	1	2	1
60–80	0	1	3
80–100	4	1	0
100–140	3	3	3
140–180	2	3	2
180–250	1	2	1
250–300	0	2	2
300–400	0	5	0
400–500	1	2	1
500–800	1	2	1
Over 800	1	1	0
Over 45	14	24	14
Total	28	36	18

[a] Market size for year ending June 1, 1974.

Sources: Civil Aeronautics Board, *Commuter Carrier—Certificated Carrier Competition, Year Ended June 30, 1974*, 1976. Fares were obtained from July 1, 1974, issue of *Official Airline Guide*.

commuters had the competitive edge in twenty-one markets, while certificated carriers had the edge in only six markets.

The general conclusion one might draw is that over the longer run, in the vast majority of less dense markets, certificated carriers cannot meet or cannot sustain as low a fare as commuter carriers.

Table 3-3

CERTIFICATED CARRIER FARES VS. COMMUTER FARES
IN COMPETITIVE MARKETS, STRATIFIED BY MARKET SIZE,
MARCH 1, 1976

Enplane-ments Per Day[a]	Com-muter Fare Lower	Certificated Carrier Fare Lower	Same Fare	Commuter Service Discon-tinued	Certificated Carrier Service Discontinued
Under 10	1	1	0	0	1
10–15	2	0	2	1	3
15–20	1	2	0	1	0
20–25	1	0	0	0	1
25–35	0	0	0	0	3
35–45	7	1	2	0	1
Under 45	12	4	4	2	9
45–60	1	1	1	1	0
60–80	0	1	2	1	0
80–100	4	1	0	0	0
100–140	1	1	7	0	0
140–180	1	2	3	1	0
180–250	1	1	0	2	1
250–300	2	1	1	0	0
300–400	0	0	4	1	0
400–500	0	2	1	1	0
500–800	1	0	1	2	0
Over 800	2	0	0	0	0
Over 45	13	10	20	9	1
Total	25	14	24	11	10

[a] Market size for year ending June 1, 1974.

Sources: Civil Aeronautics Board, *Commuter Carrier—Certificated Carrier Competition, Year Ended June 30, 1974,* 1976. Fares were obtained from March 1, 1976, issue of *Official Airline Guide.*

Monopoly Pricing

A related issue is whether unregulated commuters might charge higher fares in markets in which they enjoy a monopoly. Even where a commuter is the only carrier, the threat of entry by other carriers exists. This should tend to keep fares low enough so that only reasonable profits are earned. Further, in short-haul markets, other modes of transportation, such as motor carrier, provide significant competition.

Miller and Laney found in their random sample of commuter markets that for markets in which commuters provided the only air service the fare structure was estimated as:

$$F = 9.45 + 0.122\,M.$$

This is not substantially different from

$$F = 10.755 + 0.111\,M,$$

which was estimated in competitive markets. Thus, it would seem that competitive pressures (that is, potential entry and competing modes of transport) keep commuter fares in monopoly markets in line with fares in directly competitive markets.

These results on balance show that expected cost advantages of small aircraft in short-haul, less dense markets are realized in real world fare structures, and that commuters are unable or unlikely to charge high fares where they provide the only air service.

PART THREE

SERVICE TO SMALL COMMUNITIES: THE CROSS-SUBSIDY QUESTION

Opponents of the regulatory reform proposals for aviation argued that reduced economic regulation would disrupt service to smaller communities by eliminating the carriers' ability to cross-subsidize. According to this view, airlines were subsidizing service to unprofitable points from profits on other routes. The added competition on these profitable routes would erode the ability to serve unprofitable points, and thus carriers would be forced to withdraw from service to small communities. The three papers in this part deal with this contention.

The first paper, prepared by the Department of Transportation, examines the actual experience with service to small communities under CAB regulation. The study found that regulation seldom required carriers to fly unprofitable routes, that regulation had not been a major obstacle to carriers' abandoning service at smaller points, and that in fact many points had been abandoned by CAB-certificated carriers. In most cases, unregulated commuter carriers had filled the void left by the departure of the certificated carriers. The local service airlines prepared a response to this DOT study. The second paper in this part is a counterresponse by DOT further evaluating service to small communities. The last paper in this part is an analysis of a list of route segments that Eastern Airlines had identified as unprofitable. Here again current conditions did not support the notion that there was extensive subsidized service which would be lost as a result of deregulation.

4

AIR SERVICE TO
SMALL COMMUNITIES

Regulatory Policy Staff, U.S. Department of Transportation

Introduction

This study reviews changes in air service at small communities and
the level of service protection provided by the current system of economic regulation. The study also reviews the development of unsubsidized commuter air service and the stability of that service. The
study estimates what service losses might be expected at small communities if the existing system of economic regulation and the present
subsidy system were eliminated. Finally, this study provides estimates of the costs of providing continued air service to small communities through a more efficient subsidy system.

The present system of economic regulation of the domestic airlines was established by the Civil Aeronautics Act of 1938 and has
remained basically unchanged since that time. This regulation includes, in the manner of traditional public utility regulation, control
over prices, entry into markets, and abandonment of service.[1] Critics
of this regulation argue that it has created a great deal of inefficiency,
resulted in higher fares for passengers, and, at the same time, failed to
benefit the regulated air carriers.[2] Recently many critics, including the

---

The principal author of this study was Peyton L. Wynns, an economist on the
regulatory policy staff in the Office of the Secretary, U.S. Department of Transportation. The study is dated March 1976. In addition to the edited materials
that are included here, the original report contained an executive summary, an
extensive discussion of the obligations and restrictions imposed by the Civil
Aeronautics Board on certificated carriers, a discussion of alternatives to the
present subsidy system, and a series of appendixes.

[1] Economic regulation is vested in the Civil Aeronautics Board. In contrast, safety
regulation is the responsibility of the Federal Aviation Administration.

[2] The full range of issues relating to the economic regulation of airlines is presented in U.S. Congress, Senate, Subcommittee on Administrative Practice and

Civil Aeronautics Board's own Special Staff on Regulatory Reform, have suggested complete abolition of the present form of economic regulation.[3]

Some believe that less comprehensive regulation would result in loss of service in many markets, and they express a belief that air carriers serve many markets in which profits cannot be earned— markets which the carrier would cease serving if permitted to do so. Unless a market is unprofitable, there is ordinarily no reason to expect loss of service. With minor exceptions, markets which are capable of generating profits would continue to be served even if controls on entry and exit were completely eliminated. This study focuses on unprofitable markets which carriers might like to abandon.[4] There are two ways of identifying markets where air service might be jeopardized by the elimination or the reduction of economic regulation. One approach is to look at all markets, estimate the costs and revenues attributable to each market, and identify unprofitable markets. Unfortunately, doing so involves difficult decisions in allocating both costs and revenues and is subject to a wide margin of error. Previous studies have taken this approach and have produced misleading results.

Procedure of the Committee on the Judiciary, *Hearings on Civil Aeronautics Board Practice and Procedures*, 94th Congress, 1st session, February-March 1975 (hereinafter cited as Subcommittee Hearings). The subcommittee report summarizes the arguments both for and against changing the present regulatory system (hereinafter cited as Subcommittee Report).

[3] Civil Aeronautics Board, *Report of the CAB Special Staff on Regulatory Reform*, Washington, D. C., July 1975 (hereinafter cited as CAB Special Staff Report).

[4] It is sometimes suggested that, although not obligated to do so, air carriers voluntarily serve unprofitable markets in recognition of public service objectives. In doing so, this argument continues, the air carriers must employ substantial cross-subsidies. That is, excess profits must be earned on some routes in order to defray the losses in those unprofitable markets which the carriers choose to serve in the public interest. If this is the case, then the relaxation of entry controls would permit competitors into markets where excess profits are being earned. With the resulting elimination of excess profits, the carriers would no longer have the ability to subsidize unprofitable markets and would be forced to withdraw their service. That this situation exists to any large degree is extremely unlikely. Although the management of an airline might like to view the airline as a public service organization, it would face severe pressures not to operate in such a manner: It must withstand comparisons with other airlines, and the airline which is most profitable (rather than the one which serves the most losing routes) will be most favorably judged. Thus, management in the airline industry, as in any other industry, faces great pressure to cut losses and increase profits. Although an industry composed of very profitable firms may afford the luxury of consciously maintaining losing operations, it seems doubtful that the airline industry is in condition to do so. These factors lead us to believe that airlines do not generally and gladly subsidize losing service with profits earned elsewhere in their system.

The present study takes a somewhat different approach. Since loss of service would be expected only in markets which carriers would like to abandon but are unable to do so, we will narrow the search for unprofitable markets by restricting the inquiry to markets in which carriers cannot discontinue service. Markets where carriers could freely cease service but do not choose to do so are assumed to be profitable and in no danger of losing service.

Changes in Service Patterns: The Decline of Certificated Service to Small Communities and the Rise of Commuters

The number of points served by trunk carriers has declined for many years. Between the certification of the local service carriers in the late 1940s and 1969, there were 211 points transferred from trunk to local service carriers.[5] Since that time trunk carriers have ceased service at another 45 points. They now serve fewer than half of the points once served. The changing service pattern is shown in Table 4-1. The smaller points have been turned over to local service carriers or to commuter carriers, or they have been abandoned.

To the extent that small communities are still served by certificated carriers, they receive service from local service carriers. Local service carriers continued to increase the total number of points served until 1962. The increase in later years, however, resulted primarily from the CAB's "route strengthening" program, which permitted the local service carriers to enter larger markets; it did not represent an increase in the number of small communities served. In 1975 only sixteen airports in the continental forty-eight states received service by certificated carriers which did not receive such service in 1965. Of these sixteen airports, seven were satellite airports, new regional airports, or airports associated with the certification of Air New England and Wright. Thus, only nine new locations were added to the network served by certificated carriers during the ten-year period from 1965 to 1975.[6]

At the same time that new points were not being added to the system, smaller points were being dropped rapidly. The trend toward abandonment continues and is, if anything, increasing. As shown in Table 4-1, forty-three points were dropped between the end of 1960 and the end of 1965. By the end of 1970, service had ceased at fifty more points, and by the end of 1975, at an additional eighty.

[5] Civil Aeronautics Board, Bureau of Operating Rights, *Service to Small Communities*, March 1972, Part II, p. 9.

[6] Comparing the *Official Airline Guide* for December 1965 with the *Official Airline Guide* for August 15, 1975.

Table 4-1

POINTS SERVED BY CERTIFICATED CARRIERS IN THE 48 CONTIGUOUS STATES, 1955–1975

Year[a]	Trunk Carriers[b]			Local Service Carriers[c]			All Carriers		
	Points authorized	Points suspended	Points served	Points authorized	Points suspended	Points served	Points authorized	Points suspended	Points served
1955	376	27	349	381	18	363	583	44	539
1956	373	23	350	380	13	367	575	35	540
1957	368	25	343	387	9	378	579	33	546
1958	361	21	340	415	14	401	581	34	547
1959	332	23	309	468	29	439	610	52	558
1960	328	13	315	497	38	459	618	51	567
1961	309	13	296	494	28	466	601	39	562
1962	302	16	286	499	22	477	599	38	561
1963	251	8	243	475	11	464	562	19	543
1964	247	8	239	468	5	463	552	13	539
1965	231	8	223	472	4	468	536	12	524
1966	230	7	223	466	5	461	530	12	518
1967	229	5	224	466	7	459	526	12	514
1968	230	5	225	468	5	463	527	10	517
1969	228	5	223	469	4	465	526	9	517
1970	228	18	210	467	34	433	524	50	474
1971	228	18	210	466	34	432	522	52	470
1972	222	15	207	455	32	423	508	47	461
1973	221	19	202	445	40	405	497	56	441
1974	208	16	192	432	49	383	481	64	417
1975	198	18	180	433	53	380	464	70	394

a As of December each year.
b Includes points served jointly with local service carriers.
c Includes points served jointly with trunk carriers.
Source: Civil Aeronautics Board, Office of Facilities and Operations.

84

Counting the number of "points" served involves a number of complicated problems. The consolidation of two or more airports into regional airports and the certification of new air carriers (for example, Air New England) changes the number of points counted as being served. In addition, the number of points shown as served in Table 4-1 is calculated by subtracting the number of points suspended from the number of points authorized. Additional problems are encountered by the fact that a few points deleted from certificates have never been served at all, so no actual service was ever lost.

Many factors are associated with the decline in the number of points served. Two of the most important have been the development of the Interstate Highway System and the transition to larger aircraft by certificated carriers. The Interstate Highway System decreased travel time on the ground, made major airports attractive to much larger geographical areas, and eliminated the need for many smaller surrounding airports. The trend toward larger aircraft by certificated air carriers has decreased the attractiveness of serving small points and has increased the tendency toward regional airports.

Paradoxically, two programs designed to promote service to small communities have increased the tendency for local service carriers to acquire larger aircraft and have therefore diminished the amount of service available at small points. First, the structure of the subsidy program during the early 1960s encouraged carriers to procure larger aircraft.[7] Second, the board's route-strengthening program—designed to provide local service carriers opportunities to earn excess profits in certain markets with which to cross-subsidize service to smaller points —also encouraged carriers to buy larger aircraft.

Just as the number of points served by certificated carriers has been decreasing, the level of service at the remaining points has also been decreasing. Table 4-2 contains an analysis of changes in service available at communities with a population of fewer than 100,000.[8] Between 1970 and 1975, the number of small communities receiving service from certificated carriers decreased by 14.3 percent. During the same period of time, weekly flight frequencies decreased 24.6 percent. Since the board cannot by law control either equipment or schedules, certificated service at many points has decreased to what is usually considered the minimal level of service—two flights a day. At

---

[7] George C. Eads, *The Local Service Airline Experiment* (Washington, D. C.: The Brookings Institution, 1972), pp. 134-35.

[8] Small community air service is usually defined as service at points which generate small amounts of traffic. This definition is followed throughout this report with the exception of Table 4-2, where small communities are categorized on the basis of their population.

Table 4-2

SERVICE TO COMMUNITIES UNDER 100,000 POPULATION, POINTS SERVED AND WEEKLY FLIGHTS BY TYPE OF CARRIER, 1970 AND 1975

Size of Community [a]	1970			1975			Percent Change: 1970 to 1975		
	Trunk	Local	Commuter	Trunk	Local	Commuter	Trunk	Local	Commuter
	Number of Points Served								
0–25,000	17	126	116	12	111	149	− 29.4	− 11.9	28.4
25,000–50,000	18	80	52	16	66	60	− 11.1	− 17.5	15.4
50,000–75,000	3	12	9	2	11	11	− 33.3	− 8.3	22.2
75,000–100,000	6	16	12	5	15	10	− 16.7	− 6.3	− 16.7
Total	44	234	189	35	203	230	− 20.4	− 13.2	21.7
	Weekly Flights								
0–25,000	583	3,911	4,025	256	3,040	5,488	− 56.0	− 22.2	36.3
25,000–50,000	556	3,464	2,282	603	2,401	2,735	8.4	− 30.7	20.0
50,000–75,000	161	409	560	132	471	800	− 18.0	− 22.7	42.9
75,000–100,000	458	865	613	373	722	836	− 18.6	− 16.5	36.4
Total	1,758	8,849	7,480	1,364	6,634	9,859	− 22.4	− 25.0	31.8

a The population figures are for 1970.

Sources: The 1970 population for most locations is contained in Civil Aeronautics Board, *A Profile of Airline Service in the 48 Contiguous States, May 1, 1973*, December 1974, table 8. In most instances, population data is for the named point. In some cases, however, the population is for a standard metropolitan statistical area of other jurisdiction thought more appropriate as a measure of market size. The population data for those locations not reported in the above source have been taken from the *City and County Data Book.* The 1970 service figures are from *Official Airline Guide, Quick Reference North American Edition*, September 15, 1970. The 1975 service figures are from *Official Airline Guide, North American Edition*, September 1, 1975.

a number of other small communities, for example, Glendive, Montana, and Devil's Lake, North Dakota, only one daily flight is provided.

In summary, certificated service has been lost by many small communities, and the quality of service (measured in terms of either frequency or markets served) has been reduced at many of the small communities still served by certificated carriers. This long-term trend shows no sign of slackening and, if anything, is increasing in speed. Local service carriers have generally expressed a desire to go off subsidy and to complete the transition to all-jet fleets. As they do so, the costs of maintaining a few smaller aircraft in a predominantly jet fleet will increase, as will the costs per passenger and the subsidy needs. Thus, the long-term trend which has already resulted in most smaller points being dropped by local service carriers will continue, and pressures for withdrawal in the future will increase.

Despite the withdrawal of certificated carriers from many small points, the total number of locations receiving air service has increased. This is because of the growth of commuter air carriers. Between 1965 and 1975, commuters replaced certificated carriers at 63 of the airports abandoned by certificated carriers. Further, commuters added and dropped a variety of other airports not receiving certificated service. Eighty-two airports were added and 34 were dropped, for a net increase of 48. Thus, by the end of the decade, commuter carriers served 111 airports which would not otherwise have received service.[9] Since the future of air service to small communities—with or without changes to the regulatory environment—will depend on commuter carriers, we will briefly trace their growth and characteristics.

In 1952, the CAB exempted operators of small aircraft from economic regulation. The new class, designated as commuter air carriers in 1969, included any air taxi operator who scheduled at least five round trips per week pursuant to a published schedule. By the late 1960s, the twin-engine Beech 99 and the DeHavilland Twin Otter began to enter commuter service. These aircraft remain the backbone of the commuter fleet.

Prior to 1969, when the board imposed reporting requirements on commuter carriers, no data were collected, and little is known about the industry. Since 1970, traffic data have been available and information on the growth of commuter carriers is presented in Table 4-3. In general, they have grown much more rapidly than certificated carriers in all respects.

Between 1970 and 1975, the number of small communities served by commuter carriers increased substantially along with the number of markets served and the number of flights scheduled. Not only were commuter carriers able to increase the amount of service provided, but they did so without subsidy and in markets that were both thinner and shorter than those served by certificated carriers. As shown in Tables 4-4 and 4-5, commuter carriers serve markets which are both short and thin (77 percent of their markets are *less* than 200 miles and 77 percent enplane *fewer* than ten passengers per day). In con-

---

[9] Comparing the *Official Airline Guide* for December 1965 with that for August 15, 1975.

Table 4-3

COMMUTER AND CERTIFICATED CARRIERS:
SIZE AND GROWTH, 1970 AND 1974

	Fiscal Year 1970	Calendar Year 1974	Annual Growth Rate (percent)
Commuter Carriers			
Carriers reporting	183	213	3.4
Number of flights	807,078	1,029,479	5.6
Passengers	4,217,431	6,842,363	11.4
Cargo (pounds)	38,661,227	138,279,017	32.7
Mail (pounds)	69,532,851	156,293,120	19.7
Certificated Carriers			
Carriers reporting	26	26	0.0
Number of flights	4,750,717	3,273,736	Negative
Passengers	152,407,139	185,451,513	4.5
Cargo (pounds)	3,773,964,320	5,048,914,580	6.7
Mail (pounds)	758,172,540	1,664,752,560	19.2

Sources: For commuter carriers: Civil Aeronautics Board, Bureau of Operating Rights, Standards Division, *Commuter Air Carrier Traffic Statistics* for the years ended June 30, 1970, and December 31, 1974. For certificated carriers: Civil Aeronautics Board, *Airport Activity Statistics of Certificated Route Air Carriers,* for the 12 months ending June 30, 1970, and the 12 months ending December 31, 1974; certificated carrier data is for forty-eight states.

trast, certificated carriers tend to serve longer, denser markets (86 percent of their markets are *more* than 200 miles and 89 percent enplane *more* than ten passengers per day).

Commuter carriers have been able to serve small markets for a variety of reasons. They tend to use small aircraft tailored to the size of the market being served. They have lower costs than certificated carriers for equipment of the same type. This cost difference is partially because of greater operational efficiency (less overhead and lower labor costs, for example) and partially because of fewer federal requirements. The most costly federal requirements from which commuters are exempted are operations requirements imposed by the Federal Aviation Administration (for example, commuters need not incur security costs in screening passengers). Smaller but still significant savings arise from exemptions related to requirements imposed

Table 4-4

DISTRIBUTION OF PASSENGER MARKETS BY PASSENGERS PER DAY, 1974

Passengers Per Day	Commuter Carriers		Certificated Carriers[a]	
	Number of markets	Percent	Number of markets	Percent
Under 10	969	77.0	286	10.8
10–20	103	8.2	578	21.9
20–30	50	4.0	351	13.3
30–40	31	2.5	219	8.3
Over 40	104	8.3	1,204	45.6
Total	1,257	100.0	2,638	100.0

[a] The data refers to markets with single-plane service. Markets where connecting service only is offered were excluded in order to make the data more comparable with commuter operations.

Sources: For commuter carriers: Civil Aeronautics Board, *Commuter Air Carrier Traffic Statistics, Year Ending June 30, 1974,* July 1975, table 3. For certificated carriers: Civil Aeronautics Board, Bureau of Operating Rights, *The Domestic Route System,* October 1974, table 8.

Table 4-5

DISTRIBUTION OF PASSENGER MARKETS BY MILEAGE, 1974

Mileage	Commuter Carriers		Certificated Carriers[a]	
	Number of markets	Percent	Number of markets	Percent
Under 100	514	40.9	63	2.4
100–200	460	36.6	306	11.7
200–300	190	15.1	374	14.2
300–400	58	4.6	287	10.9
Over 400	35	2.8	1,595	60.8
Total	1,257	100.0	2,625	100.0

[a] The data refers to markets with single-plane service. Markets where connecting service only is offered were excluded in order to make the data more comparable with commuter operations.

Sources: For commuter carriers: Civil Aeronautics Board, *Commuter Air Carrier Traffic Statistics, Year Ending June 30, 1974,* July 1975, table 3. For certificated carriers: Civil Aeronautics Board, Bureau of Operating Rights, *The Domestic Route System,* October 1974, table 9.

Table 4-6

FREQUENCY OF CARRIER SERVICE BY SIZE OF POINT, 1973

Size of Point: Average Daily Passenger Enplanements	Commuter Carriers		Certificated Carriers	
	Number of points	Average weekly departures	Number of points	Average weekly departures
1.0–4.9	59	21.9	24	16.5
5.0–9.9	50	28.7	36	20.3
10.0–14.9	25	46.9	27	20.7
15.0–19.9	21	52.2	18	26.6
20.0–29.9	27	58.7	37	28.8
30.0–39.9	17	56.5	19	31.2
40.0–49.9	12	60.3	16	33.6
50 and over	51	—[a]	256	—[a]

[a] Not calculated.

Source: Calculated from the data contained in Civil Aeronautics Board, Bureau of Operating Rights, Standards Division, *A Profile of Airline Service in the 48 Contiguous States: May 1, 1973*, December 1974, table 8.

by the CAB (for example, a reduction in legal fees associated with processing route cases).

Because of their use of small aircraft and operational efficiency, commuters are able to provide frequent service into smaller points. As indicated in Table 4-6, the frequency of service provided by commuters is about twice as great as that provided by certificated carriers at points with the same volume of traffic. While providing more frequent service, the commuters are able to charge fares generally comparable to those charged by certificated carriers.[10]

Since it is clear that the future of small communities will depend upon commuter service, the question arises about what level of traffic will support such service. Any changes in the existing regulatory system may hasten the transition from certificated service to commuter service at most points and the abandonment of remaining points. Thus, the level of traffic which will support commuter service is of major importance.

---

[10] A staff study of the Council of Economic Advisers indicated that the fares charged by commuter carriers have a lower fixed component and a higher charge per mile than those charged by local service carriers. Thus, for distances up to about 100 miles, commuter fares would usually be lower than the fares charged by certificated carriers. See Miller and Laney, "Evidence on Regulated and Unregulated Air Fares."

The CAB's 1972 study of service to small communities estimated that any point enplaning seventeen or eighteen passengers a day would probably support viable and unsubsidized commuter service.[11] Since traffic statistics for commuter carriers began to be collected in 1970, historical data on the number of passengers actually needed to sustain service were not available. Therefore, the board arrived at its estimate through a consideration of operating costs, typical passenger fares, and load factors. Although this is the sort of calculation any entrepreneur must make before entering the market, it is subject to a wide range of error, and we believe that the threshold of seventeen or eighteen passengers was far too high. Data are now available that can be used to establish the volume of passengers necessary to support commuter service without having to make the type of estimates the board's staff was forced to make in 1972. We began by examining the carriers listed as providing service during 1974. These carriers were screened to eliminate those which were not headquartered in the forty-eight states or which served any point under a replacement agreement with a certificated carrier (a replacement agreement opened the possibility that a commuter was operating a different service pattern than it otherwise would). Also eliminated were all carriers who did not file timely and complete reports with the board in both 1972 and 1974. The result was a sample of forty-two carriers who had been operating for at least three years, whose system was not affected by replacement agreements, and who had collected what the board considered adequate data and submitted that data in a timely manner.

For the forty-two carriers meeting these qualifications, each of the points served was screened. Points not operated in both 1972 and 1974 were eliminated, as were all points to which a commuter carried mail.[12] Unfortunately, this eliminated many of the smallest points in the system since a commuter carrier serving, say, a large hub, a small hub, and a number of small communities, will typically carry mail from the small hub to several of the small communities, and the station least likely to be affected by mail would be the large hub. After the screening process described above, a total of ninety-three stations served by thirty-three carriers remained.

---

[11] In subsequent analyses, to be on the conservative side, the CAB used a threshold of twenty-five passengers a day.

[12] Since there is a possibility that a mail contract will induce a carrier to operate its system differently than it otherwise would, all commuter carriers who carried mail might have been eliminated as were carriers who had replacement agreements. However, since most major commuter carriers handle at least some mail, and it was not possible to eliminate a carrier completely on those grounds, only the points to or from which they carried mail were eliminated.

Having selected a sample of points voluntarily served for several years by established carriers, it was hoped that passenger traffic at those points would provide some insight into the volume of passenger traffic needed to support such service. Since the board maintains commuter data on the basis of markets served, it was necessary to add market data in order to calculate the number of average daily passenger enplanements at these points. The format in which the data were available did not identify the amount of traffic carried by each commuter in markets served by more than one commuter. Hence, points were eliminated when one or more of the markets served from that point was shared with another commuter carrier. In addition, four points served by one carrier were eliminated when it turned out that the markets served from those points included international traffic. The final result was a sample of sixty-five points served by thirty carriers. The volume of traffic enplaned at these points is shown in Table 4-7. It is clear that carriers unsubsidized and free to discontinue unprofitable operations choose to continue service to a number of very

Table 4-7
SIZE OF POINTS CONTINUOUSLY SERVED
BY SELECTED COMMUTER CARRIERS

Size of Point: Average Daily Passenger Enplanements	Number of Points	Percentage	Cumulative Percentage
2 or less	4	6.2	6.2
3 or 4	1	1.5	7.7
5 or 6	3	4.6	12.3
7 or 8	4	6.2	18.5
9 or 10	9	13.8	32.3
11 or 12	6	9.2	41.5
13 or 14	4	6.2	47.7
15 or 16	3	4.6	52.3
17 or 18	3	4.6	56.9
19 or 20	4	6.2	63.1
21 or 22	4	6.2	69.3
23 or 24	4	6.2	77.5
25 and up	16	24.6	100.0
Total	65	100.0	

Source: Data accumulated by the Regulatory Policy Staff of the Department of Transportation.

small points. It is also clear that the CAB threshold for profitable commuter service seems high—for half of these points are below the board's seventeen or eighteen threshold. However, no threshold below which commuter activity seems unlikely is apparent from the data.

A second approach to establishing a threshold where commuter service is likely to be economically viable was that of examining the payments made by certificated carriers to commuter carriers who provide replacement service in their stead. During 1975, a total of forty-four points were served by commuter carriers as replacements for two trunk and six local service airlines. These points are listed in Table 4-8. These are points where certificated carriers have suspended service but remain responsible for insuring that scheduled service is maintained. In some cases financial assistance to the commuter carrier is provided by the certificated carrier. In other instances, no financing is provided but the certificated carrier guarantees that the commuter carrier will break even for some period of time. In still other cases, no explicit financial arrangement exists but the suspension of the certificated carrier is contingent upon service being provided by a commuter. Since many of the replacement points enplane very few passengers, it was hoped that the level of payments by certificated carriers would shed some light both on the level of traffic needed for commuter viability and on the amount of financial assistance needed to continue service at the smallest points.

Allegheny Airlines, which had twenty-seven points being served by commuters under replacement agreements during 1974, does not report expenditures and revenues disaggregated by the points involved. On a system-wide basis, however, they are usually successful in having their commuter network break even. The other seven airlines, having either replacement agreements or responsibility for resuming service should the commuter service fail, reported no comparable expenditures. Thus, although it appears that commuter service is economically viable with very low levels of passenger traffic, we are again unable to establish a threshold.

A third approach, and ultimately the most useful, was that of examining the stability of commuter service over some period of time. As shown in Table 4-9, all of the 190 points which received commuter service during fiscal year 1973 also had commuter service during calendar year 1974. Thus, no point enplaning six or more passengers per day had lost service six months later. Not only is the continuity of commuter service remarkably stable during the short run, it is also stable over a longer term. As indicated in Table 4-10, only 4 of the

Table 4-8

POINTS RECEIVING SERVICE BY COMMUTER CARRIERS AS REPLACEMENTS FOR CERTIFICATED CARRIERS, 1975

Point	Certificated Carrier Replaced
Atlantic City, N.J.	Allegheny
Altoona, Pa.	Allegheny
Astoria/Seaside, Oreg.	Air West
Binghamton, N.Y.	Eastern
Bloomington, Ind.	Allegheny
Cape May, N.J.	Allegheny
Clearfield/Philipsburg/Bellefonte, Pa.	Allegheny
Clinton, Iowa	Ozark
Crescent City, Calif.	Air West
Danville, Ill.	Allegheny
Dodge City, Kans.	Frontier
DuBois, Pa.	Allegheny
Elkins, W.Va.	Allegheny
Great Bend, Kans.	Frontier
Hagerstown, Md./Martinsburg, W.Va.	Allegheny
Hazleton, Pa.	Allegheny
Hutchinson, Kans.	Frontier
Johnstown, Pa.	Allegheny
Key West, Fla.	National
Kingman, Ariz.	Air West
Kokomo/Logansport/Peru, Ind.	Allegheny
Lancaster, Pa.	Allegheny
Mansfield, Ohio	Allegheny
Massena, N.Y.	Allegheny
Moab, Utah	Frontier
Muncie/Anderson/Newcastle, Ind.	Allegheny
Natchez, Miss.	Southern
New London/Groton, Conn.	Allegheny
Ogdensburg, N.Y.	Allegheny
Oil City/Franklin, Pa.	Allegheny
Owensboro, Ky.	Ozark
Pullman, Wash.	Air West
Reading, Pa.	Allegheny
Rutland, Vt.	Allegheny
Salisbury, Md.	Allegheny
Saranac Lake/Lake Placid/Plattsburgh, N.Y.	Allegheny
State College, Pa.	Allegheny
Terre Haute, Ind.	Allegheny
Trenton, N.J.	Allegheny
Walla Walla, Wash.	Air West
Watertown, N.Y.	Allegheny
Wenatchee, Wash.	Air West
Winona, Minn.	North Central
Victoria, Tex.	Frontier

Source: Civil Aeronautics Board, "Supplemental and Replacement Commuter Air Carrier Service on Certificated Routes," unpublished table, October 1, 1975.

Table 4-9

SHORT-TERM CONTINUITY OF SCHEDULED PASSENGER
SERVICE BY COMMUTER CARRIERS BASED ON
AVERAGE DAILY PASSENGER ENPLANEMENTS (ADPE)

FY 1973 ADPE	Total Points Receiving Service during FY 1973	Points Receiving Service during both FY 1973 and CY 1974	Points Receiving Service during FY 1973 but not during CY 1974	Percentage Retaining Service
0.1–0.9	80	37	43	46
1.0–1.9	28	19	9	68
2.0–2.9	16	11	5	69
3.0–3.9	11	7	4	64
4.0–4.9	16	12	4	75
5.0–5.9	14	13	1	93
6.0–6.9	8	8	0	100
7.0–7.9	10	10	0	100
8.0–8.9	9	9	0	100
9.0–9.9	10	10	0	100
10.0–14.9	24	24	0	100
15.0–19.9	22	22	0	100
20.0 and up	107	107	0	100
Totals	355 a	289	66	81

a By CY 1974, the number of points listed as receiving commuter service had increased by more than 30 percent to 476.

Sources: Civil Aeronautics Board, *A Profile of Airline Service in the 48 Contiguous States, May 1, 1973*, December 1974, table 8; compared with Civil Aeronautics Board, *Commuter Air Carrier Traffic Statistics, Year Ending December 31, 1974*, October 1975, table 11.

190 communities enplaning as many as six passengers a day lost commuter service during the two and one-half years between the end of fiscal year 1973 and January 1, 1976.[13] The loss of service at three of these cities, however, was related to one carrier, Air South, and does not necessarily indicate that commuter service would not have been maintained in the absence of that carrier's financial difficulties. The fourth city, Fort Wayne, is a small hub served by both United and Delta. There, a commuter carrier withdrew after unsuccessfully at-

---

[13] The identity of the carrier or carriers providing service may have changed in some cases, and the service was not necessarily continuous at all communities. However, the stability of service, over both the six-month period and the longer period, seems to indicate that service was probably continuous in the vast majority of cases.

Table 4-10

LONGER-TERM CONTINUITY OF SCHEDULED PASSENGER SERVICE BY COMMUTER CARRIERS BASED ON AVERAGE DAILY PASSENGER ENPLANEMENTS (ADPE)

ADPE FY 1973	Total Points Receiving Service during FY 1973	Points Receiving Service during both FY 1973 and CY 1976	Points Receiving Service during FY 1973 but not during CY 1976	Percentage Retaining Service
0.1–0.9	80	40	40	50
1.0–1.9	28	15	13	54
2.0–2.9	16	10	6	63
3.0–3.9	11	6	5	55
4.0–4.9	16	10	6	63
5.0–5.9	14	11	3	79
6.0–6.9	8	7	1 [b]	88
7.0–7.9	10	9 [a]	1 [b]	90
8.0–8.9	9	9	0	100
9.0–9.9	10	9	1 [b]	90
10.0–14.9	25	24	1 [c]	96
15.0–19.9	21	21 [a]	0	100
20.0 and up	107	107 [a]	0	100
Totals	355	278	77	78

[a] Includes one city which "lost" commuter air service through the certification of Air New England.

[b] Previously served by Air South.

[c] Fort Wayne, Indiana, a small hub served by two trunk carriers where Skystream Airlines withdrew after attempting to compete against United in the Chicago-Fort Wayne market and against Delta in the Detroit-Fort Wayne market. Fort Wayne retains service by both United and Delta.

Sources: Civil Aeronautics Board, *A Profile of Airline Service in the 48 Contiguous States, May 1, 1973,* December 1974, table 8; compared with the *Official Airline Guide,* January 1, 1976.

tempting to compete head-to-head with United in the Chicago-Fort Wayne market and with Delta in the Detroit-Fort Wayne market. Fort Wayne continues to receive service from both United and Delta. Thus, for the most recent two-and-one-half-year period, the largest point losing service because the point did not enplane enough traffic (rather than failure of the commuter carrier itself) enplaned fewer than six passengers a day.

The stability of commuter service summarized above reflects the fact that commuter service is far more stable than generally perceived.

Some of the larger firms have operated continuously for twenty years.[14] Most have operated more than ten years. Although still tiny in comparison to certificated carriers, the larger commuters carry more passengers than several of the local service carriers did when they received permanent certification in the early 1950s.

As in any industry where the amount of capital required for entry is low and few restrictions to entry are imposed, the commuter industry is frequently entered by small firms who do not survive. But the bulk of the industry appears highly stable. Indeed, in terms of continuous operation at small communities, the commuter industry is far more stable than is the certificated portion of the industry. The perception that continued commuter service at small points is less reliable than certificated service appears to stem from the perceived guarantee that certificated service will continue to be received. As indicated in the previous section, however, this guarantee is more apparent than real.

On the basis of the data developed in the course of this study (which were unavailable in 1972), it is clear that earlier estimates of the volume of traffic needed to sustain commuter service are far too high. Although it appears that virtually all communities enplaning as few as six passengers a day will support commuter service, we will follow the precedent set by the CAB staff of selecting thresholds on the high side. For the purposes of the analyses which follow, any point enplaning fewer than six passengers a day is assumed to be incapable of supporting commuter service; points enplaning between six and ten passengers a day are assumed to be marginal (having a 50 percent chance of retaining air service and a 50 percent chance of losing air service); points enplaning between ten and sixteen passengers a day are assumed to have a 75 percent probability of retaining air service; and points enplaning seventeen or more passengers a day are assumed to be certain of retaining air service.

The Impact of a Changed Regulatory System on Small Communities

As certification provides a community little or no protection as to the quality of service it will receive, certification provides little protection that a location will continue to receive service from a certificated carrier for an extended period of time. Thus, the protection

---

[14] For the chronology of early commuter carriers, see R. E. G. Davies, *Airlines of the United States Since 1914* (Totowa, N.J.: Rowman and Littlefield, 1972), Appendix, table 25.

a community receives by virtue of being named in the certificate of an air carrier can best be viewed as the right to a continuation of service for some limited period of time. If a community protests a carrier's plan to suspend or delete service, the suspension or deletion may be delayed several years. However, the certificate will not prolong service indefinitely.

The present subsidy program for local service carriers is intended to promote service to small communities. Given an adequate subsidy program, no point should lose service because of any change in the regulatory environment. If carriers were fully compensated for the service they provide to small points, even complete deregulation would not jeopardize that service. Thus, it can be argued that abandonment of service to small communities is not an issue in the present debate over regulatory reform. Such arguments assume the present subsidy system is adequate to protect service at small points. But the present subsidy program has not protected such service, and small points have been losing certificated service for years.

Under a changed regulatory environment, trunk carriers might wish to withdraw from a number of points where they are the second or third or fourth carrier and are doing poorly. However, as outlined above, trunk air carriers have already withdrawn from most of their marginal points, and continued air service to communities involved would not be jeopardized. The withdrawal of local service carriers from small points is not yet complete.

Either total deregulation or modification of the present regulatory system would simply accelerate the trend already underway, and the transition from local service carriers to commuter carriers at smaller communities would be completed sooner. The extent to which regulatory reform would accelerate this trend is unclear. The amount of acceleration would depend on the future level of payments made under the present subsidy system, whether or not the board makes any changes to that system. The amount of acceleration would also depend on such factors as the degree to which abandonment standards are liberalized, the degree to which entry standards are liberalized, the response of aircraft manufacturers in producing aircraft both to meet the present thirty-seat exemption for commuters and any future changes in commuter limits, the extent of future traffic growth, cost changes, general economic conditions which influence the entire aviation industry, and, to a lesser extent, political factors.[15]

---

[15] Political factors arise to the extent that airlines now serve a few politically sensitive points from which they do not attempt to withdraw, but from which they would be expected to withdraw if the board's control over entry and exit were eliminated.

Because of these factors, we cannot estimate when the transition from local service to commuter service will be completed at smaller points, nor can we estimate the extent to which changes in the regulatory system might accelerate this trend. We can, however, identify those points where certificated service will eventually be replaced by commuter service or will be abandoned if the airlines are gradually deregulated, if no traffic growth occurs, *and* if all subsidies are eliminated. The third assumption—that all subsidies are eliminated—is equivalent to the assumption that local service carriers will fulfill their twin desires of gradually completing the conversion to all-jet fleets and ceasing dependence on the present subsidy program. Although making these assumptions will result in an estimate of the maximum changes expected in the air system, doing so will provide an indication of the ultimate outcome of the direction in which the system is already moving. The extent to which regulatory changes accelerate this trend must remain a matter of judgment.

In its 1972 study of air service to small communities, the board's staff estimated that any point enplaning forty passengers a day was very likely to be able to support economically viable and unsubsidized air service by the aircraft being flown by local service air carriers—predominantly twin-engine aircraft seating forty-five to fifty-five passengers.[16] This estimate was reaffirmed in 1975.[17] The CAB staff believed that this estimate was on the high side—that many points below this level might actually support such service and that few points above it would not. Although the estimate was intended to be conservative, it should be noted that this rule of thumb, like any other, is subject to a number of qualifications. Whether or not a certificated carrier would choose to retain or delete service at a point, if given the choice, would depend on the location of the point in relation to the rest of the carrier's scheduling needs, on whether or not the point generated feeder traffic, and on other factors.

For the purposes of this study, we adopt the forty-passenger-per-day estimate as the basic dividing line between those communities which are able to support certificated service with large turboprop or piston aircraft and those which are not. We also assume that a few smaller points are capable of supporting such service. These are points where any certificated carrier schedules more than four daily arrivals. Since a carrier's certificate obligation requires him, at most, to provide two daily flights, any point which receives more than twice this level of service from any carrier is assumed to be clearly profitable.

---

[16] More than a third of the aircraft in the local service fleet are still of this type.
[17] CAB Special Staff Report, p. 201.

While points enplaning forty or more passengers per day can be considered almost certain of retaining certificated service into the foreseeable future, some of these points, unless traffic growth occurs, may not support economically viable and unsubsidized service if the carrier ultimately completes the conversion to an all-jet fleet. We believe that virtually all points enplaning eighty passengers per day will support economically viable service by the jet aircraft likely to be operated by local service carriers (the smaller jet aircraft would tend to be DC-9s and Boeing 737s).[18] Indeed, local service carriers with the preponderance of smaller aircraft often schedule their larger jets into communities enplaning fewer than eighty passengers. Where local service carriers opt to use jets, these communities are assumed to be capable of supporting such service.[19] Thus, at larger communities we have two categories:

- Those points which are expected to continue to receive jet service by certificated carriers.
- Those points where scheduled service by certificated carriers will be retained into the foreseeable future, but where certificated carriers may ultimately be replaced by commuter or intrastate carriers if the local service carrier converts to all-jet fleets and no traffic growth occurs.

The first category, among the larger points, would continue to receive service regardless of changes in the regulatory system, even if protective regulation were completely eliminated. Communities in the second category will face few changes in service in the foreseeable future, but, if traffic does not grow and the local service air carriers complete their conversion to all-jet equipment, certificated service may eventually be replaced by commuter or intrastate carriers. Detrimental effects from even complete deregulation on this category would be minor. The impact would simply be a hastening of long-term trends already under way.

How can smaller points—those generally enplaning fewer than forty passengers per day—be categorized? In its 1972 study, the CAB

---

[18] The selection of the eighty-passengers-per-day criterion is based on an analysis similar to that conducted by the board in selecting the forty-passengers-per-day criterion. However, the analysis was less extensive and a high threshold was deliberately chosen. Subsequent conversations with a number of sources in both airlines and aviation manufacturing firms confirm the impression that the threshold is high.

[19] Note that the presumption that jet service is profitable applies only to local service carriers who have a choice among aircraft types. The trunk carriers now have all-jet fleets and any trunk point enplaning fewer than eighty passengers is assumed to be a candidate for commuter replacement.

staff estimated that any point enplaning seventeen or eighteen passengers a day was almost certainly capable of supporting unsubsidized and economically viable commuter service. As indicated above, we believe this estimate is far too high. Nevertheless, in the interest of estimating maximum impacts, we retain this threshold. Thus, any point is assumed capable of supporting economically viable commuter service if it generates seventeen or more average daily passenger enplanements. In addition, any point which has received commuter or intrastate service for at least three years is also assumed to be capable of supporting such service. These points, and smaller points, are locations where certificated carriers may be expected ultimately to discontinue service in any event. If protective economic regulation were discontinued, the result would be a shortening of the transition period.

Points enplaning between ten and sixteen passengers a day are regarded as probable, but not certain, of retaining scheduled service. For subsequent analysis, we will assume that 75 percent of these points will continue to receive scheduled service. We assume that half of the points enplaning between six and nine passengers per day will receive commuter service and half will lose all air service. The outlook for continued air service is bleaker at those points now receiving certificated service and enplaning five or fewer passengers per day. Although some will undoubtedly receive commuter service, we will assume that all air service would be discontinued at these points if protective regulation were eliminated.

It is conceivable that a few small points served by commuters under replacement agreements would lose service if the certificated carrier were relieved of the obligation to ensure continued service. However, certificated carriers do not report payments of any size to their replacements. Further, certificated carriers have successfully deleted replacement points where the commuter could not make money. Thus, it appears that most points receiving replacement service are economically viable and that certification provides only limited protection for those which are not. For these reasons, such points are unlikely to be affected by regulatory changes.

In summary, we have the following categories of communities where elimination of protective regulation and elimination of the present subsidy system would be expected to hasten transitions already under way:

Category A. Points which *will retain scheduled service* by certificated carriers into the foreseeable future but where certificated carriers may ultimately be replaced by commuter or intrastate carriers if local service carriers convert to all-jet fleets.

- Those points where local service carriers average between forty and seventy-nine average daily passenger enplanements (ADPE), except where a carrier that operates both jet and smaller equipment chooses to operate jet aircraft.

- Those points where certificated carriers have fewer than forty ADPE but where any certificated carrier schedules more than four daily flight arrivals.

Category B. Points served by certificated carriers where scheduled *service will be continued* and where the transition from certificated carriers to commuter or intrastate carriers may be hastened.

- Those points not qualifying for Category A but where the total ADPE by both commuter and certificated carriers is seventeen or more.

- Those points having fewer than seventeen ADPE but where commuter or intrastate service has been provided for at least three years.

Category C. Points served by certificated carriers where scheduled *service will probably be continued* and where the transition from certificated carriers to commuter carriers may be hastened.

- Those points having between ten and sixteen ADPE, unless the point has had commuter or intrastate service for at least three years.

Category D. Points served by certificated carriers where scheduled *service may or may not be continued* and the transition from certificated carriers to either commuter service or abandonment of service may be hastened.

- Those points having between six and nine ADPE unless the point has had commuter or intrastate service for at least three years.

Category E. Points served by certificated carriers where the continuation of scheduled *service is highly uncertain* and where the transition from certificated service to either commuter service or abandonment will be hastened.

- Those points enplaning fewer than six passengers per day unless the point has had commuter or intrastate service for at least three years.

The communities falling into these categories are shown in Table 4-11. We expect that all other communities would receive a continuation of air service of the type now received even if protective regulation and the present subsidy program were completely eliminated. At about eighty points, the transition from certificated to commuter service might be hastened, but the continuation of scheduled service would not be endangered. About fifty other points would face some risk of losing all air service and, with the probabilities for retaining commuter service outlined above, fewer than thirty of these points might lose service.[20]

The fifty points subject to some risk of service loss are used by about 300,000 passengers annually, or about one-sixth of one percent of the nation's passengers. The thirty points where loss of service would be expected handle about 130,000 passengers, or about one-twentieth of one percent of the nation's travelers.[21]

It is somewhat startling that the number of points involved and the number of travelers affected are so small—especially since they result from an attempt to estimate the maximum impact of eliminating both protective regulation and all subsidy payments. Fortunately, the basic conservatism of the estimates can be readily checked. The categorization of points was based initially on the traffic data for 1974 contained in Appendix B of our original report. Subsequently, it turned out that thirteen points served by certificated carriers had been dropped during 1975. One, Goldsboro, North Carolina, was an airport consolidation. Of the remaining twelve, two were airports which would have been regarded as certain to retain commuter service and both did. The three airports regarded as likely to receive commuter service actually did so, as did all four regarded as doubtful. The only loss of all air service occurred in the smallest group. There, two of the three airports regarded as certain to lose service did so. In short, loss of service occurred at only two of the airports dropped by certificated carriers during 1975, rather than the five or six airports which would have been predicted with the probabilities utilized above. On

---

[20] All sixteen points in the smallest category would be expected to lose service, as would about one-half of the seventeen points in the next category and about one-quarter of the seventeen points in the largest category. Thus, the expected number of points losing service would be about twenty-nine.

[21] Based on the average passenger enplanements at each class, doubled to reflect total passengers to and from, and applying this figure to the percentage points in the class expected to lose all air service.

Table 4-11

COMMUNITIES FACING CHANGES IN CARRIER SERVICE, BY CATEGORIES

Category A: Points which will retain scheduled service by certificated carriers into the foreseeable future but where certificated carriers may ultimately be replaced by commuter or intrastate carriers if local service carriers convert to all-jet fleets

Anniston, Ala.
Beckley, W.Va.
Bloomington, Ill.
Chisholm/Hibbing, Minn.
Clarksburg, W.Va.
Cortez, Colo.
Durango, Colo.
El Centro, Calif.
Ft. Leonard Wood, Mo.
Hickory, N.C.
Hot Springs, Ark.
Hyannis, Mass.
Jackson, Mich.
Longview/Kilgore, Tex.
Manhattan, Kans.
Martha's Vineyard, Mass.

Menominee, Mich.
Morgantown, W.Va.
Nantucket, Mass.
North Bend/Coos Bay, Oreg.
North Platte, Nebr.
Rhinelander, Wis.
Riverton/Lander, Wyo.
Rock Springs, Wyo.
Scottsbluff, Nebr.
Staunton, Va.
Steamboat Springs, Colo.
Topeka, Kans.
Waco, Tex.
Watertown, S.Dak.
Yuma, Ariz.

Category B: Points served by certificated carriers where scheduled *service will be continued* and where the transition from certificated carriers to commuter or intrastate carriers may be hastened

Alamogordo, N.Mex.
Alpena, Mich.
Athens, Ga.
Bemidji, Minn.
Brainerd, Minn.
Cape Girardeau, Mo.
Carlsbad, N.Mex.
Clarksville, Tenn.
Clovis, N.Mex.
Cortez, Colo.
Danville, Va.
El Dorado/Camden, Ark.
Elko, Nev.
Ely, Nev.
Flagstaff, Ariz.
Gadsden, Ala.
Galesburg, Ill.
Gallup, N.Mex.
Garden City, Kans.
Greenbrier, W.Va.
Gunnison, Colo.
Harrison, Ark.

Hays, Kans.
Huron, S.Dak.
Ironwood, Mich.
Jamestown, N.Dak.
Keene, N.H.
Laramie, Wyo.
Lebanon, N.H.
Liberal, Kans.
Manitowoc, Wis.
Marion, Ill.
Mattoon, Ill.
Merced, Calif.
Modesto, Calif.
Montpelier, Vt.
Montrose/Delta, Colo.
Mount Vernon, Ill.
New Bedford, Mass.
Ottumwa, Iowa
Rocky Mount, N.C.
Salem, Oreg.
Salina, Kans.
Sault Ste. Marie, Mich.

Table 4-11 (Continued)

Sheridan, Wyo.	Tyler, Tex.
Temple, Tex.	Vernal, Utah
Thief River Falls, Minn.	Waterville, Maine
Tupelo, Miss.	Worland, Wyo.

Category C: Points served by certificated carriers where scheduled *service will probably be continued* and where the transition from certificated carriers to commuter carriers may be hastened

Beloit/Janesville, Wis.	Lovell/Powell/Cody, Wyo.
Brownwood, Tex.	Moultrie, Ga.
Enid, Okla.	Norfolk, Nebr.
Fairmont, Minn.	Page, Ariz.
Hastings, Nebr.	Silver City, N.Mex.
Hobbs, N.Mex.	Sterling/Rock Falls, Ill.
Hot Springs, Va.	Williston, N.Dak.
Jonesboro, Ark.	Yankton, S.Dak.
Kearney, Nebr.	

Category D: Points served by certificated carriers where scheduled *service may or may not be continued* and the transition from certificated carriers to either commuter service or abandonment of service may be hastened

Brookings, S.Dak.	Lufkin, Tex.
Cedar City, Utah	Manistee, Mich.
Chadron, Nebr.	Mankato, Minn.
Columbus, Nebr.	McCook, Nebr.
Goodland, Kans.	Mitchell, S.Dak.
Greenwood, Miss.	Rockford, Ill.
Independence/Parson City, Kans.	Sidney, Nebr.
Kirksville, Mo.	Worthington, Minn.
London/Corbin, Ky.	

Category E: Points served by certificated carriers where the continuation of scheduled *service is highly uncertain* and where the transition from certificated service to either commuter service or abandonment will be hastened

Alliance, Nebr.	Lewiston, Maine
Blythe, Calif.	Lewistown, Mont.
Devil's Lake, N.Dak.	Miles City, Mont.
Glasgow, Mont.	Paris, Tex.
Glendive, Mont.	Ponca City, Okla.
Glens Falls, N.Y.	Sidney, Mont.
Havre, Mont.	University/Oxford, Miss.
Lamar, Colo.	Wolf Point, Mont.

Sources: The basic data for categorizing points—the volume of traffic—are contained in Appendix B of the original report. Data with respect to schedules, equipment types, and the continuity of commuter service were taken from the *Official Airline Guide,* August 15, 1975, and earlier issues.

this basis, the estimate that approximately thirty points might lose service seems overstated by a factor of two or three.

The fact that few small points would lose all air service even under complete deregulation and elimination of the present subsidy system reflects the fact that most small points have already lost certificated service. The trend toward abandonment of small points continues at a rapid pace. During the first two months of 1976, certificated carriers either withdrew or were preparing to do so from a number of other points. Indeed, based on past trends there remains only a three- to five-year stock of small points served by certificated carriers. Although a few small points may retain certificated service beyond that time, the costs of retaining one or two smaller aircraft in an otherwise all-jet fleet will also rise along with the pressure to abandon the few remaining small points. Thus, the present regulatory system is so close to the elimination of certificated service at small points and the elimination of the remaining points seems so inevitable that service to small communities would be little affected by even the complete elimination of protective regulation.

It seems paradoxical that declining service to small communities should be used to justify continuation of the present regulatory system. The present system of economic regulation has permitted a rapid decline in the number of points served and a reduction in the quality of service at remaining points. At times, it has even provided incentives to regulated carriers to move to larger aircraft and abandon small points. Indeed, most small points now receive scheduled service only from unregulated commuter carriers.

5

AIR SERVICE TO SMALL COMMUNITIES: FURTHER DISCUSSION OF THE ISSUES

Regulatory Policy Staff, U.S. Department of Transportation

On March 29, 1976, the Department of Transportation (DOT) released a report tracing the decline in air service to small communities by the nation's regulated air carriers, the growth of commuter service, and the ineffectiveness of the present program of subsidizing local service air carriers. In response, the Association of Local Transport Airlines (ALTA) submitted an "Answer" accompanying the testimony of William C. Burt, Esq., before the Subcommittee on Aviation of the Senate Commerce Committee, on June 14, 1976, disagreeing with certain aspects of the analysis in the report. Regettably, that "Answer" is full of factual errors, distortions, and inaccuracies. DOT therefore has prepared point-by-point comments on the "Answer." These comments are set forth below.

The Obligations and Restrictions Imposed on Certificated Air Carriers

The first portion of DOT's report reviewed the obligations and restrictions imposed on certificated air carriers. It showed that the requirements for service at any community are minimal, that air carrier managements have great discretion in choosing the level of service they wish to offer, and that restrictions imposed by the Civil Aeronautics Board serve principally to restrict competition rather than to guarantee service. Thus, the pattern of air service at any given community in most cases results from market demand and decisions of

This paper is edited from a report entitled *Comments of the United States Department of Transportation on the Answer of the Association of Local Transport Airlines to the Report "Air Service to Small Communities."* The report is dated July 1976. The principal author of the study was Peyton L. Wynns, an economist on the regulatory policy staff in the Office of the Secretary, U.S. Department of Transportation.

carrier managements rather than protection offered by the present regulatory system.

Beginning with discussion of Air New England, the report demonstrated that certificate restrictions imposed on air carriers serve little or no purpose in protecting service to small communities. With respect, for example, to Air New England's two-stop restriction between Boston and New York, the report observed that:

> Since Air New England cannot become a viable competitor with two-stop service, it does not attempt to participate in the market. Thus, the restriction does little to aid the four points (New Bedford, Hyannis, Martha's Vineyard, and Nantucket) which might benefit by forcing Boston-New York traffic to stop through those points. Furthermore, even if the restriction were intended to force traffic through small points, the restriction would help only two of the four points. The two smallest points, presumably most in need of protection, would receive none.[1]

Turning next to the restrictions imposed on North Central Airlines, the report demonstrated that certificate restrictions serve primarily to protect the markets of other carriers. In North Central's case, it faces restrictions at each and every one of the twenty-eight points where other airlines also serve. In contrast, North Central faces not a single certificate restriction at any of the thirty-nine points where it is the only carrier. As the report observed, "A clearer pattern of protectionism would be hard to find."[2]

As a practical matter, small communities are protected only by the carrier's obligation to provide some level of service—one or two flights per day—to each point on their route system. Further, because the board is precluded by law from controlling either equipment or schedules, carriers may use any type of equipment or arrive at any time of the day they choose. Thus, the report concluded that communities receive little in the way of guaranteed service from the present regulatory system.

The local service carriers vigorously object on two grounds. First, they assert, "The Report chooses to ignore the role of stop restrictions in assuring service to intermediate points."[3] "Because it

---

[1] U.S. Department of Transportation, Office of Transportation Regulatory Policy, *Air Service to Small Communities*, March 1976, p. 10.

[2] Ibid., p. 16.

[3] U.S. Congress, Senate, Subcommittee on Aviation of the Commerce Committee, *Answer of the Association of Local Transport Airlines to the Report "Air Service to Small Communities,"* accompanying the testimony of William C. Burt, Esq., 94th Congress, 2d session, June 14, 1976, p. 6 (hereinafter cited as ALTA Answer).

ignores the intermediate stop requirement," says ALTA, the report "reached the wrong conclusion and grossly misstates the rights of small cities to service under the present regulatory standards." [4] This allegation is factually incorrect. The nature of intermediate stop requirements was indeed discussed in DOT's report. As previously indicated, in a discussion of Air New England's intermediate stop requirements, DOT demonstrated that they contribute little or nothing to small community air service. A community's right, correctly stated, is a right to one or two flights provided at some unspecified time of the day or night to some other point of the carrier's choosing (whether or not that other point reflects a community of interest with the city being served), at least until such time as the community is abandoned by the carrier in question.

As DOT has shown, certificate restrictions do not insure a high quality of air service to small communities. Nevertheless, such communities do receive a guarantee of some minimal level of service. The local service carriers describe this guarantee as follows:

> In the new realignment certificates recently issued to most locals, the minimum service requirement was specifically embodied in the certificates. As a result, the locals today are generally required to provide two daily roundtrips to the small cities. It is this requirement which provides the *major legal assurance of adequate service* for small cities.[5]

Although the local service carriers concede that DOT's report "initially recognized that 'each point served by a certificated carrier is guaranteed some service—one or two flights per day,'" they charge: "After giving lip service to this *major guarantee of service*, the report ignores it completely in reaching its conclusion." [6] DOT did not, however, ignore this guarantee, and to charge that this guarantee was ignored is to misstate the issue. Simply stated, the issue goes to the value of the guarantee: DOT believes the guarantee is of little value in fact.

Since the issue is the value of the guarantee, it is useful to review some of the service now being provided under this guarantee. Carriers retain complete freedom with regard to scheduling of flights. Some towns are served during the morning but not during the afternoon or the evening. Others receive afternoon service, but nothing in the morning. For example, Piedmont Aviation has four flights serving

---

[4] Ibid., p. 7.
[5] Ibid., p. 4. (Emphasis added.)
[6] Ibid., p. 5. (Emphasis added.)

Newport News, Virginia, but all are scheduled in the afternoon.[7] (Newport News has service available from other carriers. The "guarantee," however, applies to each carrier separately.) Other communities are not so fortunate. Hot Springs, Virginia, is served only by Piedmont. Although Hot Springs does have three daily flights, they all depart within a three-hour period, between 11:47 a.m. and 2:40 p.m.[8] Even those points with numerous flights may have them at inconvenient times. North Central Airlines, for example, has five daily flights from Pellston, Michigan, but the first leaves at 1:16 a.m. and the second at 6:03 a.m. The other three flights are clustered within the period between 12:58 p.m. and 2:35 p.m.[9] Thus, anyone who wishes to leave between, say, 6:30 a.m. and 12:30 p.m. or after 2:35 p.m. has no air service available, despite the fact that five daily flights are offered.

The list of examples could go on and on. ALTA and DOT are in agreement that each town named in the certificate of a local service carrier is "guaranteed" one or two flights a day, five days a week, at least until such time as the carrier abandons the point. DOT has not, as ALTA charges, ignored this guarantee. Rather, it is simply that DOT, like many of the communities afflicted, does not regard this as a "major legal assurance of adequate service for small cities." The basic parameters of service quality, frequency (except for minimal frequency), scheduling, and type of equipment are not affected by the guarantee.

The ineffectiveness of the guarantee is particularly disturbing in that the locals are paid a subsidy whose apparent purpose is support of adequate service to small communities. In arguing that they are compelled to provide good service to small communities, ALTA introduces the notion that "The locals, including North Central, are paid subsidy only to the extent that they serve small cities." [10] This is factually incorrect. CAB Order 73-10-65 lists a number of large competitive markets which are, in fact, eligible for subsidy. These include, for example, Chicago-Milwaukee, Cleveland-Detroit, and Dallas-Houston. A sample of the major city-pairs eligible for subsidy which were listed by the CAB in Order 73-10-65 are presented in Table 5-1.[11] Operations in these large city-pair markets are "subsidy eligible" and the

---

[7] Piedmont Aviation timetable, May 1, 1976.

[8] Ibid.

[9] North Central Airlines timetable, October 26, 1975.

[10] ALTA Answer, p. 5.

[11] Selected market data on those city-pairs with competitive nonstop service were presented in the original report in a table which has not been included here.

110

Table 5-1

SAMPLE OF THE SUBSIDY-ELIGIBLE CITY-PAIRS WITH
NONSTOP COMPETITIVE SERVICE BY CARRIER

Frontier

Denver–Albuquerque
Denver–Colorado Springs
Denver–Grand Junction
Denver–Rapid City

Texas International

Dallas–Houston
Houston–San Antonio
Austin–Dallas
Dallas–Little Rock
Austin–Houston

Piedmont

Washington–Norfolk
Baltimore–Washington
Washington–Richmond
Atlanta–Asheville

Allegheny

Philadelphia–Pittsburgh
Washington–Philadelphia
Cleveland–Pittsburgh
Newark–Philadelphia
Cleveland–Detroit

North Central

Cleveland–Detroit
Chicago–Milwaukee
Madison–Chicago

Airwest

San Francisco–Sacramento
Los Angeles–Monterey
San Francisco–Eugene
Los Angeles–Fresno
San Francisco–Monterey
Los Angeles–Palm Springs
San Francisco–Oakland
Portland–Eugene

Ozark

Moline–Chicago
Minneapolis/St. Paul–Rochester
Cedar Rapids–Chicago
Milwaukee–Madison

Southern

Atlanta–Birmingham
Atlanta–Columbia
Atlanta–Greenville
Atlanta–Columbus

Source: Civil Aeronautics Board, Order 73-10-65, October 17, 1973.

losses contribute to the overall "subsidy need" upon which the overall
level of subsidy payments is largely based.

Although it is true that the payment formula does not include
such city-pairs, the "subsidy need" generated in these large markets is
nevertheless reflected in the overall level of payments. In 1973, when
the board first proposed making operations in such major competitive
markets subsidy ineligible, they estimated that several million dollars
in subsidy payments could be saved.[12] The local service carriers
objected vigorously to this proposal. Reviewing service in markets
such as Baltimore-Washington, a brief filed on behalf of Piedmont
asserted that "there is little need for extended analysis of these
markets. No sensible system would classify these markets as subsidy
ineligible."[13]

---

[12] Civil Aeronautics Board, Order 73-10-65, October 17, 1973, pp. 3 and 6.

[13] Civil Aeronautics Board, Docket 26009, December 3, 1963, brief filed by Piedmont Aviation, p. 18.

Not only are the local service carriers paid for serving large cities, in many cases in competition with unsubsidized carriers, but they have also fought to keep unsubsidized carriers out of their markets. During 1971, for example, when Southwest Airlines was seeking to begin operations in the intrastate markets of Dallas/Fort Worth-Houston, Dallas/Fort Worth-San Antonio, and Houston-San Antonio, Texas International took vigorous legal action in order to prevent them from doing so. Among its legal activities, Texas International appealed to the board and requested them to prevent Southwest from beginning operations. The board summarized Texas International's position as follows: "Even if Southwest's services are truly intrastate in character, the diversionary impact on TXI and Braniff will amount to an undue burden on interstate commerce which the Board can and should prohibit."[14] Here we have the ultimate absurdity: a subsidized local service carrier in a subsidy eligible market, flying between major cities in competition with unsubsidized trunk carriers, arguing that a new firm able to offer profitable unsubsidized service at substantial discounts should be prohibited from operating, even if the new firm was "truly intrastate in character," because there would be adverse financial impacts on interstate carriers. The board characterized these contentions as "legally untenable" and dismissed the motions.[15]

Regrettably, the situation has deteriorated since the board first proposed to make service in major competitive markets subsidy ineligible. The subsidies associated with such service have now risen to some $22 million per year,[16] and the board has again proposed to make such service subsidy ineligible. As the board said in April 1976, "We find it increasingly difficult to reconcile subsidization to hub-to-hub operations with our Congressional mandate to develop and maintain services to small communities."[17]

DOT believes that the board has embarked on the right course of action and supports the board's initiatives in this area. It is inappropriate public policy to subsidize large aircraft flying, for example, the 11 miles between San Francisco and Oakland, or the 247 miles between Dallas and Houston (flown profitably with lower fares by Southwest Airlines, an intrastate carrier that is not certificated by CAB). Making such large markets ineligible for subsidy would result in the local service carriers being truly "paid subsidy only to the extent that they

[14] Civil Aeronautics Board, Order 71-6-79, June 1971.
[15] Ibid., p. 6.
[16] Civil Aeronautics Board, Order 76-4-101, April 1976, p. 4.
[17] Ibid., p. 3.

serve small cities," which, although appropriate public policy, is not now the case.

The Volume of Service Provided to Small Cities

The second part of ALTA's "Answer" deals with the volume and quality of their air service currently provided to small cities. Their argument has three parts: that good quality service is being provided, that the acquisition of jet equipment has not led to the neglect of service at small communities, and that "recent" suspensions and deletions of service at small cities have been justified.

Quality of Service. ALTA argues that "by concentrating on the relatively small number of cities which have lost certificated service, the [DOT] Report serves to obscure the fact that the locals are not only providing a very substantial volume of scheduled subsidized service— they are providing substantially more than they did 10 years ago." We do not regard the locals' abandonment of 107 cities since 1965 to be "a relatively small number." Nor is this period atypical. (We have listed in Table 5-2 the cities which lost all certificated service as a result of being abandoned by a local service carrier.)

ALTA is correct in stating that the local service carriers do provide substantially more subsidized service than they did ten years ago. The increase in subsidized service does not represent travel to the small towns the subsidy program is designed to help. Rather, it results from ever-increasing numbers of passengers traveling between major points where alternative, unsubsidized service is available.

With respect to the quality of service offered to small communities, ALTA states:

> The locals are providing high quality service at the small cities. The table below sets forth the frequencies scheduled by the local service carriers during 1974 by the size of the city served:

Distribution of Local Carriers'
Stations by Population Size and Service

Population Groupings	Total Airports	Average Daily Scheduled Departures
1- 25,000	106	3.6
25,001- 50,000	65	5.1
50,001-100,000	23	6.6

Table 5-2
POINTS ABANDONED BY LOCAL SERVICE CARRIERS, 1964–1976

Point Abandoned	Year Certificated Service Discontinued	Carrier[a]
Arizona		
Kingman	1970	RW
Prescott	1970	RW
Winslow	1974	FL
Arkansas		
Jonesboro	1976	TI
Pine Bluff	1965	TI
California		
Apple Valley	1966	BAL
Crescent City	1975	RW
Inyokern	1973	RW
Long Beach	1973	BAL
Marysville/Yuba	1970	RW
Oxnard/Ventura	1973	RW
Palmdale/Lancaster	1975	RW
San Luis Obispo/Paso Robles	1973	RW
Santa Rosa	1974	RW
Colorado		
Cortez	1976	FL
Connecticut		
Bridgeport	1975	AL
New London/Groton	1973	AL
Idaho		
Burley/Rupert	1969	RW
Coeur d'Alene	1967	RW
Pullman/Moscow	1974	RW
Sun Valley/Hailey	1969	RW
Illinois		
Danville	1968	AL
Indiana		
Bloomington	1973	AL
Columbus	1965	LC
Kokomo	1969	AL
Lafayette	1974	AL
Lawrenceville	1969	AL
Marion	1969	AL
Muncie	1971	AL

Table 5-2 (Continued)

Point Abandoned	Year Certificated Service Discontinued	Carrier[a]
Indiana (continued)		
Richmond	1965	LC
Terre Haute	1973	AL
Iowa		
Clinton	1965	OZ
Kansas		
Dodge City	1968	FL
Great Bend	1970	FL
Hutchinson	1970	FL
Kentucky		
Owensboro	1975	OZ
Maryland		
Hagerstown	1970	AL
Salisbury	1969	AL
Massachusetts		
Lawrence	1965	NE
Michigan		
Cadillac/Reed City	1966	NC
Pontiac	1966	NC
Port Huron	1965	NC
Minnesota		
Mankato	1969	NC
Winona	1969	NC
Mississippi		
Natchez	1975	SO
Missouri		
Kirksville	1976	OZ
Moberly	1969	OZ
Montana		
Glendive	1968	FL
Sidney	1968	FL
New Jersey		
Atlantic City	1970	AL
Cape May	1970	AL
Trenton	1972	AL

Table 5-2 (Continued)

Point Abandoned	Year Certificated Service Discontinued	Carrier[a]
New York		
Glens Falls	1975	AL
Jamestown	1974	AL
Liberty/Monticello	1970	MO
Massena	1970	MO
Ogdensburg	1970	MO
Olean	1972	AL
Oneonta	1968	MO
Plattsburgh	1974	AL
Poughkeepsie	1970	MO
Saranac Lake	1974	AL
Watertown	1974	AL
North Carolina		
Elizabeth City	1972	PI
Southern Pines	1972	PI
Ohio		
Findlay	1965	LC
Lima	1973	AL
Mansfield	1969	AL
Portsmouth	1971	AL
Zanesville/Cambridge	1970	AL
Oklahoma		
Bartlesville	1974	FL
Duncan	1972	FL
McAlester	1968	FL
Muskogee	1975	FL
Oregon		
Astoria/Seaside	1974	RW
Baker	1973	RW
Burns	1967	WCA
Lakeview	1967	WCA
Ontario/Payette	1973	RW
Roseburg	1973	RW
Pennsylvania		
Altoona	1971	AL
Clearfield/Phillipsburg	1973	AL
Dubois	1969	AL
Hazleton	1968	AL
Lancaster	1973	AL
Johnstown	1970	AL
Oil City/Franklin	1969	AL

Table 5-2 (Continued)

Point Abandoned	Year Certificated Service Discontinued	Carrier[a]
Pennsylvania (continued)		
Reading	1973	AL
State College/Bellefonte	1973	AL
South Carolina		
Anderson	1974	SO
Greenwood	1974	SO
Tennessee		
Crossville	1974	SO
Rockwood	1966	SO
Shelbyville/Tullahoma	1974	SO
Texas		
Big Spring	1975	TI
College Station/Byron	1973	TI
Galveston	1972	TI
Lufkin	1975	TI
Utah		
Moab	1974	FL
Vermont		
Rutland	1970	MO
Virginia		
Pulaski/Radford/Blacksburg	1972	PI
Washington		
Ephrata/Moses Lake	1974	RW
Hoquiam/Aberdeen	1974	RW
Olympia	1973	RW
Port Angeles	1967	RW
Walla Walla	1974	RW
Wenatchee	1974	RW
West Virginia		
Elkins	1969	AL

[a] Airline abbreviations: AL—Allegheny; BAL—Bonanza; FL—Frontier; LC—Lake Central; MO—Mohawk; NC—North Central; OZ—Ozark; PI—Piedmont; RW—Hughes Airwest; SO—Southern; TI—Texas International; WCA—West Coast.

Source: Civil Aeronautics Board, "Unduplicated Suspensions and Deletions," unpublished table.

The assumption that locals are not fulfilling their function of serving small cities is simply not true. Even for cities with a population of 25,000 or below, the locals are averaging 3.6 departures per day. Cities between 25,000 and 100,000 population receive substantially more departures.[18]

The table suggests that quality of service is measured entirely in terms of frequencies. ALTA does not make any representation about departure times, community needs, or destinations. As previously noted, service into small communities often appears to be scheduled as an afterthought. Service is provided at undesirable times of the day when no one wants to fly elsewhere on the system and no other reasonable use can be made of the equipment involved. Flight frequencies alone do not show quality air service, even if the figures could be taken at face value.[19]

ALTA argues that the subsidy is falling when measured in terms of constant dollars. In fact, whether measured in terms of current or constant dollars, the subsidy bill has been rising in recent years. Between 1969 and 1975, it rose from slightly less than $36 million to slightly less than $70 million.[20]

A more relevant measure of change in the rate of subsidization would be the subsidy provided per unit of service. Given the structure of the subsidy program, however, it is difficult to identify those services which in fact require subsidy. ALTA does contend that "the locals' jet equipment has been utilized primarily to serve subsidy ineligible routes."[21]

Taking ALTA's contention as correct, it is possible to examine whether subsidy per unit of non-jet service is increasing or decreasing. Table 5-3 shows non-jet revenue passenger miles by year, subsidy by year, and subsidy per non-jet revenue passenger mile. This shows that subsidy cost per revenue passenger mile has nearly tripled since 1968. Clearly, subsidy costs per unit of service are increasing, not decreasing. Of course, this is an underestimate of the subsidy per unit of service requiring subsidy. Many of the non-jet aircraft used by

---

[18] ALTA Answer, p. 9.

[19] Even the data in ALTA's table cannot be verified since a source is not given. The data conflict with data presented on a similar subject by ALTA to the board in 1973. In a filing made on April 20, 1973 (Docket 25342), the local service carriers indicated that they served forty-five airports where the population was less than 25,000; seventy-two airports where the population was 25,000-50,000; and eighty-nine airports where the population was 50,000-100,000. In view of the fact that those numbers differ so radically from the ones now presented, and since no source was given in either case, no significance can be attached to the data.

[20] ALTA Answer, p. 9.

[21] Ibid., p. 11.

118

Table 5-3

SUBSIDY PER NON-JET REVENUE PASSENGER MILE (RPM)
TO LOCAL SERVICE CARRIERS, 1968–1975

Year	Non-Jet RPMs (thousands)	Total Subsidy Paid to Locals (thousands)	Subsidy per RPM
1968	3,076,855	$40,949.6	$0.013
1969	2,563,122	34,804.2	0.014
1970	2,316,916	40,339.5	0.017
1971	2,292,982	58,862.8	0.026
1972	2,357,513	64,484.4	0.027
1973	2,232,205	64,555.3	0.029
1974	1,865,795	68,508.3	0.037
1975	1,511,294	59,789.5	0.040

Source: Civil Aeronautics Board, Form 41.

locals must be profitable. Only that service being provided because of the subsidy that would not be provided in a free market is relevant.

Acquisition of Modern Equipment. ALTA argues that the acquisition of modern equipment (that is, jets) has not led to the neglect of service at small communities, but rather to a strengthened route system. DOT does not quarrel with ALTA's conclusion that the transition from smaller aircraft to larger aircraft has enabled them to "strengthen and improve length of hop, average passenger trip, and average passengers per mile." [22] As ALTA notes, the result has been that costs per available seat-mile for the local service carriers have increased relatively less than similar costs for trunks. This analysis, however, does not address the point at issue. The simple fact is that local service carriers have been making a transition from smaller piston and turboprop aircraft suited for small town service to jet aircraft. As they have made the transition to jet aircraft and deleted small points, their average length of hop and passenger trip has naturally increased. The ultimate progression is to stage lengths, passenger trips, and seat-mile costs entirely comparable to those of the trunks. Unfortunately, in the process of this transition, the local service carriers

---

[22] Ibid., p. 12.

will, as have the trunks, essentially terminate all service to small communities.

Suspensions and Deletions. ALTA argues that the suspensions and deletions of service at small cities have been economically justified and have not substantially impaired the overall quality of small city air service. ALTA notes than "in 1969, they [locals] were serving 465 cities—or 6 more than had been served in 1960." [23] These numbers are accurate. But any implication that locals were providing more service to small communities than before is inaccurate. In fact, the 1960s saw a substantial period of route strengthening with the local service carriers granted access to more and more major markets. As they moved into large towns already served by trunks, they were simultaneously departing small towns at which they provided the only service. Table 5-4 indicates the towns they dropped and the towns they entered. As can be seen, between 1960 and 1969 the locals were rapidly abandoning small towns while adding large towns which were already served by other carriers. Southern's experience is not untypical. Southern dropped Morristown, Rockwood, Corinth, Selma, and Bogalusa. They added New York, Washington, Charleston, Columbia, Anderson, Crossville, Jackson, St. Louis, and Montgomery. All of the points they dropped were small. Of the points they added, only Anderson, Crossville, and Jackson were non-hubs, and Anderson and Crossville were subsequently dropped. Only by offsetting large cities already served by other carriers against small points they abandoned are the local carriers able to make the technically accurate statement that they served six more cities in 1969 than in 1960. This statement, however technically correct, should not be used to obscure the fact that the number of small towns served is steadily declining.

ALTA argues that, for the eighty-five cities which lost service after 1969, the degradation in service was not serious. The thirty-five smallest points are dismissed without comment, and only the fifty largest (those enplaning more than six passengers a day) are discussed. There is a table purporting to show that only twenty-two (or slightly less than half of these fifty points) were more than fifty miles from another airport.[24] Although it is hard to see how these numbers prove ALTA's contention that the quality of small city air service has not been "substantially impaired," it is even harder to see how these

---

[23] Ibid., pp. 12 and 15.

[24] Since the alternative airports are not identified, the accuracy of these estimates could not be checked.

Table 5-4

POINTS ADDED AND DROPPED BY
LOCAL CARRIERS, 1960–1969

Carrier	Points Added	Points Dropped
Airwest[a]	Fresno, Calif. *Inyokern, Calif. *Lake Tahoe, Calif. *Seattle/Tacoma, Wash. Tucson, Ariz.	†Apple Valley, Calif. Bellingham, Wash. †Burns, Oreg. Coeur d' Alene, Idaho Cut Bank/Shelby, Mont. †Flagstaff, Ariz. †Hawthorne, Nev. †Kanab, Utah †La Grande, Oreg. †Lakeview, Oreg. Logan, Utah †McCall, Idaho †Newport/Toledo, Oreg. †Oceanside, Calif. Ogden, Utah Omak, Wash. Pendleton, Oreg. Port Angeles, Wash. Provo, Utah †St. George, Utah †Tonopath, Nev. Ukiah, Calif.
Allegheny[b]	Albany, N.Y. Charleston, W.Va. Clarksburg/Fairmont, W.Va. *Elkins, W.Va. Evansville, Ind. Lexington, Ky. Louisville, Ky. *Martinsburg, W.Va. Memphis, Tenn. Morgantown, W.Va. Nashville, Tenn. Newport News/Hampton, Va. Norfolk, Va. Saint Louis, Mo. *Sandusky, Ohio	Cumberland, Md. Danville, Ill. †Dover/New Philadelphia, Pa. Georgetown/Rehoboth Beach, Del. Hagerstown, Md. Hazleton, Pa. Lockhaven, Pa. Mansfield, Ohio Marion, Ohio Richmond, Ind. Salisbury, Md.
Frontier[c]	Alamogordo/Holloman, N.Mex. Bozeman, Mont. El Paso, Tex. Garden City, Kans. Goodland, Kans. *Great Bend, Kans.	‡Ada, Tex. Ainsworth, Nebr. ‡Ardmore, Tex. Beatrice, Nebr. Dickinson, N.Dak. Douglas, Wyo. Hot Springs, S.Dak.

121

Table 5-4 (Continued)

Carrier	Points Added	Points Dropped
	Hays, Kans.	Idaho Falls, Idaho
	*Hutchinson, Kans.	Imperial, Nebr.
	Las Vegas, Nev.	†Lamar, Colo.
	Manhattan/Junction	Lemmon, S.Dak.
	City/Ft. Riley, Kans.	†Lubbock, Tex.
	Missoula, Mont.	Lusk, Wyo.
	Steamboat Springs/	New Castle, Wyo.
	Hayden/Craig, Colo.	Norfolk, Nebr.
	West Yellowstone, Mont.	†Plainview, Tex.
		Prescott, Ariz.
		Rawlins, Wyo.
		Safford, Ariz.
		†Sherman/Denison, Tex.
		Sterling, Colo.
		Valentine, Nebr.
Mohawk[d]	Burlington, Vt.	Auburn/Geneva, N.Y.
	Islip, N.Y.	Bradford, Pa.
	New Haven, Conn.	‡Meadville, Pa.
	*Ogdensburg/Massena,	‡Oneonta, N.Y.
	N.Y.	
	Philadelphia, Pa.	
	Pittsburgh, Pa.	
	*Plattsburgh, N.Y.	
	*Rutland, Vt.	
	*Saranac Lake, N.Y.	
	Washington, D.C.	
North Central	Alpena, Mich.	Land O' Lakes, Wis.
	Cleveland, Ohio	Mankato, Minn.
	Denver, Colo.	‡Mobridge, S.Dak.
	Flint, Mich.	Rockford, Ill.
	Muskegon, Mich.	Spearfish, S.Dak.
	Manistee/Ludington,	‡Winona, Minn.
	Mich.	
	Pellston, Mich.	
	Saginaw/Bay City, Mich.	
	Traverse City, Mich.	
Ozark	Chicago (O'Hare), Ill.	Austin/Albert Lea, Minn.
	Dallas/Ft. Worth, Tex.	†Danville, Iowa
	Denver, Colo.	‡Moberly, Mo.
	Ft. Leonard Wood, Mo.	Pittsburg, Kans.
	Mount Vernon, Ind.	St. Joseph, Mo.
	New York, N.Y.	Wichita, Kans.
	Sioux Falls, S.Dak.	
	Sterling/Rock Falls, Ind.	
	Tulsa, Okla.	
	Washington, D.C.	
Piedmont	Atlanta, Ga.	
	Augusta, Ga.	
	Baltimore, Md.	
	*Blacksburg/Radford/Pulaski, Va.	

Table 5-4 (Continued)

Carrier	Points Added	Points Dropped
	*Chicago (Midway), Ill.	
	Columbia, S.C.	
	*Elizabeth City, N.C.	
	Florence, S.C.	
	Greenville/Spartanburg, S.C.	
	*Goldsboro, N.C.	
	*Hot Springs, Va.	
	Jacksonville/Camp Lejeune, N.C.	
	Memphis, Tenn.	
	Nashville, Tenn.	
	New York (La Guardia), N.Y.	
	Rocky Mount, N.C.	
Southern	*Anderson, S.C.	Bogalusa, La.
	Charleston, S.C.	‡Corinth, Miss.
	Columbia, S.C.	‡Morristown, Tenn.
	*Crossville, Tenn.	Rockwood, Tenn.
	Jackson, Tenn.	†Selma, Ala.
	Montgomery, Ala.	
	New York (La Guardia), N.Y.	
	St. Louis, Mo.	
	Washington, D.C. (Dulles)	
Texas International [e]	Abilene, Tex.	De Ridder, La.
	Albuquerque, N.Mex.	Ft. Stockton, Tex.
	Amarillo, Tex.	†Magnolia, Ark.
	Baton Rouge, La.	Marfa/Alpine, Tex.
	*Big Spring, Tex.	†Marshall, Tex.
	*Carlsbad, N.Mex.	†Morgan City, La.
	Clovis, N.Mex.	Natchez, Miss.
	*College Station, Tex.	†Pecos, Tex.
	Denver, Colo.	
	*Ft. Polk, La.	
	Hobbs, Ark.	
	*Jonesboro, Ark.	
	Lubbock, Tex.	
	Roswell, N.Mex.	
	*Santa Fe, N.Mex.	
	Waco, Tex.	

[a] In 1960: Bonanza Airlines, Pacific Airlines, and West Coast Airlines; in 1969: Hughes Airwest.
[b] In 1960: Allegheny and Lake Central; in 1969: Allegheny.
[c] In 1960: Central Airlines and Frontier Airlines; in 1969: Frontier Airlines.
[d] Now Allegheny.
[e] In 1960: Trans-Texas Airlines; in 1969: Texas International.
Notes: * Point deleted by carrier since 1969.
  † Points served in 1960 under a temporary agreement.
  ‡ Service not inaugurated in 1960.
Sources: Civil Aeronautics Board, *Book of Official Airline Route Maps and Airport-to-Airport Mileages,* 6th edition (1960) and 14th edition (1969).

numbers justify their conclusion that "It is hard to conceive of a program which has been more successful in providing service to small cities." [25]

ALTA also notes that commuter service is available at most of those cities having more than six passengers a day, and that commuter service is available at every city which enplanes as many as six passengers per day and which is more than fifty miles from another airport. This is, of course, to be expected. As the DOT report indicated, where local service carriers abandon points of this size, unsubsidized commuter replacement service is to be expected.

ALTA asserts that "if the DOT proposal had been in effect, 47 out of the 85 cities would have lost service under the DOT proposal itself"; [26] but this is in error. The footnote referred to by ALTA relates to DOT's estimate of loss of service if communities were abandoned by subsidized local service carriers and if an alternative subsidy proposal were not adopted. DOT's estimates are intended to be conservative in estimating the availability of unsubsidized replacement service and, as a result, overstate the loss of service. ALTA might have correctly said, "Of the 85 cities abandoned by local service carriers, DOT would estimate that unsubsidized commuter replacement service would be available in at least 38 locations and a maximum of 47 would have lost service." DOT's proposal would initially guarantee service to *all* 85 cities with no qualifications. Only those 35 cities enplaning fewer than five passengers per day would have been in any danger of losing subsidy. At those points, if traffic failed to grow to a minimum of five passengers per day, the communities would ultimately have to share in the cost of the subsidy program or face the termination of service.

Service and Fares of Commuters and the Locals

ALTA contends that local service carriers, rather than commuters, provide most of the small city air service and that there is no evidence that commuter fares are lower than those charged by local service carriers.

The Volume of Services Provided. ALTA contends that local service carriers provide far more service to small cities than commuters do. In doing so, ALTA makes several erroneous and misleading comparisons. First, the association notes that local service carriers carried

---

[25] ALTA Answer, p. 15.
[26] Ibid., p. 13.

124

more total passengers and generated more passenger miles than commuters did.[27] DOT does not dispute this. Indeed, the local service carriers are far larger than the commuters. Comparing their total traffic with the total commuter traffic says nothing, however, about service to small communities. Neither does the fact that the local service carriers provide more subsidy eligible service than the commuters provide total service. The extent of subsidy eligible service reflects the present subsidy program, which pays local service carriers to fly jets between major hubs.

ALTA contends that commuter service is limited and attaches a chart (Chart B in the "Answer") which shows the 100 largest markets served by commuters to demonstrate this point. ALTA asserts that "these markets account for 68 percent of the total commuter traffic in the 48 States. As Chart B shows, there are large areas of the country which have little commuter service."[28] Presenting a map of the top 100 markets does not, of course, show that large areas of the country have little commuter service. Showing 100 markets and arguing that these represent the only important service is no more rational than arguing that because the top twenty-six airports enplane 68 percent of the nation's air passengers there is little air service available to other parts of the country.[29]

In order to demonstrate that local service carriers provide more service than commuter carriers do, ALTA discusses traffic "carried by commuters in the 148 cities listed in Appendix B to the [DOT] Report."[30] Appendix B of the department's report listed all 615 cities in the forty-eight states which received scheduled air service in 1974. Of these cities, 190 received service only from commuter carriers, 247 received service only from certificated carriers, and 178 received service from both certificated and commuter carriers. It is unclear which 148 cities ALTA chooses to discuss. In any event, the volume of air service provided to small points is summarized in Table 5-5.

The data in this table clearly demonstrate that commuters tend to provide more service and fly more passengers at the smallest points. Commuters serve almost three times as many points enplaning fewer than ten passengers per day as the certificated carriers do. Nearly twice as many passengers are served every day. The commuters have been able to provide this service without federal subsidy. It is not

---

[27] Ibid., p. 16.

[28] Ibid., p. 17.

[29] Civil Aeronautics Board and Federal Aviation Administration, *Airport Activity Statistics, Year Ended June 30, 1975*, tables 1 and 3, pp. 1-3 and 14-15.

[30] ALTA Answer, p. 17.

Table 5-5

TOTAL POINTS AND PASSENGERS SERVED BY COMMUTERS AND CERTIFICATED CARRIERS BY NUMBER OF ENPLANEMENTS, 1974

Daily Enplanements	Total Points	Exclusively Served by Commuter	Exclusively Served by Certificated Carrier	Served by Both Commuter and Certificated Carrier	Commuter Enplanements Daily	Certificated Enplanements Daily
0–9 a	128	91	32	5	355	200
10–19	65	32	28	5	490	452
20–29	47	21	20	6	517	577
30–39	33	10	16	7	497	586
40–49	18	5	6	7	265	471
50–59	15	7	6	2	405	421
60–69	12	1	7	3	138	635
70–79	19	2	10	7	500	930
80–89	16	3	9	4	330	1,023
90–99	11	0	7	4	77	969

a Points with less than one enplanement per day are not included.

Source: Prepared from U.S. Department of Transportation, "Air Service to Small Communities," a report by the Office of Transportation Regulatory Policy, March 1976, Appendix B.

until one reaches the range of forty to fifty enplanements per day that certificated carriers begin clearly to dominate service.

ALTA argues that certificated carriers provide more flights to small cities than commuter carriers do. In doing so, they argue that the table in the department's report which appears in this volume as Table 4-2 is in error. This table is not incorrect. Certificated carriers provide more flights to small cities only if trunk and local service data are added together and 3,000 weekly commuter flights are omitted from the number actually flown.

Focusing on the number of flights flown by certificated carriers vis-à-vis commuters also ignores the trend in service to small communities. Over the past five years, trunk and local service flights into small towns have decreased by 18 percent and 15 percent, respectively, while commuter flights have increased 20 percent—a trend which ALTA does not choose to dispute.

ALTA's final contention with respect to the volume of service provided to small communities is yet another variation of the argument that certificated carriers carry more passengers to small towns than commuters do.[31] The data presented by ALTA is not sourced, so it cannot be analyzed. Nevertheless, the trend is that the certificated carriers are leaving small towns. Since 1960, all certificated service has been lost by 179 points. Commuters are serving an increasing number of small towns (about 400) and are carrying an ever-increasing proportion of the passengers.

Commuter and Local Service Fares. ALTA's "Answer" addresses the question of commuter fares compared to those charged by local service carriers. ALTA does not argue that local service fares are lower than commuter fares. Rather, they argue: "There is no basis for the assertion that commuters are charging lower fares than the locals."[32] This conclusion is based on a graph comparing commuter fares in the top fifty markets with the yield of the local service carriers in subsidy eligible markets and with the CAB rate formula.[33] The locals have, in effect, compared apples and oranges. More appropriate would be a comparison of commuter fares with local service fares, or commuter yields with local service yields. This they have not done.

ALTA admits that "the Board has permitted the locals to charge somewhat higher fares than the formula on subsidy eligible services."[34]

---

[31] Ibid., p. 19, n. 1.
[32] Ibid., p. 22.
[33] Ibid., Chart C.
[34] Ibid., p. 22.

DOT believes that the word "somewhat" should be clarified. The CAB permits the locals to charge their customers up to 130 percent of the otherwise lawful fare.[35] Indeed, if a line were added to the exhibit submitted by the locals which showed 130 percent of the formula fare in small monopoly markets, the conclusions would have been far different. In fact, it would have shown that commuter fares are generally lower than local service fares up to a distance of 200 miles. Since more than 90 percent of all commuter passengers travel less than 200 miles,[36] commuter fares for the vast majority of passengers carried would be lower than the typical local service fare over comparable distances according to the data that ALTA has submitted.

The lack of validity of the comparison of commuter fares to hypothetical CAB "Y" (or coach class) fares is highlighted by ALTA's table entitled "Top Commuter Markets of 100 Miles or Greater—CY 1974." [37] The table compares commuter fares to the CAB "Y" formula fare for eighteen markets. The computed "Y" fare is lower than the commuter fare in seventeen of the eighteen markets. This, of course, ignores the fact that fully 50 percent of commuter passengers are carried in markets under 100 miles,[38] and that it is well established that commuters do not have cost advantages in longer markets. Nonetheless, the table contains a column labeled "If Served," which lists the actual local carrier fare if a local carrier serves the market. These actual fares show that only seven of the eighteen markets are in fact served by local carriers. Further, in six of the seven markets, the local carrier fare is *higher* than the CAB "Y" formula (via the 130 percent rule explained above). And even more to the point, the actual local carrier fare was lower than the commuter fare for only *one* of the seven markets. (The commuter fare was lower for two markets and four had the same fare.)

Taking a very specific example, the CAB "Y" fare of $26.85 for the 164-mile College Station-Dallas market is shown to be less than the actual commuter fare of $29.93. But College Station was dropped by a local carrier (Texas International) in 1973. In the "order to show cause" for deletion, it is indicated that the market was also served by a commuter, Davis Airlines, which flew more passengers and

---

[35] Civil Aeronautics Board, *Domestic Passenger Fare Investigation: Phase 9—Fare Structure*, Board Order 74-3-82, decided March 18, 1974, p. 181.

[36] Civil Aeronautics Board, Bureau of Operating Rights, *Commuter Air Carrier Traffic Statistics, Year Ended June 30, 1975*, January 1976, table 3.

[37] This table, labeled "Appendix B" precedes "Chart C" in testimony for ALTA by Mr. Emory Ellis, which was presented to Congress along with Mr. Burt's testimony and ALTA's Answer.

[38] Civil Aeronautics Board, *Commuter Air Carrier Traffic Statistics*, table 3.

offered more flights at a fare of $20 than Texas International did at a fare of $21. (These were the fares as of March 1, 1973. Those indicated above were as of October 10, 1975.) Further, and most important, it was indicated that continued service by Texas International would generate a subsidy need of $41 per passenger.[39]

Fortunately, there is a considerable amount of data available on the relationship between commuter and certificated fares. First, there is a Council of Economic Advisers (CEA) study, which is discussed in DOT's report and has not been challenged by ALTA. Second, there is a more recent study conducted by DOT which shows, if anything, that the CEA results were far too conservative. It shows that commuter fares are not only generally lower than the fares charged by certificated carriers, but that commuter carriers did well when engaged in head-to-head competition with certificated carriers.[40]

There is also evidence developed in connection with the *New England Service Investigation*, prepared by the CAB Bureau of Operating Rights. ALTA states that:

> A Bureau study submitted with the *New England Service Investigation*, Docket 22973, shows that where local service was replaced by commuter carrier service, fares increased by an average of 26.8 percent. (BOR-R-501, p. 6.) [41]

ALTA is incorrect. First, commuter carriers did not generally replace local service carriers. Rather, the commuters replaced services formerly provided by two trunks, Delta and Northeast, and to a much lesser extent services previously provided by Allegheny. Thus, although the new fares charged by commuters were higher than the fares charged by the trunks they replaced, the fares were not higher than the fares which might have been charged by local service carriers had they served the points in question, and had they been able to exercise their discretion to charge 130 percent of the ordinary formula fare.

More importantly, while fares did increase 26.8 percent, the number of flights more than doubled and passenger traffic rose some 70 percent. Thus, the market seemed most responsive to the greatly improved service offered by the commuters. DOT has never argued that commuter fares are always lower than those charged by certificated carriers—only that they are generally lower. The department recognizes that, in many situations where passengers demand high-

---

[39] Civil Aeronautics Board, Order 73-4-49, Docket 25187.

[40] The study appeared as Exhibit 4 of the original version of this report, but it is not included here.

[41] ALTA Answer, p. 22.

frequency service at premium prices, commuters are often able to provide such services better than certificated carriers because they are not tied to an arbitrary pricing formula which applies equally to all markets.[42]

The fact that commuters were able to double service levels and carry 70 percent more traffic without subsidy is remarkable. It is no wonder that Administrative Law Judge Greer M. Murphy, after carefully studying the transition from certificated to commuter service in New England, wrote: "The conclusion is inescapable that commuter carriers, within the limitations of their exemptions, have provided frequent and reliable service that has met the needs of the communities and has been far superior to what they received in the past." [43]

When all evidence is considered, it is clearly evident that unsubsidized commuters do in fact generally charge prices which are comparable to or lower than those charged by certificated carriers, and that, in those cases where fares are not lower, commuters are able to provide a premium service.

The Efficiency of Commuter and Local Service Air Carriers

ALTA argues that DOT did not accurately compare the efficiency of commuter air carriers with local service carriers. ALTA's argument is divided into four parts: (1) that DOT did not use cost analyses of commuter operations as compared with local service operations, (2) that the costs of operating small aircraft are relatively high, (3) that the costs would be even higher if the commuters were given major responsibilities for small city service, and (4) that DOT's analyses of markets where commuters have historically been able to provide viable service were unsound. ALTA's contentions are erroneous and unsound. Indeed, some of the arguments raised by ALTA illustrate the greater efficiency of commuters.

The Desirability of Using Hypothetical Cost Analyses Versus Actual Operating Data. DOT's report noted at the outset the difficulty of allocating both costs and revenues in applying hypothetical cost data to forecast service patterns. The report included an appendix containing an extensive critique of previous studies which had produced

---

[42] In this case, it might be noted that the prices charged by the commuters for their premium services might have been described, in ALTA's terms, as only "somewhat" higher than the previous fare levels.

[43] *New England Service Investigation*, Docket 22973, Initial Decision of Administrative Law Judge Greer M. Murphy, July 9, 1973, p. 41.

misleading results, and it discussed the methodological problems and the resulting errors.

ALTA also recognizes the difficulties in the use of hypothetical cost analyses to ascertain the efficiency of commuter service compared with similar service provided by the locals. ALTA notes that "cost data on small airplane operations is not definitive," that the board "does not receive financial reports or audit their books," and that difficult allocations of costs are involved.[44] It was for these very reasons that DOT chose not to rely on hypothetical costs to ascertain where commuter service was viable. Rather, DOT chose to rely on actual experience with commuter service. In spite of the recognized objections to hypothetical costing techniques, ALTA's argument concludes that DOT should have used such techniques. The results of ALTA's application of such techniques (discussed in the next section) are not any improvement over the previous studies and present misleading results.

ALTA's Use of Cost Analyses. Having pointed out the difficulties inherent in cost analyses and having faulted DOT for not using such analyses, ALTA next proceeds to apply such analyses in order to determine that "recent cost analyses show that costs for operating small aircraft are relatively high."[45] By judicious adjustments of certain data developed in the course of the Air Midwest Certification Proceeding,[46] ALTA purports to show that:

> A commuter carrier, without certification, would require average enplanements of 26 passengers per day to provide one flight in each direction to an intermediate point. Initial certificated operations would require 30 passengers, and a mature certificated operations (sic) would require 34 passengers per day.[47]

The costs of operating a Swearingen Metro as originally calculated by ALTA, as revised by ALTA, and as provided by the Bureau of Operating Rights are presented in Table 5-6. These are the figures on which the passenger numbers are based.

ALTA has used costs of an aircraft rarely used by commuter operators in order to generalize about the level of traffic needed to

---

[44] ALTA Answer, pp. 23-24.

[45] Ibid., p. 25.

[46] Civil Aeronautics Board, Docket 28262.

[47] ALTA Answer, p. 26. These are revised estimates. The initial passenger thresholds were 38, 43, and 49, respectively. Letter from William C. Burt to the Committee on Public Works and Transportation, June 21, 1976.

Table 5-6

COMPARISON OF ALTA'S UNIT COSTS WITH THE
BUREAU OF OPERATING RIGHTS' UNIT COSTS

	ALTA Revised[a]	ALTA[b]	BOR[c]
Commuter Carrier Costs			
Direct cost	$0.85	$0.85	$0.85
Total cost	1.38	1.38	1.38
Return and taxes	0.53	0.60	0.20
Total economic cost	1.91	2.83	1.58
Initial Certificated Costs			
Direct cost	0.95	0.95	0.95
Total cost	1.72	1.73	1.72
Return and taxes	0.53	0.60	0.20
Total economic cost	2.25	3.28	1.92
Mature Certificated Costs			
Direct cost	1.05	1.05	1.05
Total cost	2.06	2.07	2.06
Return and taxes	0.53	0.60	0.20
Total economic cost	2.59	3.72	2.27

[a] See text, note 45.

[b] ALTA Answer, p. 26.

[c] Derived from Civil Aeronautics Board, Docket 28262, BOR-R-1, p. 1, and AMW-105.

support a commuter carrier. In fact, the Swearingen Metro is one of the newest, most expensive aircraft in the commuter carrier fleet. Only fourteen such aircraft were in service on June 30, 1975, which represented 1.5 percent of the commuter fleet.[48] The use of a relatively large commuter aircraft to calculate the level of traffic needed to support commuter service is no more relevant than using the operating costs of a Boeing 747 to determine the traffic volume necessary to support scheduled jet service.

The overwhelming majority of commuter carriers use aircraft which are capable of carrying no more than fifteen or nineteen pas-

[48] Civil Aeronautics Board, Bureau of Operating Rights, *Commuter Air Carrier Traffic Statistics*, table 14. As of July 19, 1976, twenty-two of these aircraft had been delivered domestically according to Joseph F. O'Connell, executive vice president of Swearingen Aviation Corporation.

sengers.[49] To argue that twenty-six to thirty-four enplaned passengers per day at a small point are needed for one flight in each direction means, according to ALTA's calculations, that a commuter cannot operate profitably unless it has load factors of 100 percent or more. In light of the rapid and unsubsidized growth of commuters, such assertions are patently ridiculous and again illustrate the reasons DOT chose to base its analysis of commuter viability on historical operating data rather than on hypothetical cost calculations.

Increases in Commuter Costs. Having argued that commuter costs are high, ALTA next argues that these costs will inevitably increase as commuters mature and that such increases have been ignored by DOT's report. ALTA quotes a CAB staff study, *Service to Small Communities*, as recognizing that "as a commuter carrier assumes the attributes of a certificated system, it will experience direct operating costs which closely approach those of a certificated carrier."[50] This is clearly correct. If commuters indeed develop the same inefficiencies or "assume the same attributes" of local service carriers, then costs will increase accordingly. But DOT has not recommended that commuters be certificated. Simple growth of existing commuter operations should not lead to increased costs. Metro Airlines and Air Wisconsin each transport twice as many passengers annually as North Central did during 1951. Metro Airlines and Air Wisconsin are unsubsidized and profitable. Other, far smaller commuters also operate profitably. In contrast, each local service airline (with the notable exception of Allegheny, which went off subsidy in 1974) has received federal subsidies every year since it was first certificated. Clearly, size alone does not necessarily mean either increased costs or inefficiency.

The cost increases which ALTA thinks the commuters will experience fall into four categories. The first is increased labor costs resulting from CAB price regulation. The local service carriers, as an industry, are able to practice essentially "cost-plus" pricing. Thus, their labor costs may rise more easily than other industries. Without such price regulation, similar tendencies would not be operative for commuters. A second category of cost increases mentioned by ALTA relates to safety standards applied to larger aircraft. ALTA quotes the board's staff in the *Air Midwest Certification Proceeding* to the effect that Air New England's costs rose when it moved to large aircraft operations.[51] DOT agrees that, should commuter carriers move to the

---

[49] Ibid.
[50] ALTA Answer, p. 27.
[51] Ibid., p. 29.

operation of large aircraft, their costs would increase. There is no reason, however, for commuters to do so unless traffic grows to the point that such service is warranted.

The third cost item discussed by ALTA, security costs, is also dependent upon the assumption that commuter carriers are certificated. Again, without certification, commuter carriers would not be forced to incur large security costs. The fourth and final cost category mentioned by ALTA is that of landing fees. It is ALTA's allegation that, as commuters replace certificated carriers, their landing fees will increase. ALTA claims that certificated carriers, apparently altruistically, are shouldering the burden of landing fees. But commuters have already replaced certificated carriers at many points. There is no evidence of these alleged increased costs.

In summary, ALTA's allegation that cost increases for commuters will make their costs comparable to those of local service carriers is unsupported. Certification and resulting regulation explain why the commuters have a cost advantage and why it will continue. This fact has been acknowledged by the Bureau of Operating Rights. The bureau's observations with respect to cost differences between certificated and commuter carriers were well summarized by Judge Murphy in the initial decision in the *New England Service Investigation:*

> [T]he bulk of the cost difference is due to the indirect effects of operating in a protected business environment in which there is no realistic threat of new entry, prices are set on the basis of cost, subsidy is paid on the basis of need, and the ultimate threat of unsatisfactory conduct—bankruptcy—is substantially softened, if not fully blunted, by the understanding of labor, management, and the investment community that the certificate is of sufficient value to warrant a merger or acquisition on relatively favorable terms. The net effect of this, argues the Bureau, is to raise costs over commuter carrier expenses several times and to result in subsidy being spent largely in increased costs rather than increased service.[52]

The Level of Traffic Required to Support Unsubsidized Commuter Service. The locals' final argument with respect to the efficiency of commuter carriers compared to local service carriers is an attack on portions of DOT's analysis dealing with the level of traffic required to support commuter service. DOT's report observed that "changes in the existing regulatory system may hasten the transition from

---

[52] *New England Service Investigation*, p. 49.

certificated service to commuter service at most points and the abandonment of the remaining points. Thus, the level of traffic which will support commuter service is of major importance." [53] ALTA indicates that "the locals agree with that statement." [54] Since there is agreement that the level of traffic which will support commuter service is of major importance and since DOT found that viable, unsubsidized commuter service can be provided with traffic volumes far lower than previously realized, it is worthwhile to summarize DOT's analysis.

DOT's first approach was to screen stringently both commuter carriers and the points they serve in order to select a sample of points voluntarily served for several years by well-established commuter carriers. As a result of that analysis, it was clear that unsubsidized commuter carriers, free to discontinue unprofitable operations, provided continuous service at a large number of very small points. In fact, half of the points enplaned fewer than seventeen passengers per day and fully three-quarters enplaned fewer than twenty-five passengers per day.[55] Although ALTA contends that twenty-six passengers per day is a minimal level for commuter service and that thirty-four passengers per day would be required for mature certificated commuter service, ALTA neither challenges nor even mentions this phase of DOT's analysis.

As an alternate approach, replacement arrangements among various certificated carriers and commuters were examined. During 1975, a total of forty-four points were served by commuter carriers as replacements for two trunk and six local service airlines.[56] These are points where certificated carriers have suspended service but remain responsible for ensuring that scheduled service is maintained. In some cases, financial assistance to the commuter carrier is guaranteed by the certificated carrier. In still other cases, no explicit financial arrangement exists but the suspension of the certificated carrier is contingent upon service being provided by a commuter. Since many of the replacement points enplane very few passengers, it was thought that the level of payments by certificated carriers would shed some light both on the level of traffic needed for commuter viability and on the amount of financial assistance needed to continue service at the smallest points.

Allegheny Airlines, which had twenty-seven points being served by commuters under replacement agreements during 1974, does not

---

[53] See above, p. 90.

[54] ALTA Answer, p. 30.

[55] See Table 4-7 above.

[56] These points are listed in Table 4-8 above.

report expenditures and revenues disaggregated by the points involved. On a system-wide basis, however, they are usually successful in having their commuter network break even. The other seven airlines, which had either replacement agreements or responsibility for resuming service should the commuter service fail, reported no such expenditures. As a result of this analysis, it again appears that commuter service is economically viable at very low traffic levels, although no specific threshold of commuter viability has been established.

It is regrettable that ALTA failed to mention this portion of DOT's analysis in its "Answer," for more than half of the points enplane fewer passengers than ALTA believes necessary to support viable commuter service. If twenty-six to thirty-four passengers were indeed necessary to support unsubsidized commuter service, how, it might be asked, do the locals avoid paying the commuters who serve in their stead and carry far less traffic? Either the commuters would appear to be losing their shirts, cheerfully shouldering the locals' obligations, or commuter service is economically viable with very low levels of passenger traffic.

DOT's third approach in seeking to determine a threshold where commuter service is likely to be economically viable was to examine the continuity of commuter service at all points receiving such service during fiscal year 1973.[57] As shown in Table 4-9 above, all of the 190 points with an average daily passenger enplanement of six or more which received commuter service during fiscal year 1973 also had commuter service during calendar year 1974. Thus, no point enplaning six passengers or more per day had lost service six months later.

Not only is the continuity of commuter service remarkably stable during the short run, it is also stable over a longer term. As indicated in Table 4-10 above, only 4 of the 190 communities enplaning as many as six passengers a day lost commuter service during the two and one-half years between the end of fiscal year 1973 and January 1, 1976.[58] The loss of service at three of these cities, however, involved the failure of one carrier, Air South. The fourth city, Fort Wayne, is a small hub served by both United and Delta. There, a commuter carrier withdrew after unsuccessfully attempting to compete head-to-

---

[57] Fiscal year 1973 is the earliest date for which commuter replacement data is available on a point-by-point basis.

[58] The identity of the carrier or carriers providing service may have changed in some cases, and the service was not necessarily continuous at all communities. However, the stability of service, over both the six-month period and the longer period, seems to indicate that service was probably continuous in the vast majority of cases.

head with United in the Chicago-Fort Wayne market and with Delta in the Detroit-Fort Wayne market. Fort Wayne continues to receive service from both United and Delta.

Thus, for the two-and-one-half-year period, the largest point losing service because the point did not enplane enough traffic (rather than failure of the commuter carrier itself), enplaned fewer than six passengers a day. In view of this fact, which has not been disputed by ALTA, DOT's conclusion that commuter service is economically viable with very low levels of passenger traffic seems well founded. Of the various approaches utilized by DOT to examine the economic viability of commuter service, ALTA discusses only the last, focusing on the table which has been reproduced here as Table 4-10 above. The locals object to this table on two grounds. The first is as follows:

> The first fundamental error in this table is that it is 1976 traffic which enables a city to continue to receive service, not traffic in FY 1973. For example, if a city enplaned six passengers a day in 1973, but 30 passengers in 1976, the Report concludes that commuter service can be supported by six passengers a day. In fact, the continued service is supported by 30 passengers a day—not six passengers. Table [4-10] does not show the traffic in 1976. Since this vital ingredient is missing, the table proves nothing about the level of traffic needed to sustain service.[59]

This argument is incorrect. Commuters are not subsidized and, as small operations, cannot generally finance current operations out of hopes of spectacular future growth. Certainly, not all commuter points grew—indeed, some undoubtedly remained relatively constant or even declined in terms of the volume of passenger traffic—yet only the smallest points lost service.

But what would be the implications of accepting ALTA's argument, if it were true? Suppose the points enplaning as few as six passengers could not support commuter carriers and that all such points did grow rapidly, say, to thirty daily passengers. Such rapid, unsubsidized growth within two and one-half years at small points speaks well of the efficiency of commuters vis-à-vis certificated carriers—especially in comparison with the lack of growth and abandonment of many small points by local service carriers.

ALTA's second argument is:

> Carriers, of course, do not serve individual cities as such, but operate route systems. The viability of a commuter carrier

[59] ALTA Answer, p. 31.

operation is determined not by traffic at any particular city but by the traffic characteristics of its system.

For this reason, the locals analyzed the traffic characteristics of the systems of the commuters serving the cities in Table [4-10]. The analysis reveals that commuter carriers average 31 daily passengers per city. This is over five times the six passengers a day minimum specified in the DOT Report for self-sufficient service, and it is almost twice the 16 passengers a day maximum. The system average of 31 passengers per day provides a far better index of viability.[60]

This is indeed a curious argument, for ALTA previously noted that the commuter carriers primarily serve through a "hub and spoke" type of arrangement, rather than through the linear routes characteristic of certificated carriers.[61] Thus, it is the traffic on each spoke which supports service on that spoke, rather than the system-wide average. Any spoke which does not generate sufficient traffic will be deleted, as commuters are free to do, and the amount of traffic generated in the system as a whole is largely, if not entirely, irrelevant.

In any event, it is certainly misleading and irrelevant to confuse system-wide averages with a minimum threshold needed to retain service. The speciousness of this argument is easily demonstrated if it is applied to the certificated system. The average station served by local service carriers enplanes about 200 passengers per day. The average station served by trunks enplanes over 800. Similar reasoning would seem to suggest that a town with fewer than 200 passengers per day would be marginal for local service carriers, and a town enplaning fewer than 800 passengers per day would be marginal for trunk line service.

Finally, ALTA argues that DOT's

Report concludes that each city enplaning fewer than six passengers a day is incapable of supporting commuter service, that the cities enplaning between six and 10 passengers are marginal with a 50% probability of retaining service, that cities enplaning between 10 and 16 passengers have a 75% probability of retaining air service, and that cities enplaning 17 or more passengers a day are assumed to be certain to retain air service.[62]

This was most assuredly *not* a DOT conclusion, and DOT vigorously objects to this misrepresentation by ALTA. Rather, the thresholds

---

[60] Ibid., pp. 31-32.

[61] Ibid., p. 18.

[62] Ibid., p. 30.

cited above were used by the department to estimate the *maximum* loss of service if the entire local service subsidy program were discontinued *and* if local service carriers were simultaneously free to abandon any point they chose. In fact, the department is confident, based on the analyses presented in the report and summarized above, that these thresholds are conservative and that the loss of service would be minor. In any event, DOT has proposed a subsidy program to guarantee against any loss of service.

Potential Loss of Service

ALTA objects to DOT's conclusion that, if the locals were free to abandon any point they wished and if the present subsidy program were entirely eliminated, only about thirty points would lose all scheduled air service and that only "about 130,000 passengers, or about one-twentieth of one percent of the nation's travelers" would be affected. ALTA raises two objections to DOT's calculations with respect to loss of service. First, the association argues that the department was in error in accepting the view of the board's staff that cities enplaning forty passengers per day are capable of supporting unsubsidized service utilizing aircraft of approximately fifty-five seats. ALTA's concern that locals do not operate efficiently enough to provide unsubsidized service to cities enplaning as many as forty passengers per day may or may not be valid. However, this concern is not relevant to the question of whether or not such larger points would be left without air service. As the DOT report demonstrates, points of this size would most assuredly receive unsubsidized commuter service.

ALTA's second objection is a repetition of the argument that "on the basis of the most recent cost development by the Board's Bureau of Air Operations [*sic*], small aircraft require from 26 to 34 passengers per day to cover economic costs." [63] As noted above, there are serious problems with such hypothetical cost estimates, and ALTA's calculations are erroneous. Even if ALTA had calculated them correctly, the estimates were for aircraft not typical of the commuter fleet. Such hypotheticals do not serve to replace real world experience. That the unsubsidized commuter industry is growing and thriving when fewer than 25 percent of their points are, according to ALTA's estimates, economically viable is positively remarkable.

---

[63] Ibid., p. 36.

Apparently, the locals believe the commuters are possessed with not only a deep sense of altruism but unlimited financial resources as well.

Conclusion

DOT's analysis of the decline in air service to small communities by the nation's regulated air carriers, the growth of commuter service, and the ineffectiveness of the present program in subsidizing local service carriers have not been seriously challenged by ALTA. As the board's staff has observed,

> Most locals have signaled by course of conduct that they intend to move toward trunkline status and abandon small community service. In fact, Allegheny, Airwest and Southern have announced publicly the intention of operating all-jet fleets. And no local service carrier except Piedmont (and to a lesser extent North Central) has exhibited any interest in reequipping for small community service. Such service is now provided by local service carriers with aging propeller aircraft fleets—in some cases airframes are 30 years old. While these can be operated indefinitely under prevailing safety standards, maintenance becomes more expensive over time. Hence, it is predictable, based on long-range corporate policies . . . and the age of the fleets, that the locals will seek to abandon small community service in the next few years. Paradoxically the abandonment strategy is enhanced if, as appears to be the case, subsidy payments can be *increased* in the short term by reason of the recognition of jet aircraft investment costs, while small community points can be reduced. This would repeat trunk carrier strategy in the period before the end of trunk subsidy.[64]

---

[64] Civil Aeronautics Board, *Request for Comment on Staff Report on Service to Small Communities*, Docket 29278, May 18, 1976, Appendix B, pp. 10–11.

6

ANALYSIS OF EASTERN AIR LINES' UNPROFITABLE DOMESTIC SEGMENTS

Regulatory Policy Staff, U.S. Department of Transportation

Frequently in the debate over regulatory reform of the aviation industry, industry representatives have presented lists of segments served which are "net loss" segments and receive cross-subsidization. The clear implication is that service to these segments will be abandoned in the absence of protective regulation which provides profits in certain markets to support service over losing markets.

Careful analysis of these lists usually indicates, however, that few if any of the segments are likely to be abandoned. In 1975, as part of its study of Civil Aeronautics Board practices and procedures, the Senate Subcommittee on Administrative Practice and Procedure broke down a list from United Air Lines of 327 "losing" city-pairs to twenty-nine route segments which were in fact susceptible to loss of service. These constituted one-half of one percent of United's revenue passenger miles.

This short paper is intended to analyze a similar list of 160 "losing" domestic segments provided by Eastern Air Lines (see Table 6-1; Table 6-2 contains a list of Eastern's "losing" international segments). The analysis is restricted to a consideration of the possibility of abandonment. The simple criterion utilized is to examine the question of whether the service provided in each segment is required by CAB regulation. If it is not, Eastern is free to abandon the segment irrespective of regulatory reform. The obvious question is then, Why have these "unprofitable" segments not already been dropped? The

This paper was initially prepared as a memorandum for the Air Bill Task Force. The authors of this analysis were Bruce N. Stram and Peyton L. Wynns, economists on the regulatory policy staff in the Office of the Secretary, U.S. Department of Transportation. This paper is slightly modified from the analysis which was submitted to Senator Edward M. Kennedy at his request and which later appeared in the *Congressional Record* on August 2, 1976.

Table 6-1

UNPROFITABLE DOMESTIC SEGMENTS ON EASTERN AIR LINES ON A FULLY ALLOCATED BASIS FOR 1975

Segment	Does Nonstop Eastern Service Still Exist? (1)	Other Nonstop Service (2)	Does Eastern Still Serve This Market? (3)	Additional Carriers Serving This Market (other than nonstop service) (4)	Type of Segment[a] (5)
Akron/Canton–Cleveland	Yes	None	Yes	None	SH–LH
Akron/Canton–Detroit	No	None	No	None	SH–LH
Akron/Canton–Pittsburgh	No	AL, UA	No	None	SH–LH
Allentown/Bethlehem/Easton–Washington (DCA)	Yes	AK[b]	Yes	None	SH–LH
Atlanta–Baltimore	Yes	DL	Yes	None	LH–MH
Atlanta–Birmingham	Yes	DL, SO	Yes	None	LH–MH
Atlanta–Charlotte	Yes	DL	Yes	SO	LH–MH
Atlanta–Chattanooga	Yes	DL, SO	Yes	None	LH–SH
Atlanta–Chicago (O'Hare)	Yes	NW, DL	Yes	None	LH–LH
Atlanta–Columbus, Ga.	Yes	DL, SO	Yes	None	LH–SH
Atlanta–Dallas/Ft. Worth	Yes	DL	Yes	None	LH–LH
Atlanta–Fort Lauderdale	Yes	DL, NW, UA	Yes	None	LH–LH
Atlanta–Greenville/Spartanburg	Yes	DL, SO	Yes	None	LH–SH
Atlanta–Indianapolis	Yes	DL	Yes	None	LH–MH
Atlanta–Jacksonville	Yes	DL, UA	Yes	None	LH–MH
Atlanta–Los Angeles	Yes	DL	Yes	None	LH–LH
Atlanta–Louisville	Yes	DL	Yes	None	LH–MH
Atlanta–Macon	Yes	DL	Yes	None	LH–SH
Atlanta–Memphis	Yes	DL	Yes	SO	LH–MH
Atlanta–Miami	Yes	DL, NW, UA	Yes	SO	LH–LH
Atlanta–Montgomery	Yes	DL	Yes	None	LH–SH
Atlanta–Nashville	Yes	SO	Yes	None	LH–MH
Atlanta–Newark	Yes	DL	Yes	UA	LH–LH
Atlanta–New Orleans	Yes	DL	Yes	SO	LH–LH
Atlanta–New York (Kennedy)	Yes	DL	Yes	UA	LH–LH
Atlanta–New York (LaGuardia)	Yes	DL, UA	Yes	PI	LH–LH
Atlanta–Orlando	Yes	DL	Yes	SO	LH–MH
Atlanta–Philadelphia	Yes	DL	Yes	None	LH–LH
Atlanta–Tampa	Yes	DL, NW, UA	Yes	None	LH–LH
Augusta–Charlotte	Yes	None	Yes	None	SH–MH
Baltimore–Boston	No	AA, AL, DL	No	None	MH–LH
Baltimore–Hartford	Yes	AL	Yes	None	MH–MH
Baltimore–Newark	Yes	None	Yes	None	MH–LH
Baltimore–Phliadelphia	Yes	AA, AK[b] AL, DL, YN[b]	Yes	None	MH–LH
Baltimore–Raleigh/Durham	Yes	None	Yes	None	MH–MH
Baltimore–Washington (DCA)	Yes	AL, NA, PI, NO[b]	Yes	None	MH–LH

142

Table 6-1 (Continued)

Segment	Does Nonstop Eastern Service Still Exist? (1)	Other Nonstop Service (2)	Does Eastern Still Serve This Market? (3)	Additional Carriers Serving This Market (other than nonstop service) (4)	Type of Segment[a] (5)
Baltimore–Washington (Dulles)	No	None	No	None	MH–LH
Birmingham–Mobile	Yes	SO	Yes	None	MH–SH
Birmingham–Nashville	Yes	SO	Yes	None	MH–MH
Birmingham–New Orleans	No	DL	Yes	SO	MH–LH
Birmingham–New York (LaGuardia)	Yes	DL	Yes	None	MH–LH
Birmingham–Pensacola	Yes	None	Yes	None	MH–SH
Boston–Charlotte	Yes	None	Yes	None	LH–SH
Boston–Hartford	Yes	AL, DL	Yes	None	LH–MH
Boston–Miami	Yes	DL	Yes	NA	LH–LH
Boston–Newark	Yes	AA, DL	Yes	None	LH–LH
Boston–New York (Kennedy)	Yes	AA, NA, TW	Yes	None	LH–LH
Boston–Philadelphia	Yes	AL, DL	Yes	None	LH–LH
Boston–Providence	No	AL, NF[b]	No	None	LH–SH
Boston–Tampa	Yes	DL, NW	Yes	None	LH–LH
Buffalo–Philadelphia	Yes	UA	Yes	AL	MH–LH
Buffalo–Pittsburgh	No	AL, UA	No	None	MH–LH
Charleston, S.C.–Charlotte	Yes	None	Yes	None	SH–MH
Charleston, S.C.–Chicago (O'Hare)	No	None	Yes	DL	SH–LH
Charlotte–Chattanooga	Yes	None	Yes	None	MH–SH
Charlotte–Columbia, S.C.	Yes	None	Yes	None	MH–SH
Charlotte–Columbus, Ohio	Yes	None	Yes	PI	MH–MH
Charlotte–Daytona Beach	Yes	None	Yes	None	MH–SH
Charlotte–Detroit	Yes	None	Yes	None	MH–LH
Charlotte–Greensboro	No	DL, PI	Yes	None	MH–MH
Charlotte–Greenville/ Spartanburg	Yes	PI, SO, WR[b]	Yes	None	MH–SH
Charlotte–Newark	Yes	DL	Yes	PI, UA	MH–LH
Charlotte–Raleigh/Durham	Yes	PI, UA	Yes	None	MH–MH
Chicago (O'Hare)–Cincinnati	No	AA, DL	No	None	LH–MH
Chicago (O'Hare)–Detroit	No	AA, DL, NW, UA	No	NC	LH–LH
Chicago (O'Hare)–Fort Lauderdale	Yes	DL, NW	Yes	SO	LH–LH
Chicago (O'Hare)–Greensboro	Yes	DL	Yes	None	LH–MH
Chicago (O'Hare)–Miami	Yes	DL, NW	Yes	SO	LH–LH
Chicago (O'Hare)–Nashville	Yes	DL	Yes	None	LH–MH
Chicago (O'Hare)–Orlando	Yes	DL	Yes	SO	LH–MH
Chicago (O'Hare)–Raleigh/ Durham	Yes	DL	Yes	None	LH–MH
Cincinnati–Fort Lauderdale	Yes	None	Yes	DL	MH–LH
Cincinnati–Milwaukee	Yes	NC	Yes	None	MH–MH

143

Table 6-1 (Continued)

Segment	Does Nonstop Eastern Service Still Exist? (1)	Other Nonstop Service (2)	Does Eastern Still Serve This Market? (3)	Additional Carriers Serving This Market (other than nonstop service) (4)	Type of Segment[a] (5)
Cincinnati–Minneapolis/ St. Paul	Yes	None	Yes	NC	MH–LH
Cleveland–Detroit	No	DL, FW, NC, NW, UA	No	None	LH–LH
Cleveland–Fort Lauderdale	No	UA	No	None	LH–LH
Cleveland–Pittsburgh	Yes	AL, NW, UA	Yes	None	LH–LH
Columbia, S.C.–Newark	No	None	Yes	None	SH–LH
Columbia, S.C.–Washington (DCA)	Yes	None	Yes	PI	SH–LH
Columbus, Ohio–Toledo	Yes	DL	Yes	None	MH–SH
Corpus Christi–Houston	Yes	BN, TI	Yes	None	SH–LH
Corpus Christi–New Orleans	Yes	None	Yes	None	SH–LH
Dallas/Ft. Worth–Miami	Yes	BN	Yes	None	LH–LH
Daytona Beach– Fort Lauderdale	No	None	No	None	SH–LH
Daytona Beach–Jacksonville	Yes	NA	Yes	None	SH–MH
Daytona Beach–Melbourne	No	None	No	None	SH–SH
Daytona Beach–Miami	Yes	NA	Yes	None	SH–LH
Detroit–Greensboro	Yes	None	Yes	None	LH–MH
Detroit–Miami	Yes	DL	Yes	None	LH–LH
Detroit–Orlando	Yes	DL	Yes	None	LH–MH
Detroit–Pittsburgh	Yes	NW, UA	Yes	AL	LH–LH
Detroit–Tampa	Yes	DL	Yes	None	LH–LH
Evansville–Louisville	Yes	None	Yes	None	SH–MH
Evansville–St. Louis	Yes	None	Yes	None	SH–LH
Fort Lauderdale–Miami	Yes	NA	Yes	None	LH–LH
Fort Lauderdale–Orlando	Yes	DL, SO	Yes	None	LH–MH
Fort Lauderdale–Philadelphia	Yes	DL	Yes	None	LH–LH
Fort Lauderdale–Sarasota	No	FE[b]	No	None	LH–SH
Fort Lauderdale–Tampa	Yes	BN, DL	Yes	None	LH–LH
Fort Lauderdale–West Palm Beach	Yes	NA	Yes	None	LH–MH
Gainesville–Jacksonville	No	FE[b]	No	None	NH–MH
Gainesville–Miami	Yes	None	Yes	FE[b]	NH–LH
Greensboro–Greenville/ Spartanburg[c]	Yes	None	Yes	PI	MH–SH
Greensboro–Pittsburgh	Yes	None	Yes	None	MH–LH
Greensboro–Raleigh/Durham	No	DL, PI	No	None	MH–MH
Greensboro–Roanoke	Yes	PI	Yes	None	MH–SH

144

Table 6-1 (Continued)

Segment	Does Nonstop Eastern Service Still Exist? (1)	Other Nonstop Service (2)	Does Eastern Still Serve This Market? (3)	Additional Carriers Serving This Market (other than nonstop service) (4)	Type of Segment[a] (5)
Hartford–Newark	Yes	AL, DL	Yes	None	MH–LH
Hartford–New York (Kennedy)	Yes	AA, AL, DL, TW	Yes	None	MH–LH
Hartford–New York (LaGuardia)	No	None	No	None	MH–LH
Hartford–Philadelphia	Yes	AA, AL, DL	Yes	None	MH–LH
Hartford–Providence	Yes	AL	Yes	None	MH–SH
Houston–New Orleans	Yes	CO, DL, NA, TI	Yes	None	LH–LH
Houston–New York (Kennedy)	Yes	None	Yes	BN, DL	LH–LH
Houston–San Antonio	Yes	AA, BN, CO, WN[d]	Yes	None	LH–MH
Huntsville–Nashville	Yes	SO	Yes	None	SH–MH
Huntsville–St. Louis	Yes	None	Yes	SO	SH–LH
Indianapolis–Louisville	Yes	AL, DL, OZ	Yes	None	MH–MH
Jacksonville–Melbourne	Yes	None	Yes	None	MH–SH
Jacksonville–Miami	Yes	DL, NA	Yes	None	MH–LH
Jacksonville–Orlando	No	DL, NA	No	None	MH–MH
Jacksonville–Sarasota	Yes	None	Yes	NA, FE[b]	MH–SH
Melbourne–Miami	Yes	NA	Yes	None	SH–LH
Melbourne–Orlando	Yes[c]	None	Yes	None	SH–MH
Melbourne–Tampa	Yes	NA	Yes	None	SH–LH
Miami–Minneapolis/St. Paul	Yes	NW	Yes	None	LH–LH
Miami–Orlando	Yes	DL, NA, SO	Yes	None	LH–MH
Miami–Sarasota	Yes	None	Yes	FE,[b] NA	LH–SH
Miami–Tampa	Yes	BN, DL, NA, QH,[b] TW	Yes	None	LH–LH
Miami–West Palm Beach	Yes	DL, NA	Yes	None	LH–MH
Minneapolis/St. Paul–Tampa	Yes	NA	Yes	None	LH–LH
Mobile–Montgomery	Yes[c]	None	Yes	None	SH–SH
Montgomery–Pensacola	Yes[c]	None	Yes	None	SH–SH
Nashville–St. Louis	No	OZ	No	None	MH–LH
Newark–Philadelphia	Yes	AA, AL, DL	Yes	None	LH–LH
Newark–Providence	No	AL	No	None	LH–SH
Newark–Raleigh/Durham	Yes	UA	Yes	None	LH–MH
Newark–Richmond	Yes	None	Yes	None	LH–SH
Newark–Washington (DCA)	Yes	BN	Yes	AL	LH–LH
Newark–Washington (Dulles)	Yes	AA, BN, NW	Yes	None	LH–LH
New Orleans–New York (LaGuardia)	Yes	DL	Yes	SO	LH–LH
New Orleans–Pensacola	Yes	NA	Yes	None	LH–SH

Table 6-1 (Continued)

Segment	Does Nonstop Eastern Service Still Exist? (1)	Other Nonstop Service (2)	Does Eastern Still Serve This Market? (3)	Additional Carriers Serving This Market (other than nonstop service) (4)	Type of Segment[a] (5)
New Orleans–San Antonio	Yes	None	Yes	None	LH–MH
New York (Kennedy)–Philadelphia	Yes	NA, TW, YN[b]	Yes	None	LH–LH
New York (Kennedy)–Providence	Yes	AA, NA	Yes	None	LH–SH
New York (Kennedy)–Richmond	Yes	None	Yes	None	LH–SH
New York (Kennedy)–Washington (Dulles)	Yes[c]	AA, BN, TW	Yes	None	LH–LH
New York (LaGuardia)–Philadelphia	No	AA,[c] DL[c]	No	None	LH–LH
New York (LaGuardia)–Richmond	Yes	None	Yes	None	LH–SH
Omaha–St. Louis	Yes	None	Yes	FL	MH–LH
Orlando–Sarasota	Yes	None	Yes	NA	MH–SH
Orlando–Tampa	Yes	DL, NA	Yes	None	MH–LH
Orlando–West Palm Beach	No	DL, NA	Yes	None	MH–MH
Philadelphia–Syracuse	Yes	None	Yes	None	LH–MH
Philadelphia–Washington (Dulles)	Yes	UA, TW	Yes	None	LH–LH
Philadelphia–West Palm Beach	Yes	None	Yes	DL, NA	LH–MH
Portland–Seattle	Yes	BN, CO, NW, RW, UA, WA	Yes	None	MH–LH
Raleigh/Durham–Richmond	Yes	None	Yes	None	MH–SH
Sarasota–Tampa	Yes	FE,[b] NA, YX[b]	Yes	None	SH–LH
Tampa–West Palm Beach	Yes	DL, FE[b]	Yes	None	LH–MH
Washington (DCA)–Wilkes Barre/Scranton	Yes	None	Yes	AK[b]	LH–NH

[a] LH—Large Hub; MH—Medium Hub; SH—Small Hub; NH—Non Hub.

[b] Commuter carrier.

[c] One-way only.

[d] Intrastate.

Sources: Data for columns (1)-(4) was obtained from the *Official Airline Guide*, April 15, 1976. Data for column (5) was obtained from Civil Aeronautics Board and the Federal Aviation Administration, *Airport Activity Statistics of Certificated Route Air Carriers,* for the 12 months ended June 30, 1974.

Table 6-2

UNPROFITABLE OVERSEAS AND INTERNATIONAL SEGMENTS ON EASTERN AIR LINES ON A FULLY ALLOCATED BASIS FOR 1975

Acapulco–Atlanta
Acapulco–Mexico
Antigua–Fort-De-France
Antigua–New York (Kennedy)
Antigua–St. Lucia

Antigua–St. Maarten
Antigua–San Juan
Aruba–Curacao
Atlanta–San Juan
Baltimore–Kingston

Baltimore–Montreal
Baltimore–San Juan
Barbados–Port of Spain
Bermuda–Chicago
Boston–San Juan

Buffalo–Toronto
Fort-De-France–Pointe-Au-Pitre
Fort-De-France–Port of Spain
Fort-De-France–St. Lucia
Fort Lauderdale–Nassau

Freeport–Miami
Freeport–Nassau
Kingston–Montego Bay

Kingston–Port-Au-Prince
Miami–Toronto

Montego Bay–Miami
Newark–San Juan
New York (Kennedy)–Mexico
New York (Kennedy)–
   Montego Bay
New York (Kennedy)–Montreal

New York (Kennedy)–San Juan
New York (LaGuardia)–Montreal
Ottawa–Montreal
Philadelphia–Montreal
Philadelphia–San Juan

Philadelphia–Toronto
Pittsburgh–Toronto
Port-Au-Prince–San Juan
Port of Spain–Pointe-Au-Pitre
Port of Spain–St. Lucia

Ponce–San Juan
St. Thomas–St. Croix
San Juan–St. Croix
San Juan–St. Maarten
San Juan–St. Thomas

answer, provided by Frank Borman, president of Eastern, in testimony before the House, is that the segments are not truly unprofitable, despite the fact that fully allocated costs are not covered by ticket revenues over the segment.

As a first step, the logical question to ask is what portion of that losing service is in fact required by Eastern's certificate obligations. Using the abandonment criterion, one must suppose that, if Eastern may voluntarily eliminate and reduce service on the losing segments and does not, they are proceeding rationally, and that the 1975 losses are expected to be temporary or to misrepresent the true situation.

The air carrier's certificate is constituted by a listing of authorized points which constitute a route. The carrier has freedom to operate as much capacity as it may wish in the exercise of sound business judgment—subject only to the minimum level of service required by the certificate obligation and the adequacy provision of the Federal

Aviation Act.[1] Minimum adequate service appears to imply at least one or two daily flights from and to a named point.

There are several points on Eastern's authority which receive only two flights daily (Allentown, Pennsylvania, and Macon, Georgia, for example). Clearly, losing service to any segment whose end points both receive two or more other profitable flights to and from other points is being provided voluntarily by Eastern. For example, the Atlanta-Chicago segment is indicated as unprofitable. However, both Atlanta and Chicago have numerous other profitable Eastern flights to other points. Thus, Eastern could discontinue the Atlanta-Chicago service if they chose, without any CAB interference. Similarly, if there are a number of losing segments being served from a single point, only two of those segments must be served; the others clearly may be abandoned (even if only one flight is provided for each segment). For example, Eastern shows three losing segments served from Akron/Canton in 1975. There is one Akron/Canton segment not on the list of losing segments (to Charlotte) which is presumably profitable. Therefore, the one profitable segment (with one flight daily) plus one losing segment (with one flight daily) constitute minimum adequate service and two of the three losing segments may be dropped at Eastern's discretion. In fact, this is exactly what has happened. Eastern has voluntarily terminated from Akron/Canton to Pittsburgh and to Detroit. The existence of this management discretion is verified by the fact that Eastern has already dropped 24 of the 160 unprofitable segments without any proceedings before the board whatsoever (see Table 6-1). As a general rule, Eastern needs to go before the board only if it desires to drop completely all service to a point on its certificate. All of these 24 segments were dropped without abandoning Eastern service to any point.

Analyzing Eastern's discretionary control over the domestic losing segments, we find that only twenty segments include a point in danger of falling below minimum adequate service if the segment in question is dropped (Tables 6-3 and 6-4). This analysis proceeded as follows: All the points included in losing segments were tabulated (Table 6-3). Eastern's segments not on the list of losers (presumably profitable segments) were also tabulated.[2] Then the number of profitable segments served by Eastern from each point included in a losing segment and the total number of daily flights flown by Eastern on

---

[1] Civil Aeronautics Board, Bureau of Operating Rights, *The Domestic Route System: Analysis and Policy Recommendations*, October 1974, p. 39.

[2] The table of segments which were profitable on a fully allocated basis for 1975 has not been included here.

Table 6-3

PROFITABLE AND UNPROFITABLE SEGMENTS SERVED BY EASTERN FROM UNPROFITABLE POINTS

Unprofitable Points	Number of Unprofitable Segments	Profitable Segments	Total Number of Daily Flights on Profitable Segments
Akron/Canton	3	1	1
Allentown/Bethlehem/Easton	1	None	—
Atlanta	25	26	107
Augusta	1	None	—
Baltimore	8	3	4
Birmingham	6	2	2
Boston	2	7	25
Buffalo	2	3	5
Charleston	2	None	—
Charlotte, N.C.	12	12	29
Chattanooga	2	None	—
Chicago	9	4	10
Cincinnati	4	2	2
Cleveland	4	4	4
Columbia	2	None	—
Columbus, Ga.	1	None	—
Columbus, Ohio	2	2	3
Corpus Christi	2	None	—
Dallas/Fort Worth	2	1	2
Daytona Beach	5	2	6
Detroit	8	2	2
Evansville	2	1	1
Fort Lauderdale	11	6	19
Gainesville	2	2	4
Greensboro	7	4	10
Greenville/Spartanburg	3	2	2
Hartford	7	5	10
Houston	4	3	15
Huntsville	2	1	1
Indianapolis	2	3	3
Jacksonville	7	4	7
Los Angeles	1	None	—
Louisville	3	3	4
Macon	1	None	—
Melbourne	5	2	5
Memphis	1	None	—
Miami	15	20	62

Table 6-3 (Continued)

Unprofitable Points	Number of Unprofitable Segments	Profitable Segments	Total Number of Daily Flights on Profitable Segments
Milwaukee	1	1	3
Minneapolis/St. Paul	3	1	3
Mobile	2	1	4
Montgomery	2	None	—
Nashville	5	None	—
Newark	12 ⎫	14 ⎫	66
New York	14 ⎭	⎭	
Omaha	1	1	2
Orlando	10	10	14
Pensacola	3	1	5
Philadelphia	11	8	20
Pittsburgh	5	7	18
Portland	1	1	1
Providence	4	3	3
Raleigh/Durham	4	3	15
Richmond	3	1	4
Roanoke	1	1	1
St. Louis	3	8	15
San Antonio	2	1	5
Sarasota	4	2	6
Seattle/Tacoma	1	2	3
Syracuse	1	3	5
Tampa	7	11	22
Toledo	1	None	—
Washington	9	20	62
West Palm Beach	5	4	11
Wilkes Barre	1	None	—

those segments were calculated (Table 6-3). Using the criterion stated above, that two daily flights constitute minimum adequate service, any losing segment whose end points receive at least two other profitable daily flights (from Eastern) may be abandoned at Eastern's discretion. All such segments which Eastern still flies are therefore eliminated as candidates for cross-subsidy. Further, even if all segments flown from a given point are losers, only two daily flights are required. For example, five segments are flown from Nashville by Eastern; all are on the list of losing segments. However, minimum required service to Nashville is provided by Eastern's five daily flights to Atlanta. Service requirements for Nashville, therefore, do not constrain Eastern to serve the other four segments. (In all such cases, the segment with the largest number of flights was included in the list of twenty and the others were excluded.) The exclusion of segments under this reasoning, plus exclusions indicated above, leaves twenty segments. Of these twenty, twelve segments receive service in excess of the minimum only if the segment is, in the relevant sense, profitable. This leaves eight segments whose service provided exactly meets the minimum service required under Eastern's certification. Of these eight, one, Corpus Christi-New Orleans, was added in 1975, over and above the one daily flight offered from Corpus Christi all through 1974, and so could presumably be dropped at Eastern's discretion. One, Huntsville-St. Louis, has a load factor of 70.1 in 1974, and two more, Allentown-Washington and Greensboro-Roanoke, ran load factors of 59.7 and 57.8, respectively, in 1974. No additional competition has surfaced on these routes, so one would expect that at least the Huntsville-St. Louis segment would be profitable in normal times and perhaps the other two as well. This leaves four to six markets which may be subject to cross-subsidy.

Of these four to six markets, three, Houston-Corpus Christi, Greensboro-Roanoke, and Macon-Atlanta, are served by competitors (Braniff and Texas International, Delta, and Piedmont, respectively). These competitors provide sufficient service to Eastern's constraining point in each case (Corpus Christi, Macon, and Roanoke), so that the competitors' service to the segment in question is clearly voluntary and these segments are therefore not cross-subsidized by those carriers. Thus, even if the cross-subsidy exists in the case of Eastern's service, it is not necessary to maintain certificated service to the segments in question. Even if one accepts the validity of providing cross-subsidies in order to maintain service at small points, it is clearly foolish to require one carrier to cross-subsidize while exactly similar service can be provided on a profitable basis by other carriers. If Eastern is indeed providing cross-subsidies to these points, rational public policy requires that Eastern be permitted to drop these points from its certificate.

This leaves a net of two or three segments which may be receiving Eastern cross-subsidies and may require them to continue receiving service (depending on whether one accepts the Allentown-Washington load factor as high enough to suggest the existence of profitable service). These three segments are: Akron/Canton-Cleveland, Allentown-Washington (DCA), and Washington (DCA)-Wilkes-Barre. In the Allentown-Washington segment, a commuter competes with East-

Table 6-4
SEGMENTS EASTERN IS CONSTRAINED TO SERVE BY CERTIFICATE REQUIREMENTS

Segment	Daily Flights	Potential Constraining Point	Minimum Required Flights	1974 Load Factor	Remarks
Akron/Canton–Cleveland	1	Akron/Canton	1	40.5	One nonlosing daily flight from Akron to Charlotte
Allentown–Washington (DCA)	2	Allentown	2	59.7	Two flight minimum requirement
Atlanta–Columbus, Ga.	3	Columbus, Ga.	2	34.6	Two flight minimum requirement
Atlanta–Los Angeles	4	Los Angeles	2	50.9	Two flight minimum requirement
Atlanta–Macon	2	Macon	2	28.1	Two flight minimum requirement
Atlanta–Memphis	3	Memphis	2	52.2	Two flight minimum requirement
Atlanta–Montgomery	5	Montgomery	2	—	Two flight minimum requirement
Atlanta–Nashville	5	Nashville	2	71.1	Two flight minimum requirement
Augusta–Charlotte	3	Augusta	2	28.4	Two flight minimum requirement
Charleston–Charlotte	4	Charleston	2	67.2	Two flight minimum requirement
Charlotte–Chattanooga	4	Chattanooga	2	29.5	Two flight minimum requirement
Charlotte–Columbia	2	Columbia	2	53.8	Two flight minimum requirement
Columbus, Ohio–Toledo	4	Toledo	2	24.9	Two flight minimum requirement
Corpus Christi–Houston	1	Corpus Christi	1	28.9	These two flights constitute the only Eastern service to Corpus Christi
Corpus Christi–New Orleans	1	Corpus Christi	1	—	

Evansville–St. Louis	2	Evansville	1	42.0	One nonlosing daily flight from Evansville to Atlanta
Greensboro–Roanoke	1	Roanoke	1	57.8	One nonlosing daily flight from Roanoke to Pittsburgh
Huntsville–St. Louis	1	Huntsville	1	70.1	One nonlosing daily flight from Huntsville to Orlando
Portland–Seattle	3	Portland	1	31.0	One nonlosing daily flight from Portland to St. Louis
Washington (DCA)–Wilkes Barre/Scranton	2	Wilkes Barre	2	46.4	Two flight minimum requirement

ern, providing five daily flights to Eastern's two,[3] at a fare of $31.00 as opposed to Eastern's $29.00. The three constraining points, for Eastern, on each segment receive substantial service to other points from other carriers. Even for these points, one may question whether Eastern's cross-subsidy, if it exists, should in fact be provided since substantial other service exists.

---

[3] Commuter airlines typically provide daily flights five or six days a week as opposed to certificated carriers' seven.

PART FOUR

U.S. AIR CARRIER ROUTE AUTHORITY AND THE ADJUSTMENT TO A LESS REGULATED ENVIRONMENT

A major objective of the Aviation Act and other aviation reform proposals was to reduce the legal barriers to entry into air transportation. The Aviation Act contained several provisions designed to liberalize entry into the industry. It directed the CAB to encourage the entry of new firms and to give greater weight to competitive policy considerations. It allowed supplemental air carriers to provide scheduled service, removed restrictions on charter service and commuters, and facilitated entry through sale and purchase of certificates. The act sought to increase the operating flexibility of carriers in three major ways: (1) all certificate restrictions were to be removed by 1981; (2) beginning in 1981, carriers could increase their route mileage by approximately 5 percent per year; and (3) carriers were free to provide nonstop service between cities not receiving such service from certificated carriers. How the carriers would respond to the entry flexibility provided by these three provisions and the amount of entry which might result from them became an important issue in the debate on aviation reform.

The first paper in this part is drawn from a study done for DOT, examining the nature and extent of the restrictions found in each carrier's operating authority and analyzing the use carriers were making of their existing authority. The study found that in many markets carriers were not exercising the full or the best operating authority which they possessed. In fact, in only 21 percent of the markets were carriers utilizing their best available authority. Carriers were found to be providing nonstop service in only 16 percent of the markets where they held such authority. The study attracted considerable attention in the Congress, and it played a significant part in the development of the legislative proposal by Congressmen Glenn M. Anderson (Democrat, California) and M. Gene Snyder (Republican, Kentucky) which provided, among other things, for liberalized entry into any market in which carriers were not utilizing the authority they possessed.

The second paper is the summary from a three-volume study prepared for DOT examining on a carrier-by-carrier basis the likely pattern of entry and exit in a less regulated environment. The study also assessed the impact of the new route structures on each carrier's operating efficiency.

7

AN ANALYSIS OF U.S. AIR CARRIER ROUTE AUTHORITY

Simat, Helliesen and Eichner, Inc.

The Aviation Act of 1975, if approved by Congress in its current form, would instruct the CAB "to undertake a proceeding to phase out all the existing restrictions in such certificate or certificates authorizing interstate air transportation . . . giving due consideration to the effects of elimination of restrictions on each carrier." The phasing out of restrictions is to be completed by January 1, 1981. As a result of this phasing out of certificate restriction, each carrier, on or about January 1, 1981, would have unrestricted nonstop authority between all U.S. points named in its certificate as of January 1, 1975.

In order to assess the number of markets that would be affected by restriction removal, we have undertaken to quantify the existing authority of each of the trunk and local service carriers, in terms of the total number of markets authorized, the number of markets for which a carrier has nonstop authority, and the extent to which a carrier is utilizing this authority.

The data compiled in this analysis are from three basic sources:

(1) The Certificate of Public Convenience and Necessity issued by the Civil Aeronautics Board to each carrier.

(2) The certificate authority matrix, produced from a computerized route authority program initially developed by Simat, Helliesen and Eichner under contract to the Civil Aeronautics Board.[1] The CAB subsequently modified and improved the pro-

---

Only the introduction and conclusions of this report have been included here. The detailed data for each carrier are available with the initial report, which was prepared for the Office of Transportation Regulatory Policy, U.S. Department of Transportation, March 1976.

[1] The program was developed in conjunction with Operations Research, Inc. (ORI), and Aviation Planning Systems, Inc. (APSI).

gram. The matrices used for this study represent, for the most part, authority effective as of early 1976.[2]

(3) The system timetables published by each carrier, showing the level of service that a carrier is providing over its system. For this study, timetables for the fall or winter of 1975 were used.

Air Carrier Authority

The primary source of authority for a scheduled U.S. air carrier to engage in the carriage of persons, property, and mail is the Certificate of Public Convenience and Necessity issued to a carrier by the Civil Aeronautics Board. Each certificate represents a specific route and is identified by a unique number. Each carrier has been issued at least one such certificate, though most carriers hold two or more. All certificates specify the cities a carrier is authorized to serve and the conditions or restrictions upon that service.

The Route Authority Program

As the air transportation industry has grown over time, the problem of analyzing and understanding each carrier's certificate authority has also increased, both in magnitude and in importance. This is because, as the industry expanded, each carrier's authority has become more complex. The merging of carriers, in most cases, has magnified that complexity; for example, the Allegheny/Mohawk merger produced a single route certificate with thirty-three different segments. Furthermore, the CAB has found it necessary to issue orders providing temporary modifications to the authority described in the various certificates.

The complexity of the air transportation system has made the computerization of the authority described in the various certificates and related orders an invaluable tool for analysis of the existing system. The airline certificate authority system, developed for the CAB, represents the most comprehensive computerization of airline operating authority available today. This system converts each carrier's certificate authority into a machine-readable format and stores this authority in a single file on a city-pair basis for all carriers.

---

[2] Exceptions are Air New England, Frontier Airlines, Hughes Airwest, North Central Airlines, Pan American Airlines, Texas International Airlines, Trans World Airlines, and United Air Lines, for which the available matrices represent authority as of January 1, 1975.

The system consists of one basic data bank and two basic subsystems—a data bank generation system and a search and retrieval system. The data bank generation system was designed to produce a maximum amount of output with a minimum amount of input. The search and retrieval system was designed to isolate selected portions of the data bank according to one or more of the following categories: (1) a specific city-pair, (2) a specific city, (3) a specific carrier, and (4) a range of certificate authorities. The format of the data bank was designed to facilitate sorting according to any or all of these categories.

For purposes of this study, we have chosen to use the data contained in the certificate authority matrix as the basis for each carrier's authority. The reasons for this are twofold. First, the matrix shows only a carrier's *best authority* for a given market. Second, no more concise or understandable format for the display of an air carrier's authority has yet been devised.

Summary of Findings

Twenty U.S. certificated air carriers (eleven trunks and nine local service carriers) were examined in this study. For each carrier, the certificate authority matrix was used in conjunction with the carrier's system timetable to produce, on a market-by-market basis, a comparison of available single-plane authority with that actually used. The detailed, city-by-city results for each carrier are summarized in Table 7-1.

At the industry level, these twenty carriers are authorized to serve 45,198 markets on a single-plane basis, out of a possible 49,392 directional city-pair combinations on the carriers' systems. This means that 92 percent of the possible markets on carriers' systems are actually authorized for single-plane service by either trunk or local service carriers (Table 7-2).

It should be noted that for the purposes of this report, a "market" is a carrier/city-pair/direction combination; that is, each direction is counted separately and, in addition, each city-pair appears in the total as many times as there are carriers on whose certificate it appears. This is necessary because service by a carrier in one direction between two cities may differ from that in the other, and different carriers may have different authority or may operate different levels of service between two cities. Thus, the percentage relationships are more significant than the absolute number of markets in any particular category.

Table 7-1

SUMMARY OF DOMESTIC SINGLE-PLANE AUTHORITY AND SERVICE OF TRUNK AND LOCAL SERVICE CARRIERS

Carrier/Number of Cities (1)	Total Possible City-Pair Combinations (2)	Number of City-Pairs Authorized for Service		Number of City-Pairs Receiving Service	Number of City-Pairs for Which Best Service Is Equal to Best Authority	
		Total (3)	Nonstop (4)	Total (5)	Total (6)	Nonstop (7)
Trunks						
American (44)	1,892	1,662	832	498	343	284
Braniff (33)	1,056	906	348	314	173	139
Continental (28)	756	660	268	268	165	116
Delta (67)	4,422	3,696	1,422	964	541	442
Eastern (67)	4,422	4,122	1,856	829	550	469
National (31)	930	836	490	338	146	138
Northwest (33)	1,056	1,008	604	363	174	168
Pan Am (11)	110	22	22	14	12	12
Trans World (34)	1,122	1,026	782	391	265	256
United (85)	7,140	6,898	2,546	934	640	556
Western (32)	992	948	296	290	180	143
Subtotal[a]	23,898	21,784	9,466	5,203	3,189	2,723
Percent of Total		91.2	39.6	21.8	13.3	11.4

Locals

Allegheny	(50)	2,450	2,448	1,716	600	377	279
Air New England	(13)	156	156	152	63	44	42
Airwest	(47)	2,162	2,160	1,820	475	221	187
Frontier	(89)	7,832	7,826	7,486	632	260	224
North Central	(67)	4,422	2,610	1,376	693	302	237
Ozark	(47)	2,162	2,120	1,730	380	219	204
Piedmont	(47)	2,162	2,158	1,872	680	298	267
Southern	(48)	2,256	2,050	792	423	213	170
Texas Int'l	(44)	1,892	1,886	1,722	352	144	126
Subtotal[a]		25,494	23,414	18,666	4,298	2,078	1,736
Percent of Total			91.8	73.2	16.9	8.2	6.8

All Carriers

Grand Total[a]		49,392	45,198	28,132	9,501	5,267	4,459
Percent of Total			91.5	57.0	19.2	10.7	9.0

[a] Totals are of carrier/city-pair/direction combinations; that is, each city-pair is counted separately in each direction and appears in the total as many times as there are carriers authorized or serving that city-pair.

Source: For each carrier the certificate authority matrix, the Certificate of Public Convenience and Necessity, and the system timetable.

Table 7-2

COMPARISON OF TOTAL CITY-PAIR COMBINATIONS TO
CITY-PAIRS AUTHORIZED FOR SINGLE-PLANE SERVICE

	Total City-Pair Combinations (1)	City-Pairs Authorized for Single-Plane Service (2)	Column (2) as a Percentage of Column (1) (3)
Trunks	23,898	21,784	91.2
Locals	25,494	23,414	91.8
All carriers	49,392	45,198	91.5

Source: Table 7-1.

Table 7-3

COMPARISON OF CITY-PAIRS AUTHORIZED FOR
SINGLE-PLANE SERVICE TO CITY-PAIRS AUTHORIZED
FOR NONSTOP SERVICE

	City-Pairs Authorized for Single-Plane Service (1)	City-Pairs Authorized for Nonstop Service (2)	Column (2) as a Percentage of Column (1) (3)
Trunks	21,784	9,466	43.5
Locals	23,414	18,666 [a]	79.9
All carriers	45,198	28,132	62.2

[a] The number of possible nonstop city-pairs for the local service carriers is somewhat misleading because the majority of the city-pairs have a minimum service requirement which must be met before they can be served on a nonstop basis.
Source: Table 7-1.

The trunk and local service carriers hold nonstop authority in 28,132 markets. Thus, nonstop authority exists in 62.2 percent of the markets authorized for single-plane service (Table 7-3). The twenty trunk and local service carriers are actually providing some type of single-plane service in 9,501 markets, or 21 percent of all markets authorized for single-plane service (Table 7-4). We have analyzed the extent to which the carriers are providing service equal

Table 7-4

COMPARISON OF CITY-PAIRS AUTHORIZED FOR
SINGLE-PLANE SERVICE TO TOTAL CITY-PAIRS
RECEIVING SERVICE

	City-Pairs Authorized for Single-Plane Service (1)	Total City-Pairs Receiving Service (2)	Column (2) as a Percentage of Column (1) (3)
Trunks	21,784	5,203	23.9
Locals	23,414	4,298	18.4
All carriers	45,198	9,501	21.0

Source: Table 7-1.

Table 7-5

COMPARISON OF CITY-PAIRS RECEIVING SERVICE EQUAL
TO BEST AUTHORITY WITH CITY-PAIRS AUTHORIZED
FOR SINGLE-PLANE SERVICE

	City-Pairs Authorized for Single-Plane Service (1)	Total City-Pairs Receiving Single-Plane Service Equal to Best Authority (2)	Column (2) as a Percentage of Column (1) (3)
Trunks	21,784	3,189	14.6
Locals	23,414	2,078	8.9
All carriers	45,198	5,267	11.7

Source: Table 7-1.

to their best authority in their various markets. The results of this analysis are as follows:

- The carriers are serving 5,267 markets using the best authority available, or 11.7 percent of all markets authorized for single-plane service (Table 7-5).

- The carriers are providing nonstop service in 4,459 markets for which they have nonstop authority. This represents 9.9 percent of the markets authorized for single-plane service and 15.9 percent of the markets with nonstop authority (Table 7-6).

Table 7-6

ANALYSIS OF NONSTOP AUTHORITY AND SERVICE OF
TRUNK AND LOCAL SERVICE CARRIERS

Carrier	Number of Nonstop Markets Authorized	Number of Nonstop Markets Served	Percentage Served of Authorized
Trunks			
American	832	284	34
Braniff	348	139	40
Continental	268	116	43
Delta	1,422	442	31
Eastern	1,856	469	25
National	490	138	28
Northwest	604	168	28
Pan Am	22	12	55
Trans World	782	256	33
United	2,546	556	22
Western	296	143	48
Subtotal	9,466	2,723	29
Locals			
Allegheny	1,716	279	16
Air New England	152	42	28
Airwest	1,820	187	10
Frontier	7,486	224	3
North Central	1,376	237	17
Ozark	1,730	204	12
Piedmont	1,872	267	14
Southern	792	170	21
Texas Int'l	1,722	126	7
Subtotal	18,666	1,736	9
Total all carriers	28,132	4,459	16

Source: Table 7-1.

Limitations of the Analysis

Since the development of the route authority data bank in 1973, the
CAB has been engaged in a continuing effort to update and refine the
route authority program. In their work with the program thus far,

they have been able to isolate and solve many of the problem areas associated with the program. However, there are still minor problems inherent in the machine generation of the air carrier matrix, stemming from the complex nature of carrier route authorization.

The following are some examples of the shortcomings of the matrix output, the correction of which was beyond the scope of this project:

(1) Some isolated cases occur where one-stop authority, instead of two-stop authority, is indicated on a matrix. This is especially true in the cases of Delta Air Lines and American Airlines. Apparently, although data input indicated two-stop, the computer has generated one-stop authority in certain cases where a new program routine was utilized. This error occurs both on junction authority and on multistop markets on a segment.

(2) The matrix for United Air Lines was run prior to the use of the new system which generates up to nine junction routings. Therefore, the matrix shows manually entered junction authority to the two-stop level, as designed by the CAB. Although the listed routings are correct, they are not comprehensive (that is, they include some, but not all, of the routings authorized to United), and they do not follow any circuity or backhaul guidelines.

(3) In the most recent runs, there are inaccuracies in some of the local service carrier markets. In restricted markets for which the computer is unable to generate a viable routing within circuity and backhaul constraints, inaccurate output is being generated. For example, Charleston, West Virginia–Lexington, Kentucky, is a one-stop market. However, since no possible routing can be generated with less than 150-mile circuity (the limit of the run), it should theoretically appear as a blank space on the matrix. However, the program apparently overrides the circuity backhaul factor and generates a legend.

Despite these occasional discrepancies, the matrices are generally accurate in showing nonstop or other general types of authority. To the extent possible, whenever we found a problem in a carrier's matrix, it was double-checked against the carrier's certificate. The correction was manually entered on the matrix and included in the updated analyses presented here. Thus, we believe that the matrices used in this analysis are correct to at least a *90-95 percent accuracy level* for the system as a whole.

Table 7-7
COMPETITIVE AUTHORITY IN AMERICAN'S
TOP TWENTY NONSTOP SEGMENTS, 1974

Market	Carriers Providing Service	Carriers Authorized but Not Providing Service
Los Angeles–New York	AA, TW, UA	None
Dallas–Los Angeles	AA, DL	CO [a]
Chicago–New York	AA, TW, UA	NW [b]
Dallas–New York	AA, BN	None
Chicago–Los Angeles	AA, CO, TW, UA	None
Dallas–San Francisco	AA, DL	None
Chicago–Phoenix	AA, TW	None
New York–San Francisco	AA, TW, UA	None
Chicago–San Francisco	AA, TW, UA	None
Detroit–Los Angeles	AA, UA	TW [c]
Los Angeles–Washington	AA, TW, UA	None
Chicago–Dallas	AA, BN	None
Boston–Los Angeles	AA, TW	UA [c]
Dallas–Phoenix	AA, DL	None
Detroit–New York	AA, NW, TW [d]	UA [c]
Detroit–San Francisco	AA, UA	TW [c]
Cleveland–Los Angeles	AA, UA	TW [c]
Dallas–Washington	AA, BN	None
Chicago–Washington	AA, TW, UA	None
Chicago–San Diego	AA, UA	None

[a] Authority temporarily suspended at carrier's request.
[b] Not permitted to operate turnaround service; provides one-stop service.
[c] Has nonstop authority.
[d] Not permitted to carry local traffic.
Note: The segments are ranked by revenue passenger miles (RPMs).

Analysis of Unused Nonstop Authority

As shown in Table 7-1, the trunks are presently authorized to serve 91 percent of the directional city-pair combinations in their systems. Of those markets in which they have authority, the trunks are authorized to serve 43 percent on a nonstop basis. However, they only provide nonstop service in 29 percent of such markets, amounting to

Table 7-8

TOP-RANKED MARKETS WITH UNUSED NONSTOP AUTHORITY

Market	Rank	Annual O&D Passengers
New York–Washington	3	1,638,310
Chicago–Detroit	13	590,490
Boston–Washington	15	579,360
Buffalo–New York	19	526,670
Boston–Philadelphia	27	409,360
New York–Rochester	28	408,030
Los Angeles–Seattle	31	376,670
Miami–Philadelphia	57	260,600
Boston–Los Angeles	62	252,900
New Orleans–New York	63	252,860
Boston–Miami	69	238,970
Detroit–Los Angeles	71	237,600
Miami–Washington	72	236,680

Source: Civil Aeronautics Board, *Origin and Destination Survey,* 12 months ended March 31, 1975, table 6.

11 percent of all their potential markets. The lack of utilization of almost three-quarters of the available nonstop authority is attributable to two major factors:

(1) There are a substantial number of small markets which cannot support nonstop service because of low traffic volumes. The majority of markets lacking nonstop service fall into this category.

(2) There are a number of sizeable markets in which nonstop authority exists (usually for more than one carrier), but this authority is not fully utilized. This is presumably because of the determination by individual carriers that additional competitive service would be uneconomical. For example, in seven of American's top twenty nonstop markets, there is another carrier authorized to provide nonstop service which has decided, on its own, not to provide such service (see Table 7-7).

In order to assess the extent to which nonstop authority is not fully utilized in large markets, we have analyzed the authority of each carrier between all city-pairs involving a large hub on the one hand, and a large or medium hub on the other. Current schedules were checked for all such markets in which nonstop service is authorized to determine the extent to which the authority is being used. As shown in Table 7-8, there are thirteen markets in the top seventy-five domestic markets in which carriers have unrestricted nonstop authority, but have opted not to provide service or to provide service inferior to that authorized.[3] Thus, the availability of authority does not by itself ensure that carriers will provide service, even in high- and medium-density markets. Rather, carriers have exercised discretion in selecting the markets they will serve and in determining the level of service they will provide in each market. Presumably, they base their choices on the likely financial impact of the various service options, as influenced by traffic volumes and integration opportunities, the availability of resources and the competitive environment.

[3] Markets are ranked by passenger volume, as shown in Civil Aeronautics Board, *Origin-Destination Survey of Airline Passenger Traffic*, for the 12 months ended March 31, 1975, table 6.

8

THE EFFECTS OF ROUTE RESTRICTION REMOVAL AND DISCRETIONARY AUTHORITY

Simat, Helliesen and Eichner, Inc.

This study examines the consequences of greater market entry and exit flexibility among existing domestic air carriers during the period of transition from the current regulatory scheme to a less regulated environment. The conditions studied are those contained in the proposed Aviation Act of 1975, which provides for the gradual (phased) removal of all the certificate restrictions the CAB has placed on existing carriers and, simultaneously, a limited (5 percent) and discretionary expansion of the carriers' existing route structures.[1] The transition period studied encompasses the short-term, or initial adjustment period (from three months to one year) when carriers are attempting to establish themselves on new routes, and the intermediate term, or equilibrium period (from one to two years), when carrier capacity and share become relatively stable and subject to the normal dynamics of a competitive market.

Many opponents of regulatory reform have argued that to permit the degree of market flexibility envisioned in the 1975 act would threaten the stability of the aviation industry, especially during the transition period. It is the purpose of this study to test this "chaos" hypothesis by projecting, on the basis of historical carrier behavior and expert judgment, how carriers will respond to the changed conditions. If anything, the study projects a more abrupt transition than

---

This paper is edited from the preface and the executive summary in the first volume of a three-volume report entitled *An Analysis of the Effects of Route Restriction Removal and Discretionary Authority: The Transition to a Less-Regulated Environment*, prepared for the U.S. Department of Transportation, Office of the Secretary, January 1977.

[1] This study does not consider the impact of fare flexibility and entry by new carriers, both of which are provided for to a limited extent by the proposed Aviation Act of 1975.

would occur under the Aviation Act of 1975 or other reform measures being considered. The assumption is made here that all route restrictions are removed simultaneously, whereas the act phases restriction removal specifically to ease the transition.

Methodology

The analytic portion of the study was performed in two stages. In stage one, the route systems of each trunk line and local service carrier were surveyed to identify those segments over which a given carrier is likely to face additional, or greater, competition as a result either of removal of other carriers' route restrictions or of additions of other carriers' discretionary route extensions. In addition to these segments, which can be considered the carrier's areas of vulnerability, the opportunities made available to each carrier as a result of liberalized market entry provisions were identified. Using an extensive data base (CAB Service Segment/ER-586 and Origin-Destination Survey Data) and knowledge of the industry (carriers' current operating strategies, announced filings for new routes, traffic flows on existing systems, and airport capacity), a set of scenarios was developed based on the probable behavior of existing carriers under the entry and exit provisions contained in the act. Although individual entry or exit decisions that have been predicted may be disputed, it is believed that the overall balance of risk and opportunity inherent in these choices is representative of the reality that will confront each carrier.

In stage two, the consequences of these choices were projected for each carrier, for each of the markets it serves, in terms of load factors, revenue passenger miles, and flight frequencies. Each carrier's market-by-market performance was then summed to yield carrier system aggregates (the effect of both the new markets a carrier enters and the existing markets of the carrier that are entered by other carriers pursuing their opportunities). Carrier system profitability was also calculated by means of a simplified accounting formula.

Assumptions Underlying the Study

Four assumptions, based on perceived historical patterns in the aviation industry, are key to this study.

- Airline services would not be concentrated in the largest markets and would not be drastically reduced in smaller markets.
- Carriers have only limited vulnerability to additional competition.

- Carriers' resources are limited.

- Competition does not result inevitably in excess capacity.

Corollary to these assumptions is the assumption that carrier managements will continue to display rational behavior; that is, to enter those markets offering the greatest profit potential while transferring resources from less profitable markets. Carrier behavior in the past supports this assumption as well as the other four. For example, out of the top 500 markets in the United States, 124 had at least one carrier with dormant authority in 1974 and these same carriers have chosen to serve less dense markets. This strongly suggests that carriers choose among markets on grounds other than density and that many less dense routes offer greater profit potential than some of the most heavily traveled routes.

Stage One Results: Markets Receiving Additional Competition

The scenarios developed in stage one of the analysis yield a set of markets whose incumbent carriers are subject to competition from additional and/or stronger competitors. Some of these are monopoly markets which would receive competition for the first time. Others are already competitive markets which would receive additional competition. The process of entry and exit clearly offers a potential for improvement in both system and carrier profitability, since one would expect that carriers would be transferring resources from their least profitable markets to markets offering greater profit possibilities. However, the extent to which this potential is achieved depends also on the performance of the new and incumbent carriers in these markets in terms of load factors and revenue passenger miles (RPMs) generated.

Stage Two Results: Impact of Additional Entry by Carrier

In projecting the impact of stage one scenarios on individual carriers, use was made of the best available evidence on (1) markets receiving additional competition over the last nine years and (2) the relation between load factors and number of competitors in a market.

In general this evidence suggests that during the initial period (from three to twelve months), when the entry actually occurs, traffic will be stimulated. But, with new competitors adding to the total number of flights in the market, market load factors will tend to be lower than system averages for both incumbents and new competitors. During the intermediate term (from one to two years), however, carriers will readjust flight frequencies, available seats, and traffic flows in response to new conditions. At the end of this period, therefore, new competitors in all markets, and incumbent carriers in originally competitive markets (except for short-haul and entry segments) generally will achieve load factors comparable to those observed in their overall system. Incumbent carriers in former monopoly markets will achieve load factors similar to those for their overall system, but lower than those they achieved with monopoly service.

It is impossible, of course, for carriers to enter all of the markets opened to them by removal of certificate restrictions. Since carriers have limited capacity and resources available, they would be forced to select markets for entry and exit carefully with a view to long-term profitability. Nor will all markets opened to new competition necessarily receive competition. Considerations such as market density, traffic flows, and carriers' capacity would figure in the entry and exit choices. Overall it would appear that most markets (from 70 to 80 percent) are immune to additional competition as a consequence of the restriction removal and discretionary mileage provisions of the act.

Table 8-1 summarizes these market-by-market projections for the trunk carriers. As the table shows, RPMs increase by 4.9 percent over the base 1974 in the intial term,[2] and by 8.3 percent in the intermediate term. The initial term load factor is projected to be 51.8 percent, while the intermediate term load factor is 56.1 percent (versus the 1974 base load factor of 55.7 percent).

Table 8-2 summarizes projections for the local service carriers. RPMs are projected to increase by 24.7 percent in the initial term and by 40.8 percent in the intermediate term. Initial and intermediate term load factors are 49.5 percent and 53.6 percent compared to 52.7 percent in the 1974 base.

Carrier Profitability

The calculations by which aggregate market performance measures for each carrier were converted into profitability estimates are presented in detail in chapter 4 of the first volume of the original report. A summary of profit estimates for the "Big Five" carriers is provided

---

[2] Projections do not include any secular growth; they reflect underlying conditions in base year 1974.

Table 8-1

SUMMARY OF IMPACT ON DOMESTIC
TRUNK CARRIER INDUSTRY

(in millions)

Item	Revenue Passenger Miles		Available Seat Miles	
	Initial term	Inter-mediate term	Initial term	Inter-mediate term
Industry current base [a]	117,646	117,646	211,067	211,067
New competition on vulnerable monopolies	(2,955)	(1,023)	. . . .	. . . .
Carrier withdrawal from weak routes	(1,319)	(1,319)	(3,452)	(3,652)
Routes with improved competition	(558)	(2,399)	. . . .	(4,379)
Routes with additional competitors	(2,118)	(6,342)	. . . .	(11,533)
Routes where carrier replaces weak carrier or improves restricted authority	2,604	4,049	6,579	7,524
Routes where carrier becomes an additional competitor	5,711	9,987	14,567	17,514
Linear extensions	4,441	6,795	9,759	10,600
Total	123,452	127,394	238,320	227,141
Percentage change from base	4.9%	8.3%	12.9%	7.6%
Industry current load factor	55.7%			
Industry load factor after shifts	51.8%	56.1%		

[a] The industry base revenue passenger miles differ by a small percentage from actual calendar year 1974 because FY 1974 was used as National's base year for estimating changes because of the carrier's lengthy strike in the second half of 1974.

Note: Pan American Airlines is not included.

Source: Simat, Helliesen and Eichner, Inc., *An Analysis of the Effects of Route Restriction Removal and Discretionary Authority*, vol. 2, *Trunk Carrier Profiles*.

here in Table 8-3. Tables 8-4 and 8-5 show profit levels for the "Small Five" trunk carriers and for the local service carriers.

The conditions that yielded these results are the projected load factors and the RPMs for each carrier in the initial and intermediate

Table 8-2

SUMMARY OF IMPACT ON LOCAL SERVICE
CARRIER INDUSTRY

(in millions)

Item	Revenue Passenger Miles		Available Seat Miles	
	Initial term	Inter-mediate term	Initial term	Inter-mediate term
Industry current base	10,858	10,858	20,612	20,612
New competition on carrier vulnerable monopolies	(70)	(31)	. . . .	. . . .
Carrier withdrawal from weak routes	(46)	(46)	(115)	(115)
Routes with improved competition	(23)	(68)	. . . .	(125)
Routes with additional competitors	(29)	(99)	. . . .	(181)
Routes where carrier replaces weak carrier or improves restricted authority	321	590	689	957
Routes where carrier becomes an additional competitor	1,743	2,896	4,255	5,176
Linear extensions	790	1,193	1,918	2,231
Total	13,544	15,293	27,359	28,555
Percentage change from base	24.7%	40.8%	32.7%	38.5%
Industry current load factor	52.7%			
Industry load factor after shifts	49.5%	53.6%		

Source: Simat, Helliesen and Eichner, Inc., *An Analysis of the Effects of Route Restriction Removal and Discretionary Authority,* vol. 3, *Local Service Carrier Profiles.*

terms (from tables similar to 8-1 and 8-2 for each carrier) together with the following additional assumptions:

- A short-term 7.5 percent increase in yield (fares) over the base year and a 1.0 percent decrease in available ton-mile cost for the initial term.

- No change from 1974 base levels in either yield or productivity for a "worst case" intermediate term.

Table 8-3

IMPACT OF ENTRY FLEXIBILITY ON PROFITABILITY OF "BIG FIVE" TRUNK CARRIERS

(domestic annual profit before taxes in millions)

Carrier	Base Year/ 1974	Initial Term	Inter- mediate Term: Worst Case	Intermediate Term: Expected Results
American	$ 17.4	$ 48.2	$ 21.7	$ 97.9
Eastern	33.7	21.5	40.5	103.9
Delta	150.1	174.8	139.5	198.7
TWA	(0.4)	26.3	31.6	90.5
United	201.5	271.7	196.9	301.6
Total profit before tax	$402.4	$542.5	$430.2	$792.6

- No change in yield from 1974 base levels, and a gain in productivity equal to a 5.0 percent decrease in available ton-mile costs, for the expected intermediate result.

Public statements by carrier officials and carrier fare applications make it clear that the carriers desire fare increases. For purposes of this study, carrier statements and applications have been accepted as representative of company policy. The assumption has been made, therefore, that in the initial term carriers will increase fares by an average of 7.5 percent above 1974 levels.[3]

As entry continues over time, however, competition and threat of competition, coupled with more efficient operations, will cause fares to decline from these levels. It is believed that, in the intermediate term, market forces will bring fares, on average, at least back down to 1974 levels (in real terms). Close study of intrastate markets suggests that substantial fare reductions in many markets could result in traffic stimulation, offering additional profit potential over and above that suggested by this study. However, it is useful to separate the impact of market entry flexibility from that of fare flexibility and, as noted, fare flexibility was excluded from this study for this and other reasons. Therefore, 1974 fare and yield levels have been used as a lower limit here.

[3] The base year for this study is 1974. The assumption is, however, that fares would increase by 7.5 percent in the initial stage of the transition period, whenever that begins. In fact, by the end of 1976, carriers had already received fare increases amounting to 14.7 percent over 1974 levels.

Table 8-4

IMPACT OF ENTRY FLEXIBILITY ON PROFITABILITY OF "SMALL FIVE" TRUNK CARRIERS

(domestic annual profit before taxes in millions)

Carrier	Base Year/ 1974	Initial Term	Inter- mediate Term: Worst Case	Intermediate Term: Expected Results
Braniff	$ 24.5	$ 33.8	$ 70.1	$ 93.9
Continental	13.5	25.1	42.2	67.8
National	47.4[a]	67.3	66.2	89.0
Northwest	76.3	120.8	129.2	158.1
Western	37.5	31.9	39.2	66.1
Total profit before tax	$199.2	$278.8	$346.8	$474.9

[a] The base year is year ending June 30, 1974, because of National's lengthy strike in the second half of 1974.

Production efficiency was examined in detail in chapters 2 and 4 of the first volume of the original report. In the initial term, a 1 percent gain in efficiency is forecast. In the intermediate term, a combination of route rationalization and market forces is likely to result in some carriers, particularly the "Big Five," achieving more efficient operations and reducing available ton-mile costs by 5 percent. Since this is not certain, intermediate term results, with and without the expected 5 percent efficiency gain, have been calculated.

The following results were derived from these calculations and are shown in Table 8-3 for the "Big Five":

(1) During the initial period, the most difficult part of the transition, when load factors are projected to decrease slightly, profits are up more than 34 percent from the 1974 base ($542 million versus $402 million).

(2) The intermediate-term expected result, when yields are stabilized and unit costs have declined because of greater operating efficiency, produces total profits of almost $800 million versus $402 million for the base year 1974.

(3) Even the worst-case intermediate term produces total profits slightly higher than those for the 1974 base year; that is, $430 million versus $402 million.

Table 8-5

IMPACT OF ENTRY FLEXIBILITY ON PROFITABILITY OF LOCAL SERVICE CARRIERS

(annual profit excluding subsidy and before taxes in millions)

Carrier	Base Year/ 1974	Initial Term	Intermediate Term
Allegheny	$ 6.1	$ 20.4	$ 39.1
Frontier	3.3	9.4	16.7
Airwest	(0.1)	(10.4)	7.6
North Central	3.6	4.3	23.7
Ozark	(0.8)	2.2	8.2
Piedmont	1.4	3.3	9.5
Southern	(3.4)	0.9	9.0
Texas International	(6.8)	(4.0)	—a
Total profit excluding subsidy and before taxes	$ 3.3	$ 26.4	$113.8

a Profit but less than $500,000.

Because the smaller trunks at present are operating both efficiently and profitably, their potential gains from market entry flexibility are largely from increased revenues. The profits are estimated to increase from less than $200 million to $475 million (Table 8-4). Profits of local service carriers, before taxes and before subsidy, are projected to increase by $110 million (Table 8-5).

Conclusion

The basic finding of this study is that the increased market entry which would result from the lifting of restrictions and the limited discretionary mileage for existing carriers would not lead to chaos for the aviation industry. Rather, these steps are foreseen to have results which would be significantly and distinctly beneficial for the carriers and for the public. The improvement in route systems because of the removal of route restrictions and discretionary extensions is expected to result in added services, greater traffic volumes, somewhat higher load factors, and increased carrier efficiency and profits.

PART FIVE

THE FINANCIAL IMPACT OF DEREGULATION ON AIR CARRIERS

Another major issue in the debate over the aviation reform proposals was the ability of the firms to adjust to the heightened competitive forces in the industry. The concern was expressed in some quarters that deregulation would mean financial collapse and bankruptcy for several carriers—that many carriers would not be able to attract capital and that the industry as a whole would suffer severe financial losses. Proponents of the reform proposal argued that regulation itself was threatening the financial condition of the industry and that increased managerial flexibility in setting prices and service would improve the industry's financial performance. The papers in this part deal with these issues.

The first paper is an analysis by James C. Miller III, then on the staff of the Council of Economic Advisers, of the likely financial impacts on the individual carriers from the Aviation Act. This paper was prepared before the Aviation Act of 1975 was submitted to Congress, in response to the concern of those preparing the administration's proposal about whether they could bear the burden of proof on the financial impact on given carriers resulting from the proposal. The next paper is a discussion by Paul W. MacAvoy of the financial effects on the aviation industry over a longer period—the coming five to ten years—resulting from reduction of CAB controls. This discussion is drawn heavily from Mr. MacAvoy's testimony before the House Aviation Subcommittee given on May 12, 1976. A member of the Aviation Subcommittee, Congressman Elliott H. Levitas (Democrat, Georgia), subsequently raised the question of whether the administration saw higher or lower air fares resulting from deregulation. The final paper is Mr. MacAvoy's response to Mr. Levitas's inquiry.

9

THE EFFECTS OF
THE ADMINISTRATION'S
DRAFT BILL ON
AIR CARRIER FINANCES

James C. Miller III

(Although the domestic airlines will experience fuel price increases over the next few months and little traffic growth this year and next, fuel prices are expected to level out shortly and traffic is expected to grow at higher-than-normal rates during the latter part of the decade. The airlines should become sound financially by 1977 or 1978.)

It is difficult to determine whether deregulation would increase or decrease industry profits. The indication is that the effect would probably be small. The draft bill would have a relatively negative impact on the "Big Four" carriers (American, Eastern, Trans World, and United) as opposed to the other domestic trunks and Pan American (which would benefit from acquiring domestic routes). Since negative impacts on individual carriers would be manifest primarily in terms of excess aircraft capacity, the ease with which aircraft can be sold when the industry is depressed moderates significantly the degree of variations among carriers.

The timing of the bill is a key factor. Neither the fare flexibility nor entry provisions would have much effect prior to the time when it is predicted that the industry will have realized financial restoration and increased growth.

Introduction

Depending upon extent and how it is phased, deregulation could have a positive or negative impact on the profits of the airline industry; it

This paper was originally prepared as a memorandum to the Economic Policy Board. A revised version of the paper was presented at a session of the American Economic Association, Transportation and Public Utilities Group, Dallas, Texas, December 29, 1975; the revised version appeared in *Transportation Journal*, Spring 1976.

could also have differential financial impacts on individual air carriers. This analysis, limited to the (larger) trunk airlines, attempts to project these effects and assess them in the context of the Ford administration's proposed Aviation Act of 1975. It begins, however, with a description and analysis of *other* factors affecting the industry's future profit performance.

Recovery of the Economy. It is generally accepted that the demand for air travel is positively related to the growth of the economy.[1] Nearly all studies have concluded that air travel demand is income-elastic, meaning that for a given percentage increase in income, quantity demanded rises a greater percentage (and vice versa).

Projections of real disposable income and of annual rates of growth provided by the Council of Economic Advisers are given in Table 9-1. Also shown are the implied rates of growth in airline demand under various assumed income elasticities. Although empirical estimates of income elasticity range somewhat, they tend to center around 2 percent. This suggests little growth in demand this year and next, but a rise to approximately 11 percent annual growth through 1980.

Fuel Price Increases. Aviation fuel used in domestic operations rose from 22.5 cents per gallon in June 1974 to 27.2 cents per gallon in June 1975. At present, fuel accounts for approximately 20 percent of trunk-airline average operating cost in domestic operations. The Federal Energy Administration estimates that by the end of the year the price of aviation fuel will have risen another three cents per gallon but that subsequently there will be no further increases in the (real) price of fuel (this assumes total decontrol of old oil, recision of the oil import tariff, and no change in the prices set by the Organization of Petroleum Exporting Countries). A one-time fuel price increase of three cents per gallon would raise (permanently) the trunk airlines' cost level by approximately 2.2 percent, making fuel expense approximately 21.7 percent of total cost. On a projected total annual cost for domestic operations of approximately $10 billion, this represents a profit reduction of approximately $220 million annually.

The airlines could respond to such a change in two ways. First, they might slow the rate of expansion until demand had caught up to the higher break-even load factor. An educated guess is that this

---

[1] Most analysts attribute the present depressed state of some carriers to two causes: the current recession and increases in fuel prices. Of the two, the former is believed to have had the more significant effect.

Table 9-1

PROJECTIONS OF REAL DISPOSABLE INCOME, ITS RATES OF GROWTH, AND RATES OF GROWTH IN AIR TRAVEL DEMAND, BY INCOME ELASTICITY

Year	Real Disposable Income (in billions of dollars)	Annual Rate of Growth in Real Disposable Income	Annual Rate of Growth in Airline Demand, Assuming Income Elasticity Equal			
			1.0	1.5	2.0	2.5
1975	1,062	(3.0)	(3.0)	(4.5)	(6.0)	(7.5)
1976	1,077	1.4	1.4	2.1	2.8	3.5
1977	1,136	5.5	5.5	8.2	11.0	13.8
1978	1,198	5.5	5.5	8.2	11.0	13.8
1979	1,261	5.3	5.3	8.0	10.6	13.2
1980	1,329	5.4	5.4	8.1	10.8	13.5

Source: Council of Economic Advisers.

would take approximately two years.[2] Or, as was recommended to the CAB by the administration on August 19, 1975, the airlines could "pass through" the increase in the form of higher fares.[3] Under this recommended procedure, each carrier would be allowed to raise its fares in individual markets a maximum of the percentage increase in total cost brought about by increases in fuel prices. Because of demand price elasticity, this would not mean revenue increases sufficient to offset totally cost increases; however, because carriers would raise fares in the least elastic markets, the resulting burden on the carriers would be much less than the $220 million figure mentioned above.[4]

[2] Much depends on orders for new equipment and on how flexible the contracts for delivery are. As of the end of 1974, the trunk carriers had aircraft on order totaling $1.8 billion. Recently, several airlines (for example, Eastern) have been successful in postponing deliveries.

[3] Joint Petition of the U.S. Department of Transportation, the Federal Energy Administration, and the Council on Wage and Price Stability for Emergency Procedures to Deal with Fuel Cost Increases (Civil Aeronautics Board, Docket 28191, August 19, 1975).

[4] Total cost recovery through uniform fare increases would be possible only if the board's conclusion that demand is price-inelastic is correct—a conclusion subject to much criticism (see below). If one assumes the board's estimated demand elasticity of −0.7, the (full) cost-recovery fare increase for a cost increase of 2.2 percent is 7.3 percent—that is, percent fare increase = percent cost increase/$(1-e_d)$, where e_d = demand elasticity. However, assuming the airlines responded to fuel price increases by reducing scheduling, and counting the

Table 9-2

ACTUAL UNIT COST PER AVAILABLE TON-MILE AS
PERCENTAGE OF STANDARD UNIT COST, 1962–1970,
BY DOMESTIC TRUNK CARRIER

Carrier	1962	1963	1964	1965	1966	1967	1968	1969	1970
American	115	113	112	113	102	99	100	98	95
Eastern	93	92	96	103	113	107	113	108	104
Trans World	115	111	113	112	114	113	111	112	109
United	103	106	101	101	107	103	103	99	97
Braniff	93	96	99	107	106	109	113	112	106
Continental	84	88	90	75	70	76	87	89	90
Delta	105	105	102	100	100	101	100	93	84
National	88	89	89	86	86	91	88	89	99
Northeast	115	127	118	119	116	120	100	119	116
Northwest	97	86	86	80	81	77	78	77	94
Western	95	89	96	101	102	a	108	108	113

a Not computed because of Western's merger with Pacific Northern in 1967.
Source: George W. Douglas and James C. Miller III, *Economic Regulation of Domestic Air Transport: Theory and Policy* (Washington, D.C.: The Brookings Institution, 1974), p. 143.

Relative Carrier Efficiency. From enactment of regulation in 1938 the CAB has unswervingly protected the "grandfather" trunk carriers from new competition, and until ten years ago the board was reasonably successful in protecting the trunk carriers from competing with each other. However, during the growth period of the middle and late 1960s, the board certificated additional competitors into many markets, so that today more than three-quarters of trunk line traffic is generated in competitive markets. This makes it difficult for the board effectively to insulate the carriers from competition. Thus, it may not be possible in the future for the board to prevent the kind of bankruptcies (or failing-firm mergers) that accompany normal business enterprise.

savings that would be realized on passenger servicing (as a result of carrying fewer passengers because of the fare increase), the full cost-recovery fare increase might well be only half that amount.

As the administration's petition pointed out, a particular difficulty in following the full cost-recovery methodology is that it raises fares so far that the break-even load factor is lowered beyond what it was before the cost increase. Over the long run this leads to greater excess capacity. Under the administration's proposal, the fare increase would leave break-even load factors unchanged.

Table 9-3

OPERATING PROFIT (LOSS) IN DOMESTIC SERVICE
BY TRUNK CARRIER, 1970–1974

(in millions of dollars)

Carrier and Group	1970	1971	1972	1973	1974
American	(19.1)	23.0	29.9	(44.4)	29.8
Eastern	26.3	38.3	53.0	3.5	81.5
Trans World	(91.8)	(3.3)	57.6	40.6	21.1
United	(21.0)	34.7	75.9	150.1	179.5
Big Four	(105.5)	92.8	216.5	149.8	311.9
Braniff	1.5	14.0	14.8	23.7	39.6
Continental	20.2	30.4	34.9	16.5	49.4
Delta	78.9	63.1	100.5	123.7	161.8
National	(11.3)	23.9	40.0	44.9	43.6
Northeast	(4.8)	(8.8)	.6	—	—
Northwest	31.1	10.0	14.1	34.7	68.8
Pan American	1.1	(5.5)	(4.7)	(11.7)	(28.5)
Western	5.5	9.6	17.2	33.1	33.5
Other Trunks	122.2	136.7	217.5	264.9	368.2
Total	16.7	229.5	434.1	414.7	680.0

There is evidence that some carriers are consistently better performers than others. This appears to have little to do with size of firm (although the larger firms do tend to perform relatively poorly) or degree of competition. For example, indexes of relative carrier efficiency over the years 1962 through 1970 are shown in Table 9-2. Note that Trans World (TWA) and Northeast are chronic poor performers, whereas Continental and Northwest consistently do well.

Domestic service operating profit for 1970 through 1974 for each of the trunk carriers (including Pan American) is shown in Table 9-3.[5] Shown in Table 9-4 is carrier rate of return on overall investment for the same period. Note again that there are steady good performers, such as Braniff, Continental, Delta, and Northwest, and steady marginal or poor performers such as Pan American, Trans World and Northeast.[6]

---

[5] Operating profit is before taxes and before interest payments on debt.

[6] Northeast merged into Delta on August 1, 1972.

Table 9-4

RATE OF RETURN ON INVESTMENT IN DOMESTIC SERVICE BY TRUNK CARRIER, 1970–1974

(percent)

Carrier	1970	1971	1972	1973	1974
Big Four					
American	0.60	3.46	2.88	−1.64	4.05
Eastern	3.97	5.51	6.36	1.36	8.31
Trans World	5.08	3.35	8.44	7.31	5.63
United	0.16	2.90	4.12	6.34	8.76
Other Trunks					
Braniff	2.37	6.16	7.74	9.70	12.59
Continental	5.70	6.66	6.71	6.92	9.20
Delta	12.37	9.50	12.09	16.45	15.89
National	1.62	6.74	9.46	9.75	9.75
Northeast	−16.90	−52.56	1.54	—	—
Northwest	10.22	4.21	5.29	8.55	11.27
Pan American	2.21	−0.16	0.47	−2.68	−10.37
Western	4.19	5.66	7.43	11.36	12.79

Effects of Total, Immediate Deregulation on the Industry

Total, immediate deregulation is *not* what the administration's bill envisions, but it is a useful starting point for analysis.

Complete deregulation would lead to a sizeable reduction in the overall level of fares. The question is whether the new (higher) level of load factor would exceed or fall short of the new (higher) break-even load factor. Another way of posing this question is to ask whether a fare decrease would lead to a higher or a lower equilibrium level of capacity. If that new equilibrium level were less, then carriers would be made worse off (giving them the incentive to contract invest-ment); on the other hand, if that new equilibrium level of investment were greater, then the industry would be made better off and might earn excess profits until which time industry investment expanded to the equilibrium level.

The equilibrium level of investment will increase when fare is decreased if and only if

$$e_d(1 - c/F) < -1,$$

where

$$e_d = \text{"full-price" elasticity of demand,}$$
$$c = \text{per-passenger "traffic cost," and}$$
$$F = \text{average fare (that is, price of ticket).}[7]$$

Otherwise, the equilibrium level of investment will be less when there is a fare decrease. If this condition holds, short-run airline (industry) profits will be greater after deregulation than before.[8]

The ratio c/F, on average, ranges between 0.201 and 0.236, depending on how much overhead expense is included in traffic cost.[9] (For short-haul markets, it is somewhat higher; for long hauls, somewhat lower.) This implies that for the industry to earn greater (short-run) profits under deregulation, (full-price) demand elasticity must be greater than 1.25 to 1.36.

There has been extensive analysis of airline demand price elasticity. Fortunately, for the instant purpose, most contain a methodological error which makes the price variable measure the response to changes in "full-price" rather than simply changes in fare.[10] However, these estimates tend to fall near the figures mentioned above and vary widely.[11] In the board's Domestic Passenger Fare Investiga-

---

[7] See George W. Douglas and James C. Miller III, *Economic Regulation of Domestic Air Transport: Theory and Policy* (Washington, D.C.: The Brookings Institution, 1974), p. 60.

[8] This condition can be explained intuitively as follows: Demand must, of course, be price elastic so that a fare decrease raises total revenue. But total cost will increase too, because more passengers will be carried on each flight. Thus, demand must be *sufficiently* elastic to offset this increase in total cost. In other words, demand elasticity, deflated by the multiplier $(1 - c/F)$ must exceed unity, in absolute value terms.

[9] Douglas and Miller, *Economic Regulation of Domestic Air Transport*, pp. 37 and 60.

[10] In other words, a change in fare also has an impact on waiting time—the additional component in the full price of service. (That is, the total "cost" of service as perceived by the passenger is the ticket price plus an imputation for the cost of "waiting" for a flight [the difference between desired departure time and actual departure]; increasing the fare leads to greater excess capacity [greater frequencies, lower load factors] and hence to lower waiting time.) Most time-series analyses use no smaller increments than a year, and this is probably sufficient for the industry to make capacity (and thus waiting time) adjustments. Cross-section observations presumably measure equilibrium combinations of simple price and waiting time. Thus, the simple price elasticity estimates are really estimates of "full price" elasticity.

[11] The most widely cited "estimate" is the board's finding in the Domestic Passenger Fare Investigation (DPFI): —0.7. This finding should not be given much weight, as it was little more than a judgment, trying to reconcile conflicting points of view. Also the board's resultant fare "methodology" was predicated on a finding of inelastic demand. See Civil Aeronautics Board, Order 71-4-59 and Order 71-4-60, April 9, 1971.

tion (DPFI) some of the carrier parties presented studies which purported to show that air travel demand is inelastic (that is, $e_d > -1$). This result, however, conflicts with most academic studies which conclude that the demand for air travel is elastic (that is, $e_d < -1$). The board's staff, for example, has compiled both time-series and cross-section estimates which conclude that $e_d \approx -1.3$.[12] Studies by Arthur S. De Vany,[13] Philip K. Verleger,[14] and others show demand elasticity ranging from just in excess of unity to well over 2.0 (absolute value terms).

Based on this sketchy evidence, it is not possible to conclude with great confidence whether sudden and complete deregulation, unaccompanied by cost changes, would result in an increase or a decrease in short-run industry profits. What one might conclude with a bit more confidence is that the difference in profit would be small. Some affirmation of this conclusion comes from the results of Lockheed's route model portrayed in the Air Transport Association's recent report, *Consequences of Deregulation of the Scheduled Air Transport Industry* (see Figure 9-1 for adaptation).[15] Based on 1973 yields and an average load factor of 55 percent, the industry was earning approximately $1 million per day. Based on my work with George Douglas,[16] it can be estimated that (for that period) total deregulation (with no changes in the cost function) would have resulted in an average fare reduction of approximately 16 percent and a new (actual and) break-even load factor of 65 percent. As indicated on the chart, under these circumstances the industry's earnings would be approximately the same (that is, $1 million per day).[17]

---

[12] See Samuel L. Brown and Wayne S. Watkins, "Measuring Elasticities of Air Travel from New Cross-Sectional Data" (Paper delivered at the annual meeting of the American Statistical Association, 1971).

[13] Arthur S. De Vany, "The Revealed Value of Time in Air Travel," *Review of Economics and Statistics*, February 1974, pp. 77-82.

[14] Philip K. Verleger, Jr., "Models of the Demand for Air Transportation," *Bell Journal of Economics and Management Science*, Autumn 1972, pp. 437-57.

[15] This report has been criticized by several academics and others for drawing conclusions not based on the model. The model itself, however, while not perfect, is useful for the purpose described above.

[16] Douglas and Miller, *Economic Regulation of Domestic Air Transport.*

[17] Deregulation might be expected also to increase the quality of service by making more direct service available and by providing a stronger competitive spur for carriers to make genuine improvements in quality dimensions such as baggage speed, loss, damage, et cetera. Deregulation would also be expected to lead to cost reductions because of less circuitous routings, easier matching of equipment to routes, and the effect of competition in holding down labor costs. Both effects (that is, quality improvements and cost reductions) would lead to greater (short-run) profits.

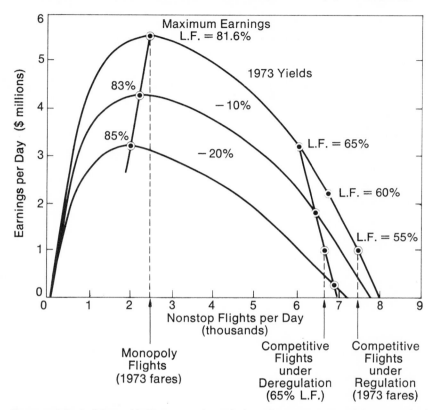

Figure 9-1

EFFECTS OF AIRLINE DEREGULATION: A ROUTE MODEL

Maximum Earnings
L.F. = 81.6%

1973 Yields

83%

−10%

85%

−20%

L.F. = 65%

L.F. = 60%

L.F. = 55%

Earnings per Day ($ millions)

Nonstop Flights per Day
(thousands)

Monopoly
Flights
(1973 fares)

Competitive
Flights
under
Deregulation
(65% L.F.)

Competitive
Flights
under
Regulation
(1973 fares)

Source: Adapted from Air Transport Association, *Consequences of Deregulation of the Scheduled Air Transport Industry: An Analytical Approach*, April 1975, figure 8.

Another indication of the effect of deregulation on industry profit rates can be obtained from the sensitivity analysis portrayed in Table 9-5. This table shows the effects of a 16 percent fare decrease on industry profits under various assumed demand elasticities. Even if the board's estimate of − 0.7 were correct and the carriers made no adjustments whatsoever in capacity in anticipation of complete deregulation, the short-run yearly loss would only be $660 million, or 6.6 percent of total revenue. On the other hand, if demand is as elastic as − 2.5, the industry could experience a windfall of $1,189 million, or 11.9 percent of total revenue.

Table 9-5

SENSITIVITY OF SHORT-RUN INDUSTRY PROFITS TO DEMAND ELASTICITY

(assuming sudden, complete deregulation; 16 percent fare decrease; $10 billion total industry revenue and cost; and 0.22 c/F ratio)

Demand Elasticity Assumption	Change in (Short-Run) Industry Profit Rate (millions of dollars per year)	Change in (Short-Run) Industry Profit Rate as Percentage of Initial Industry Total Revenue and Cost
$e_d = -.7$	-660	-6.6
$e_d = -1.0$	-352	-3.5
$e_d = -1.3$	-44	-0.4
$e_d = -2.0$	$+675$	$+6.8$
$e_d = -2.5$	$+1,189$	$+11.9$

It must be noted, however, that the regulatory reform program incorporated in the administration's proposal is a gradual one. This means that carriers would have ample time to adjust capacity to changing market conditions, including competitive forces that alter the level of fares. Thus, competition among carriers might be expected to result in normal profits within a broad range of demand elasticities. Also, it would appear that the lower estimates are based on methodologies which reveal short-run demand elasticities, whereas the higher estimates are based on methodologies revealing long-run estimates. Since under the proposal's provisions the price reductions would take place over a period of years, it would seem appropriate to rely on the higher estimates. For these reasons it appears extremely doubtful that the regulatory reform program incorporated in the administration's proposal would have any significant adverse impact on short-run industry profits.

Effects of Deregulation on Individual Carriers

The previous discussion centered around the effects of deregulation on the industry as a whole. Although the effects on individual carriers could vary, the most important consideration with respect to the impact on individual firms would appear to be the projection of *industry* profits. The reason is that the differential carrier impacts would show up primarily in terms of excess (or insufficient) flight equipment. When the industry is sound, flight equipment can be bought and sold at rates reasonably consistent with book value. Thus, even though the industry may not be able to expand or contract capacity quickly, individual firms are indeed in a position to do so. Thus, the differential impacts described below may be moderated considerably by voluntary contractions or expansions by individual carriers.

Fare Flexibility. There is considerable lethargy in the airlines with respect to pricing. Since individual fare changes have been very costly, the industry has concentrated on across-the-board increases and some system-wide discounts. Because of inertia, during the first phase of pricing flexibility (probably six to eighteen months) there would be few significant variations from existing pricing policies. However, as traffic began to pick up and as uncertainty began to subside, carriers would begin to experiment with fares on a market-by-market basis. It is likely that carriers would use their discretion to raise fares on many of their "monopoly" routes. As shown in Table 9-6, this would tend to benefit Eastern, United, Braniff, Delta, Northwest, and Western—all of which generate at least approximately one-quarter of their traffic in monopoly routes. Less advantaged would be American, Trans World, Continental, and National.

Fare decreases would depend primarily on four factors: (1) degree of competition, (2) average length of haul, (3) average market density, and (4) carrier aggressiveness. For obvious reasons, decreases would more likely obtain in competitive markets. This would imply that a higher incidence of fare decreases would be experienced by American, Trans World, Continental, and National than by the other carriers. (See Table 9-6.)

It would appear that existing fares are particularly excessive in markets that are long-haul and/or have high density. Fares in such markets would be the most likely to fall as the carriers began to exercise pricing freedom. As shown in Table 9-6, on the basis of average trip length this would imply a higher incidence of fare reductions for American, Trans World, United, Continental, and Pan American; Eastern, Braniff, and Delta would experience a lower incidence of fare reductions. On the basis of route density (Table 9-6), the "Big Four" carriers (American, Eastern, Trans World, and United) plus National would likely experience a greater incidence of fare reductions than would Braniff, Continental, Northwest, Pan American, and Western.

Table 9-6

ANALYSIS OF MONOPOLY MARKETS, BY TRUNK CARRIER

Carrier	Percentage of Revenue Passenger Miles (RPMs) in Monopoly Markets, 1970	Average Length of Passenger Trip, 1972 (miles)	Average Route Density, 1972 (RPMs/route miles/ 1,000,000) [a]
Big Four			
American	17.0	908.9	1.37
Eastern	23.4	593.3	1.16
Trans World	8.9	1,044.0	1.60
United	32.5	873.7	2.00
Other Trunks			
Braniff	34.0	619.2	0.30
Continental	20.6	879.4	0.66
Delta	32.1	600.2	0.94
National	10.9	805.4	1.36
Northwest	36.5	759.1	0.35
Pan American	—	2,506.1	0.22
Western	26.6	763.6	0.60

[a] Route-mile data is system-wide, whereas traffic data is domestic only.

Finally, some carriers have become known in the industry as "mavericks," and these may be expected to be more aggressive with respect to price competition than others. As shown in Table 9-7, mavericks such as Continental, Delta, and Northwest may be expected to have a depressing effect on the fares charged by American, Trans World, Eastern, and United.

Entry. The draft bill contains three major provisions on entry. First, the revision in the "Declaration of Policy" (section 102) admonishes the board to consider the benefits of competition and the public's need for service in deciding upon entry cases. How much this would mean in terms of the entry by existing carriers into new markets and the entry of new carriers is difficult to judge since the board would retain wide discretion. However, given the board's proclivity to protect existing carriers it would appear unlikely that significant entry would flow from this provision during the first five years.

Second, the draft bill requires the board to eliminate all restrictions on carrier routes by January 1, 1981. The board can be relied

Table 9-7

NUMBER OF CITY-PAIRS IN COMMON AMONG TOP 135
AUTHORIZED-SERVICE DOMESTIC TRUNK CARRIERS, 1970

Carrier		AA	BN	CO	DL	EA	NA	NE	NW	TW	UN	WA	City-Pairs Authorized
AA	American	—	11	10	39	37	19	14	24	47	45	3	70
BN	Braniff	11	—	10	19	18	5	3	8	11	14	1	27
CO	Continental	10	10	—	11	7	3	0	10	10	17	9	26
DL	Delta	39	19	11	—	44	26	13	23	41	46	1	68
EA	Eastern	37	18	7	44	—	21	21	27	33	44	1	64
NA	National	19	5	3	26	21	—	15	10	22	30	4	35
NE	Northeast	14	3	0	13	21	15	—	10	16	18	0	21
NW	Northwest	24	8	10	23	27	10	10	—	30	50	10	52
TW	TWA	47	11	10	41	33	22	16	30	—	63	8	75
UN	United	45	14	17	46	44	30	18	50	63	—	18	100
WA	Western	3	1	8	1	1	4	0	10	8	18	—	20

Source: U.S. Department of Transportation, *Executive Branch Criteria for Domestic Airline Merger Proposals*, Washington, August 31, 1971, p. 4.

upon to orchestrate this entry relaxation in such a way as to minimize adverse impact on the industry and on individual carriers. In order to assess the impact of this certificate restriction removal program, an examination was made of the top 100 city-pair markets, which (alone) represent approximately one-third of all domestic traffic. The additional opportunities for new entry made possible by the route restriction removal program are summarized in Table 9-8. The main beneficiaries would appear to be Northwest, Delta, Eastern, and American, in that order. On the other hand, the program would generate relatively few opportunities for Western and Continental.[18]

The maximum potential effect of this entry decontrol on incumbent carriers is summarized in Table 9-9. Potentially, the worst impact could be experienced by the "Big Four" carriers (American, Eastern, Trans World, and United), plus Delta and Northwest. The rest would be relatively less impacted.

Under the third major entry provision, each year after January 1, 1981, trunk carriers would be allowed to expand into new markets and provide up to one billion seat-miles of service without CAB restraint.[19] Total available seat-miles (ASMs) by carrier are shown

---

[18] Not highlighted in the table is the fact that Pan American stands to gain considerably through the acquisition of "fill-up" rights for domestic portions of international flights.

[19] This is approximately 5 percent of the average carrier's available seat-miles.

Table 9-8

MAXIMUM POTENTIAL ENTRY CREATED BY PROPOSAL'S ROUTE RESTRICTION REMOVAL PROGRAM, BY TRUNK CARRIER, TOP 100 MARKETS

Carrier	Nonstop Markets Now Served		Markets Converted from Restricted Service to Nonstop Service		New Markets (markets not previously served)	
	Number	Passenger-miles (thousands)	Number	Passenger-miles (thousands)	Number	Passenger-miles (thousands)
Big Four						
American	40	15,040	4	7,377	15	3,342
Eastern	26	6,740	2	2,722	42	9,884
Trans World	39	14,701	0	0	27	8,178
United	42	16,977	2	132	35	7,219
Other Trunks						
Braniff	11	3,894	2	684	23	6,082
Continental	10	3,418	3	1,258	8	2,143
Delta	27	6,544	1	112	39	14,639
National	14	3,894	4	1,294	16	8,840
Northwest	22	5,921	2	1,439	36	15,063
Pan American	5	4,255	0	0	9	6,315
Western	13	3,817	1	228	3	284

Table 9-9

MAXIMUM ADDITIONAL COMPETITION CREATED BY PROPOSAL'S ROUTE RESTRICTION REMOVAL PROGRAM, BY CARRIER, TOP 100 MARKETS

Carrier	Number of Competitors per Market	Additional (Potential) Competitors per Market Converting from Restricted to Nonstop Service	Additional (Potential) Competitors per Market from New Entry	Maximum (Potential) Competitors per Market
Big Four				
American	1.83	0.18	2.58	4.59
Eastern	2.38	0.23	2.62	5.23
Trans World	1.82	0.15	2.69	4.66
United	1.81	0.19	2.79	4.79
Other Trunks				
Braniff	3.00	—	1.91	4.91
Continental	3.20	—	1.90	5.10
Delta	2.11	0.19	2.44	4.74
National	2.86	—	2.07	4.93
Northwest	2.36	—	2.77	5.13
Pan American	4.20	—	3.00	7.20
Western	2.62	0.23	1.85	4.70

Table 9-10

SCHEDULED AVAILABLE SEAT-MILES (ASMs) AND MAXIMUM (POTENTIAL) RATE OF EXPANSION

(billion seat-miles)

Carrier	Carrier ASMs[a] (billions)	Percentage of Total ASMs	Allowable Rate of Expansion as Percentage of 1975 ASMs[b]
Big Four			
American	32.74	15.1	3.1
Eastern	24.69	11.4	4.1
Trans World	26.97	12.4	3.7
United	47.23	21.7	2.1
Other Trunks			
Braniff	9.75	4.5	10.3
Continental	10.88	5.0	9.2
Delta	28.38	13.1	3.5
National	7.27	3.3	13.8
Northwest	15.91	7.3	6.3
Pan American	3.25	1.5	30.8
Western	10.21	4.7	9.8

[a] Domestic service for the twelve-month period ending in April 1975.
[b] Under the proposed act's discretionary entry provision.

in Table 9-10. Also shown is the proposed allowable discretionary expansion as a percentage of 1975 ASMs (right column). Clearly the relative opportunities for new entry are inversely related to the size of the carrier.

Of course, the entry opportunities summarized in Tables 9-8 and 9-10 are maximums, and there is little reason to believe that each carrier would exercise its discretion to the full amount. In order to obtain some idea of carrier attitudes toward new entry, calls were placed to senior executives representing each of the trunk carriers. Surprisingly, the carriers generally appeared cautious about route expansion. Although they expect to address the issue in responding to the board's proposed deregulation experiment and the administration's legislation, they do not seem to have a position well thought out at this time. Some are still recoiling from the entry experience of the late 1960s, and some even feel that there would be less entry if entry were free (vis-à-vis the present entry regime, which precipitates a

Table 9-11

ENTRY PROPOSALS NOW PENDING BEFORE THE
CIVIL AERONAUTICS BOARD BY TRUNK CARRIER

Carrier	Docket Number	Date Filed	New or Improved Domestic Authority Sought
American	24574	6/26/72	Miami/Ft. Lauderdale–Los Angeles/Ontario
	21247	7/28/69	Los Angeles–Cincinnati; Indianapolis
	20789	3/4/69	Detroit–Atlanta; Cleveland–Atlanta
Eastern	27912	6/6/75	Atlanta–Wichita–San Francisco
	27942	6/12/75	Route 10, Atlanta–Wichita–Denver
	27981	6/23/75	Route 10, Atlanta–Denver
	23977	11/11/71	Miami/Ft. Lauderdale–Los Angeles
	23915	10/15/71	Route 5, Akron/Canton–Atlanta
	21248	7/28/69	Philadelphia–Cincinnati, Columbus, Dayton, Indianapolis; Los Angeles–Cincinnati, Columbus, Dayton, Indianapolis; Indianapolis–Pittsburgh; Indianapolis–Cleveland
Trans World	24579	6/29/75	Miami–Los Angeles/Long Beach
	23484	6/8/71	San Diego–Kansas City
United	26953	8/15/74	Detroit–Denver
	26890	7/22/74	Denver–Grand Rapids
	21806	1/15/70	Las Vegas–Seattle
	21243	7/28/69	Dayton–Columbus–Los Angeles
	20788	3/4/69	Atlanta–Detroit
Braniff	27812	5/7/75	Amend Certificate to add Louisville
	26927	8/5/74	Add Orlando to Route 9
	26521	3/30/74	Amend Route 9 to serve Dallas/Ft. Worth–Atlanta
	23387	5/11/71	Orlando between St. Petersburg–Clearwater and Miami/Ft. Lauderdale
	23024	1/1/71	Miami/Ft. Lauderdale–Los Angeles/Ontario/Long Beach
	21504	10/9/69	Detroit–Nashville
	21471	9/29/69	Denver–Tulsa
Continental			Continental has only three domestic route applications pending before the board. Two of these applications involve removal or modification of beyond area service requirements. The third application seeks to add Las Vegas to segment 8 of its certificate.

Table 9-11 (Continued)

Carrier	Docket Number	Date Filed	New or Improved Domestic Authority Sought
Delta	27646	3/21/75	Memphis–Minneapolis
	27814	5/7/75	Memphis–Louisville
	27935	6/11/75	Houston–Cincinnati; Houston–Louisville
	21939	2/20/70	Boston–Atlanta
	21244	7/28/69	Los Angeles–Cincinnati/Columbus/Dayton/Indianapolis; Philadelphia–Cincinnati/Columbus/Dayton/Indianapolis
National	27239	Pending	Ft. Meyer–Atlanta
	21208	7/18/69	Philadelphia–Cincinnati/Dayton/Indianapolis; Los Angeles–Cincinnati/Columbus/Dayton/Indianapolis; Indianapolis–Pittsburgh; Indianapolis–Cleveland
Northwest	22682	10/27/70	Spokane–Los Angeles
	21505	10/9/69	Spokane–Denver, Salt Lake City
	21245	7/28/69	Philadelphia–Cincinnati/Dayton, et cetera
	20930	4/21/69	Seattle/Portland–Fairbanks
	20766	2/26/69	Cleveland–Atlanta; Detroit–Atlanta
Pan American	—	—	Miami–Los Angeles
	27626	—	Domestic fill-up rights
Western	27123	10/29/74	Honolulu–Kodiak–Anchorage
	23441	5/27/71	Amend Route 35, Denver–Chicago

"run to the courthouse"). In any event, predictions by industry trade associations that, under free entry, carriers would immediately concentrate on the handful of "lucrative" markets and abandon numerous marginal points does not square with the results obtained in these telephone interviews.

Additional evidence on individual carrier attitudes toward new entry can be gleaned from a survey of route extension proposals now before the board. (See Table 9-11.) From this information, as well as the telephone interviews, one may conclude that the carriers are likely to adopt a moderate policy of "rounding out" their existing route networks and making logical extensions for "feed" traffic before embarking upon programs of significant entry into new territory.

Summary. A subjective summary of the bill's impact on individual carriers is displayed in Table 9-12. For each of the pricing and entry

Table 9-12

SUBJECTIVE SUMMARY OF DRAFT BILL'S IMPACT ON INDIVIDUAL CARRIERS: RANK ORDERING FROM MOST FAVORABLE TO LEAST FAVORABLE

Carrier	Pricing				Entry			Overall Average
	Percentage monopoly routes	Average length of trip	Average route density	Exposure to mavericks	Certificate restriction removal (potential) entry created	Certificate restriction removal (potential) competition created	Discretionary entry program	
American	8	9	9	7	4	6	10	9
Eastern	6	1	8	8	3	7	7	7
Trans World	10	10	10	9	6	8	8	11
United	3	7	11	10	7	10	11	10
Braniff	2	3	2	5	8	3	3	1
Continental	7	8	5	2	10	2	5	5[a]
Delta	4	2	6	4	2	5	9	4
National	9	6	7	6	5	4	2	5[a]
Northwest	1	4	3	3	1	9	6	2
Pan American	n.a.	11	1	n.a.	9	11	1	8
Western	5	5	4	1	11	1	4	3

[a] Continental and National have the same ranking.

elements discussed above there is a ranking in order of most favorable to least favorable. These rankings were averaged by individual carrier in order to obtain an overall ranking (right column). It should be stressed that these rankings (especially the overall average) are subjective and do not necessarily tell the whole story. In particular, Pan American's ranking on entry grossly understates the importance of the "fill-up" rights it would acquire under the bill. But based on this subjective array, it would appear that the major beneficiaries would be the smaller trunks, as opposed to the industry giants.

Conclusion

The administration's draft bill, if enacted, would have little impact on the financial viability of the industry, but could accelerate a "shaking out" of inefficient firms—a process that would appear inevitable even without regulatory reform.

The timing of the bill's provisions is key. Although limited pricing flexibility would commence with enactment, carrier inertia with respect to pricing policy would probably mean little fare-cutting at first. Since the entry provisions would not come into full play until 1981, and since what entry does obtain by that time would be under board supervision and control, the carriers will have abundant opportunity to reconfigure their operations to the new regime.

Except for the three-cents-per-gallon increase projected for this year, no further fuel price increases are anticipated. And, although traffic will grow little this year and next, the projected economic recovery will mean a significant, higher-than-normal rate of growth in traffic starting in 1977 and continuing through the rest of the decade. Thus, at the time when the bill's major pricing and entry provision come into play, the industry should be in a position of much greater strength than exists today.

10

THE FINANCIAL NEEDS OF THE AVIATION INDUSTRY AND REGULATORY REFORM

Paul W. MacAvoy

A wide range of regulatory reform initiatives in sectors as diverse as surface transportation, retailing, financial services, and energy have been undertaken in recent years in order to remove many serious regulatory constraints which either impose on consumers billions of dollars in cost increases every year or else restrict the quantity or quality of service available. In the last few years in the railroad business, we have had the opportunity to observe the adverse effects of regulation on shippers and transporters both, and in the near future we will have the chance to take advantage of the gains to be made from the regulatory reform in the Rail Revitalization Act of 1975. The Rail Act has begun the deregulation process in the railroad industry, but only after the railroads had virtually ceased to operate. The damage had advanced so far that many shippers had been driven to other modes of transport and those who continued to use rails have had to endure extremely poor service. Similarly, Federal Power Commission regulation of natural gas has produced a serious shortage which has disadvantaged many consumers and increased our dependence on foreign oil. In both cases Congress has had to begin a reform movement or otherwise the industry would, itself, "deregulate" by simply withdrawing capital and going out of business.

Conditions in aviation are not entirely dissimilar. We need aviation regulatory reform to prevent CAB controls from running down this industry as similar controls did the railroad and gas industries. To indicate that this is the present problem, a discussion follows of the nature of industry response to change under regulation as compared to deregulation. In particular, future pricing problems and the

This paper is edited from testimony before the U.S. Congress, House, Subcommittee on Aviation of the Committee on Public Works and Transportation, May 12, 1976.

timeliness of the bill in solving these problems are evaluated. The conclusion is that this bill provides means for preventing the onset of "declining industry" conditions in airline service in the next few years.

The first concern, however, is with the way in which unregulated markets would operate. The widespread fear is that there will be an outbreak of predatory pricing resulting in the elimination of all but a few of the largest airlines from service.[1]

Market and Regulatory Responses to Change

Many of the problems associated with regulation are the result of the inflexibility of the process. Not only are regulators slow in adjusting to changing conditions, but no amount of improvement in management is likely to change this situation. The very nature of the regulatory process is to control prices based on historical rather than on future costs, so that even the most current case decisions are backward looking and lag behind the investment process. Moreover, regulating bodies often resist change because change invariably hurts some members of the industry. For example, the Interstate Commerce Commission (ICC) is widely held responsible for the fact that technology in the railroad industry remained substantially unchanged in the 1950s. A similar result is possible in aviation given that the economy experienced substantial price inflation and capital cost increases and that the commission process lags behind these changes.

Up to the present time, CAB regulation has been quite specific and detailed compared to that of other agencies. Existing route structures were essentially planned by the CAB, and these route structures have been major determinants of costs of operation for an individual airline. A poorly planned route structure results in poor utilization of equipment and duplication of facilities, which means higher costs and ultimately higher fares. Consequently, minimization of cost should be the primary consideration in design of route structures. However, routes in general have been awarded not on the basis of which airline is most efficient but on the basis of which airline needs the revenue from a new route the most.

The more efficient airlines provide too little and the less efficient too much service. Awarding the most attractive routes to the least efficient carriers has had the effect of giving the most efficient carriers the lowest load factors. This effect has been further increased because all carriers have substantial unused route authority. The more efficient

---

[1] The section of the testimony dealing with this assertion is not included here.

carriers have expanded into more unattractive routes than the other carriers because for them they are profitable. This further reduces their average load factors. This, of course, raises average costs and ultimately fares.

The proposed act's flexible pricing provisions and the gradual relaxation of entry and exit constraints would result in the most efficient route structure for each particular operation. Any one airline would exit from any one market, and enter or expand in others. For example, American Airlines flies from Chicago to Salt Lake City on weekday afternoons and returns to Chicago in the morning. Continuing on to Los Angeles would be a sensible extension of the route from the consumer's viewpoint and would increase utilization of equipment. What is now prohibited would eventually produce more efficient use of aircraft in this and many other markets. There will be a tendency in the next few years for load factors to increase for the most efficient carriers as they adjust their structure by shifting to more attractive markets where consumers can get the benefit of their greater efficiency through lower prices, not by traveling on empty planes. The result will be lower costs which competition will pass on in benefits to consumers.

Current restrictions on entry and exit are one source of rigidity. The board's pricing policies are another.

The CAB set standard fares for routes with widely varying characteristics. This simplification is required to keep the CAB from being mired down in route detail. But the board recognized the complexity of the problem in the recent Domestic Passenger Fare Investigation (DPFI), and it adopted a formula which gives the fare for each market based on (1) a 55 percent load factor, (2) a standard seating configuration, (3) a reduced per-mile charge for longer distances, and (4) the average cost of operating an aircraft. This procedure was an advance over previous rate making.

However, the average costs used here are not those of the most efficient line for the reasons noted above. This raises average costs and ultimately fares. The open pricing provisions of the act will lead to growth by the more efficient airlines and to contraction by the less efficient until they reach a profitable operating scale.

To delve into the effects of these pricing policies requires a bit more explanation. The board sets economy and first-class fares; it allows only limited price competition through discount fares of restricted availability. Unlimited competition is allowed in scheduling and in other aspects of quality competition. Where competition exists, service expands until profits are driven to the competitive level.

One effect of this pattern is that markets with relatively higher priced service consistently have lower load factors. In the late 1960s the price for longer trips was high relative to shorter ones, with the result being substantially lower load factors on many long-haul routes. This result from regulation was recognized and the "fare taper" increased, so that the situation is now much improved, although we are not sure that the taper is steep enough yet to reflect relative costs.

An even more costly regulatory distortion occurs in relative fare levels between high- and low-density markets. The simple economics of any transportation system state that for a given market the greater the volume of traffic, the lower the per-passenger average costs. In intrastate air passenger markets, the economies of greater volume have resulted in lower fares on high-density as compared to low-density routes of the same distance. The study by Simat, Helliesen and Eichner, Inc.,[2] graphically illustrates the greater efficiencies achieved in both revenue miles per employee and passengers boarded per employee by higher density operations. Productivity of carriers on the most dense intrastate routes has been more than double the productivity of interstate carriers with the same distance for operations. For example, Pacific Southwest Airlines carries 80,000 revenue ton-miles per employee annually while Allegheny, the most similar interstate airline, carries only 46,000. But regulated rates do not reflect these volume savings.[3] The failure to adjust rates for volume has

---

[2] Chapter 2, above.

[3] The question might well be asked as to whether the relation between costs per unit volume and prices holds, even though it is not given in the rates. This could occur if discounting varied between city-pairs sufficiently to establish lower relative prices per trip on the larger volume city-pairs.

We tested the relation of yields to the average amount of passenger traffic per airport for the domestic trunks. The yield per revenue ton-mile was regressed on average trip length and average number of passengers boarding a plane per airport served. We would predict that there would be no relation between yields and the number of passengers boarding a plane per station if the restriction on charging lower fares on high-volume routes was effective. The regression had significant T statistics and a very small R squared. Our hypothesis was confirmed.

Yield + 699.3 + −0.9 average trip length + 40.3 average number of
$\quad\quad\quad\quad\quad\quad$ (−0.4) $\quad\quad\quad\quad\quad\quad\quad\quad$ (0.39)
passengers boarding a plane. (The figures in parentheses are T statistics.)
$R^2 = 0.05$.

To provide a further test, we regressed system revenues on system passengers carried for each carrier and on a number of transformations of passengers carried, such as passengers squared, the log of passengers, and the like. Adding the transformations of passengers increased the explanatory power of the regression, only very slightly indicating a linear relation between passengers and revenue. This is significant since the carriers with high revenue and passenger levels are the ones with relatively more of their traffic originating in stations with high average number of passengers boarding a plane. Again, it indicates that there are not reduced prices to passengers in high-volume markets.

probably had diverse market implications. For example, it may well have impaired service to smaller communities.

Regulated fares set on the basis of average volume for all city-pairs the same distance apart would be set too low to cover costs on service to smaller cities or towns with lower volumes of service. To adjust to the high costs, the airlines must have to offer limited service frequency. For some markets this may result in no service at all. The administration's bill, by allowing flexible prices and entry, would work to correct this problem. It would tend to improve flight frequency in all markets and would keep fares down in high-density markets.

The Immediate Pricing Problems in the Years Ahead

These problems have to do with the CAB's, or any commission's, limited ability to plan. The experience of the past few years points to a more important problem. As I indicated above, rigid regulations can destroy the health of a regulated industry. In 1973 and 1974, increases in fuel prices and rapid overall inflation were accompanied by a slowdown in demand growth, and there was apparently some lag in the upward adjustment of regulated fares. Schedules were curtailed and other services were reduced, apparently because inflexible fares lagged behind costs, but also because of significant demand reductions. If this phenomenon had continued, there would have been continually declining service and schedules as the industry sought to reduce costs and bring them in line with prices.

We have seen an example of this problem in the electric utility industries. The natural gas industry is a much more serious instance of the same problem. The failure to raise natural gas rates appropriately has already led to shortages. The railroads are perhaps the most serious instance of the problem. The ICC failed to respond to changed circumstances over the course of two decades and, as a result, the railroads of the United States are in a sad state and Congress has been required to step in with a very expensive salvage program.

The airlines have not yet been caught in such a cycle of decay. The potential for such a situation, however, continues to exist because it is built into the regulatory process. The board, by nature, makes fundamental misjudgments that affect the health of the industry because of the backward-looking "cost of service" rate-setting procedures. And the CAB's current policy forces operations with little margin of error.

The proposed act would add some badly needed flexibility. Prices could be much more the critical determinant of the conditions of the industry in the last part of the 1970s than they were in the 1960s. Then airline productivity rose rapidly for most of the decade, causing steadily declining unit costs. Interest rates and inflation rates were low throughout most of the decade so that a fairly constant regulated price level implied constant or gradually increasing profit margins for most of the carriers. In these circumstances it was difficult for the CAB to make a serious error in setting rates too low, thereby damaging the finances of the carriers. But conditions in the near future are not likely to be the same.

Large productivity increases are unlikely because of slower rates of expansion and because of increasingly strict noise and pollution standards which have changed the nature of investment. Inflation rates, while declining, are still going to be substantially greater than in the same period of the 1960s. In its annual report the Council of Economic Advisers predicted continued moderation in the inflation rate, but it emphasized that there was considerable risk of higher rates. Partly as a result of inflation, interest rates are higher now so that capital is more expensive. This has eroded the margin between the 12 percent allowed rates of return and the market cost of capital. The failure to adjust the rate of return for future inflation-induced changes in the cost of capital could cause serious problems. There would not be such problems within the context of the flexible rate-setting and entry provisions of the administration's bill.

The Need for Increased Reliance on Market Behavior

An increased reliance on competition in the market is not only feasible, but it could possibly lead to significant improvements in industry performance in the coming decade. Furthermore, I do not believe that, as a practical matter, fundamental problems in present regulation can be resolved by improvements in CAB management. This is because the basic source of inflexibility is the board's way of doing business. Regulatory agencies must observe the requirements of both substantive and procedural due process. All affected parties must be heard and, because regulatory decisions often affect vital interest, the regutory process must be fair and highly formal. The result is delay. Regulators are slow to decide and slow to adjust to change. Furthermore, it is the very nature of the regulatory process to control prices based on historical rather than future costs, so that even the most current case decisions are backward looking or lagging behind the investment process. Moreover, regulatory agencies often protect their industries from change because change invariably hurts some members of the industry. Such a result is possible in aviation if the economy experiences substantial price inflation, capital cost increases, and the commission process lags behind these changes.

The proposed act would eliminate much of the inflexibility that is built into current regulation. It would permit more flexible pricing and permit the airlines to adapt their route structures to changing circumstances.

The bill is timely because an extended period of prosperity is now beginning. Excess capacity is rapidly declining because of board policy, the business cycle, and the fact that no major equipment orders are presently on the books. The council projects that real gross national product (GNP) will grow at 6.4 percent in 1976 and 7.5 percent in 1977. Immediate implementation of the bill would allow an orderly transition free of cyclical losses and a path towards solution of the more fundamental problems raised here.

11

THE EFFECTS OF THE AVIATION ACT ON AIR FARES

Paul W. MacAvoy

There seems to be little disagreement among analysts and econo-mists that the effect of regulation on air fares in the recent past has been to increase fares over what they would have been in the absence of controls. If controls were removed over a lengthy period of time, and if there were no inflation, price competition from the removal of entry and rate regulation would result in substantial fare reductions for most travelers, although not necessarily in all markets. However, my view is that current inflationary pressures will continue for a number of years, because we have yet to develop in this country a system for controlling federal expenditures and for enfolding those expenditures in increased monetary aggregates. With substantial in-flation—at an annual rate exceeding that in the past decade—we can expect that cost increase trends will outweigh the greater efficiencies possible with less regulation and that in the absence of regulation fares will rise above today's levels. With substantial inflation in a con-tinuation of present regulation, fares may not rise much above today's levels because the lag structure in the regulatory process itself tends to dampen price flexibility substantially. That is, the comparison takes two parts: (1) present unregulated fares will be lower, and (2) future unregulated fares may be higher.

These predictions of "real price" reductions relate specifically to dense markets and may not apply to smaller markets. Nevertheless, since most trips are flown in relatively dense markets, the potential reductions would clearly be beneficial to most passengers. The experi-ence in smaller markets, however, relates to the elasticity of demand for passenger service.

This paper is edited from a response to an inquiry of Congressman Elliott H. Levitas (Democrat, Georgia). The response is dated August 10, 1976.

My expectation is that elasticities of demand will vary substantially from market to market, depending on distance, the percentage of business travel, and other factors. But in some smaller short-haul markets the demands will be inelastic, and there may very well be price increases as a result of removal of regulation. The extent of these increases will be limited by the threat of potential entry. Also, some upward rate flexibility in these markets will provide incentives for increasing the quality of service, particularly in the provision of well-timed connections to important high-volume routes. This occurred, for example, when commuter carriers replaced trunk carriers in New England—fares were raised by more than 25 percent, but the number of flights more than doubled as well. There the response of the traveling public was highly positive, and the number of passengers rose by 70 percent. Thus, a combination of higher fares and higher quality of service could be expected in some smaller markets, and it would be beneficial to most potential passengers in these markets.

This last point is relevant for an evaluation of my long-run predictions as well. In the long run I expect that the level of air fares will likely be higher in the absence of regulation than in the presence of continued rate controls based upon the CAB's Domestic Passenger Fare Investigation (DPFI). This is because DPFI is the most inflexible of regulatory response mechanisms, and it causes considerable lag of prices behind costs in periods of high inflation, low productivity growth, and expanding demands. The invocation of DPFI would likely lead to a reduction of the quality of service and in many cases to the curtailment of flights and the introduction of informal rationing of seats as demand exceeds supply in the early 1980s.

This phenomenon of informal rationing has already been encountered in the electricity-generating industry, the natural gas industry, and the railroad industry (passenger service as well as freight service) in this country—all in response to rigid rate controls in the face of rising costs and demands. The resulting shortages and reduced service have not benefited the economy.

There is reason to believe that, absent a significant technological breakthrough, this will occur in air passenger service as well. The resulting degradation of service will be a signal for subsidies and for eventual nationalization of the poorest run airlines first. From my view, it is better to have a more flexible upward movement of rates than a continuation of DPFI in the next few years, because the market guarantees a response to demand increases while reduction of entry controls guarantees that the response will be competitive.